Matthew Collin has worked as a magazine editor, a foreign correspondent, a broadcast journalist and a features writer. He has been the editor of *The Big Issue*, the *Time Out* website and *i-D* magazine, and has worked in news for the BBC World Service. He has also written for a wide range of newspapers and magazines, including the *Guardian*, the *Daily Telegraph*, the *Observer*, the *Independent*, *The Moscow Times*, *The Face* and *Mojo*. His previous books, *This is Serbia Calling* and *Altered State*, were also published by Serpent's Tail.

Praise for Matthew Collin's earlier books

This is Serbia Calling

'Matthew Collin captures the conviction of a generation whose culture and identity were under siege. Real pop stars can inspire a revolution – B92's soundtrack of resistance ends in a triumphant celebration of the power of protest' *Independent on Sunday*

'Collin has not only found a way into the psyche of intelligent, tolerant young people suddenly swamped by a tide of fascist hate... he also shows how pop music can still ignite change, or quietly save souls, when life arrives at its most extreme' *Uncut*

'*This is Serbia Calling* should sit proudly as the latest addition to the people's history of the world... People power has never been so readable or so credible' *Big Issue*

'As the author of *Altered State*, you'd expect Collin to have a keen eye for pop cult detail, but *This Is Serbia Calling* also has its fair share of incisive political analysis. An essential read' *Jockey Slut*

'This story of a literal fight for the truth through music makes a particularly stirring read' *Metro London*

'Any jaded types who yawn at the idea of music's ability to influence social change should read this brilliantly written and researched book' *Mojo*

'A truly excellent and accessible read' *Buzz*

'Collin provides a vivid snapshot of a moment in time' *The Wire*

Altered State: The Story of Ecstasy Culture and Acid House

'At last somebody has written the real history of the last ten years, and written it with such wit, verve, empathy and profound intelligence. If you've been part of the scene in any way, this brilliant book will serve as positive affirmation. If you haven't, yet still feel moved to pontificate about it, you will no longer have the excuse of doing so from a position of ignorance. I can't recommend this marvellous piece of work enough and in a sane world it would sell more copies than any other book written over the last decade' Irvine Welsh

'The first full history of the dance boom which, fuelled by Ecstasy, has transformed British culture over the past decade: here you will also find the drive to transcendence, or oblivion, that is at the heart of British pop' Jon Savage

'Not just timely; it was crying out to be written' *Independent*

'*Altered State* remains the definitive story of the last decade's love affair with MDMA and mucking about in fields just off the M25' *Q*

The Time of the Rebels

Youth Resistance Movements and 21st Century Revolutions

Matthew Collin

A complete catalogue record for this book can be
obtained from the British Library on request

The right of Matthew Collin to be identified as the author
of this work has been asserted by him in accordance
with the Copyright, Designs and Patents Act 1988

First published in 2007 by Serpent's Tail,
an imprint of Profile Books Ltd
3A Exmouth House
Pine Street
London EC1R 0JH
website: www.serpentstail.com

Designed and typeset at Neuadd Bwll, Llanwrtyd Wells

Printed and bound in Great Britain by Clays, Bungay, Suffolk

10 9 8 7 6 5 4 3 2 1

CONTENTS

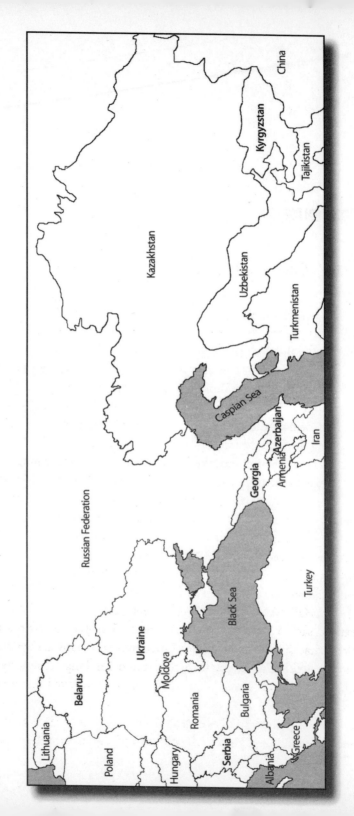

INTRODUCTION

THE YOUNG PIONEERS

It was twenty minutes past eight in the evening and the city was already in darkness when one of the leaders of the youth resistance sent a text message to my mobile phone. The temperature was eight degrees below zero and I was standing in October Square in the centre of the Belarussian capital, Minsk, where thousands of people had gathered on the frozen grey stones for another tense night of protest against the country's indomitable president, Alexander Lukashenko. A late winter breeze was chilling our bones, and my Belarussian friends were stamping their feet in time to the heavy rhythms thrashing out of the sound system in an attempt to keep themselves warm and raise their spirits high enough to beat back the fears about what might happen next, at least for as long as they could manage it.

'City Hall. Near pyramid of glass near trees. In 15 mins,' read the text message. I knew he wouldn't wait if I was even a few minutes late; he had said as much earlier. There were too many armed police on the streets that night to hang around for long, especially for someone who was under surveillance: he truly believed that he was a wanted man.

As he emerged from the gloom into the frosty silence of the deserted park, I recognised him immediately, even though he wasn't wearing any opposition badges or stickers; this would have been far too risky for someone involved in organising protests which the authorities had warned could be prosecuted as terrorist acts. He was a tall, dark youth in his early twenties, and he was extremely edgy, gabbling nervously about some of his comrades who had gone missing a couple of days beforehand, presumably detained by the police after the night's demonstration had ended. Nobody knew where they were being held; the police were saying nothing; their parents were frantic with worry. Such stories were not so unusual, that week in Minsk.

He led me on a long, twisting route through the city's snow-covered backstreets, sometimes doubling back, sometimes changing direction abruptly as if to confuse anyone following him, flitting in and out of bars and restaurants, scanning the tables for plain clothes state security officers or off-duty policemen enjoying an evening refreshment. When we finally found a café where he felt secure enough to talk quietly, he demanded to see my passport to check that I was who I said I was. He was apologetic, but insisted that it was necessary: in this country, not everyone is who they seem, he said. At the time, I thought him a little paranoid, but as it turned out, they were out to get him. A few days after we met, he was arrested by the secret police.

Minsk was the final destination on a series of journeys through turbulent times, through days of chaos and uncertainty and nights of hope and wonder, and this young Belarussian was just the latest of many who had committed themselves to the cause of peaceful resistance. At the start of the twenty-first century, a wave of revolution began to sweep across former Communist states, from Serbia to Georgia, Ukraine and Kyrgyzstan. Dramatic images filled the television screens of the world: fresh-faced youths marching proudly under brightly-coloured banners; rows of hardy tents pitched on grand boulevards, flying flags of justice and freedom; revellers chanting and dancing amidst gusts of tear gas and the fierce crack of plastic bullets; crowds of jubilant insurgents bursting into parliament buildings, the police unable to hold them back… At first these fairytale uprisings looked like a sequel to the 'velvet revolutions' which hastened the fall of Communism across eastern Europe at the end of the 1980s: 'people power' revolts which challenged the might of an authoritarian state not with weapons, but with the pure force of righteousness. They sang to soldiers, laid flowers upon riot shields, met repression with defiant humour. *Freedom can't be stopped*, they declared.

But although they targeted the old functionaries who had held on to power since the fall of Communism, this was not simply 1989 revisited; at the heart of all these revolutions was a new kind of youth movement, a product of its own time and place. In Serbia, Otpor set the template which the others were to follow: a tiny faction of disaffected students which grew into a subversive network spanning the entire country. Otpor had one simple goal: complete democratic transformation. Its activists had learned from the liberation movements of 1989, but their methods were resolutely modern: the marketing techniques of the advertising industry, the new technologies of the internet and the mobile telephone, the graphic possibilities of desktop publishing, the seductive signs and symbols of popular culture. This was politics with a smart logo and a pulsing beat. It made regime change fun.

There were also echoes of 1968, the last mass outbreak of student unrest in Europe, when hundreds of thousands of young people took to the streets of Paris, Berlin, London and other cities to protest against the Vietnam War and demand socialist liberation. But this time, the fight was for liberal democracy and the values of 'the West', at least as they were imagined: free speech and free markets. The new student revolutionaries didn't consider themselves militants or radicals, but noble dissidents and genuine patriots. Otpor's members had seen other former Communist countries move towards the promised land of the European Union while their own, Yugoslavia, regressed into isolation and armed conflict. They wanted, they said, to reverse the decline, to 'become part of the world' again, to 'live a normal life'.

My first direct contact with Otpor came in January 2000, when one of its leading members, a literature student, visited the apartment where I was staying in Belgrade. We talked about rock music and the nature of betrayal that day, and about the fury she was feeling about Serbian bands who were collaborating with record companies which had links to the government of Slobodan Milošević. It was a time for taking sides, she said, and they had chosen the path of darkness, sold out their own generation – her generation – for some small ugly reward. 'They are giving an alibi to the corrupt,' she insisted. She said she didn't join Otpor when it started because she thought it would be just another pointless political project – she hated politicians and their sordid posturing – but she quickly realised that this was something very different; that it had an enthusiasm and a sense of purpose which the Serbian opposition had lacked for years.

Over the coming months, as the fall of Milošević approached, I got to know more of the Otpor activists, and came to appreciate the sheer imaginative daring which put them one step ahead of the authorities. They were great storytellers, too, with a powerful sense of the absurd. One of them recalled an incident when their office was raided, and one policeman – lacking anything else to seize – tried to confiscate a pair of her trousers, as if they were some kind of subversive talisman. It was this sort of everyday idiocy which kept them in fine spirits and nourished their sense of destiny. The authorities were serious, but the Otpor youths were just laughing at them, as if the whole thing was just a ludicrous movie spooling ever faster towards the final credits.

Every few years, an idea comes along which connects with a generation in a deep and powerful way, setting off reactions which could never, even with the best of foresight, have been predicted. Otpor was like a viral explosive which detonated in the consciousness of like-minded youths; a thrilling flash of revelation which set them dreaming and scheming. The Serbian youth movement was followed by Kmara in Georgia and then Pora in Ukraine, both using similar logos, T-shirts, stunts and pranks, as the virus spread into the former Soviet Union. I already knew about Pora when I arrived in snow-covered Kiev during what would become known as the Orange Revolution – like the others, they had an English-language website – so I headed straight for their office. It was a dusty basement near the foreign ministry, cluttered with posters, stickers and half-finished cups of coffee, with muffled rock music playing from a computer somewhere in the background, like a scruffy student common room. It almost could have been Otpor's old office on Knez Mihailova street in central Belgrade. A short walk away, thousands of Pora activists were camping out on the city's main street – until victory, they insisted. It was clear that after the revolutions in Serbia and Georgia, the emergence of Pora was more than a coincidence: a new phenomenon had arrived.

After the Orange Revolution, I spent the next year tracing the story through the region, meeting hundreds of brave and determined young people. They were bound together not just by their audacious struggles for democracy, but by their commitment to the philosophy of non-violent resistance. It was, they explained, all about targeting and undermining what they called the 'pillars of the regime'. They believed that authoritarian governments were not impregnable monoliths but a series of vulnerable institutions which depended on individuals who could be convinced or shamed into defecting. 'Even a dictator can't collect taxes on his own,' one of the Serbs told me. 'He can't deliver the mail, he can't even milk a cow: someone has to obey his orders or the whole thing shuts down. The task is to convince them to disobey. When they change sides, the government starts to fall.' The other decisive factor they all spoke about was the need for meticulous strategic planning: 'It won't happen without a strategy, without structure, without unity,' a young Georgian explained. 'You need... well, it's like Lenin said, it's all about *organisation, organisation, organisation*.'

Around the same time, the international media became entranced by this new phenomenon. Most press commentators fell into one of two camps: those who took the slogans at face value – the 'brightest and the best' versus the dinosaur dictators; a Hollywood morality show with a happy ending – and those who thought the young rebels were part of some kind of global conspiracy directed by George W. Bush and a crack squad of neo-conservative Svengalis; puppet soldiers in the battle for power, influence and energy resources in the former Soviet Union – a continuation of Cold War shadow play by other means. As the bitter propaganda war shifted from state to state, Western politicians feted the youths as wholesome avatars of freedom, while their own governments sought to portray them as puppets of the Bush administration, advancing Washington's liberal capitalist agenda abroad: treacherous hirelings or, at the very least, credulous dupes. Such accusations reached feverish highs when President Bush began to speak of promoting the spread of democracy throughout the world.

Although it became evident that the truth was more complex and nuanced than both these viewpoints allowed, there were uncomfortable questions which all these youth movements had to face: who was paying the bill, who was giving the orders, and who stood to gain? Most of them received money directly or indirectly from Western governments, and those that didn't would have liked some. But they all argued that change could not be imposed from outside; a diktat from the White House could not mobilise the masses in a country far away. The revolution has to begin here, they insisted, at home. Neither were they unequivocally pro-American. Some had ideological differences with Washington's military adventures, particularly in Yugoslavia and Iraq, as they clashed with the sacred creed of peaceful, indigenous resistance.

Youth movements like Otpor, Kmara and Pora were not traditional political campaigns, at least not in the sense of party politics; there were no candidates or policy programmes, not at first anyway. Their desires were more abstract and universal: free speech, human rights, fair elections. They declared themselves non-partisan – nobody trusts these politicians with their bad suits and their opportunist promises, they reasoned – although they maintained strong links with the more progressive opposition leaders and, once the crisis in their countries reached its critical stage, they all supported opposition parties against the authorities. But by distancing themselves from the orthodoxies of traditional politics and focusing on one simple mission – the end of the old order – they were able to unite a wide range of people, sometimes with opposing political opinions, creating a motley coalition of the discontented... It is also, perhaps, why most of them couldn't manage to retain their unity or their mass support after they had achieved their goal.

Like the students of 1968, the young people who started these movements were mostly middle-class, well-educated and well-travelled, unlike many of their compatriots. They came from the digital generation and understood the motivational power of new media and rock music. They had good connections with veterans of previous lost struggles for liberty and with international foundations dedicated to promoting democracy and Western values, which in turn supplied them with resources and training.

Beyond their righteous certainties, there were also contradictions. They said they had no leaders but were extremely well-regimented; they said they were non-partisan but effectively aided the political opposition; they said they were completely open but were often wary of saying exactly where their finances came from. They had good reasons for blurring the facts, they believed, but at the height of their struggles, these contradictions left them vulnerable to attack.

In a globalised world of instantaneous digital communication, their ideas have continued to ripple outwards. After the revolutions in Serbia, Georgia and Ukraine, youth movements based on the strategies and iconography of Otpor, Kmara and Pora have appeared in the most unlikely places: the Middle East, Africa, and all across the former Soviet Union. Wherever there were grievances about democracy, there were youths with colourful T-shirts and protest websites preaching the philosophies of non-violent resistance. An informal network also began to emerge, with veterans of these twenty-first century uprisings travelling the world, sharing their experiences and expertise with like-minded young people in other countries: a new revolutionary international.

But success had its drawbacks: their tactics no longer had the element of surprise which once gave them the edge, and their revolutions convinced other former Soviet countries to reinforce their defences against internal subversion. Many would spend time in jail. And amidst the spectacular victories, there were sobering failures. Sometimes the state proved too strong, sometimes the opposition too weak or too compromised. Sometimes the people themselves were not ready or willing. As even the most hardcore evangelists for non-violent resistance admit, the time and the conditions have to be right. Strategy, solidarity, money; none of these is enough on its own.

I was not looking for deep political analysis when I set out on this journey through spectacular times. I was searching for stories; the illumination of the personal and the minutiae of lives lived in the intoxication of the moment. I wanted to know how they felt, what they saw; about the jokes they told and the songs they sang, about their doubts and fears. Sometimes this approach met with incomprehension, particularly from those who believed it was enough to repeat the 'official history' of their movement, the party line, in the desiccated jargon favoured by international democracy foundations; with drab phrases like 'capacity building' and 'informational-educational work' stripping their narratives of all their passionate energy. But others got it instantly. For them, it had been an almost spiritual experience; it had transformed them. It had been, in the phrase they so often used, a 'revolution of the mind'.

It is important not to exaggerate the contribution these youth movements made to the political changes in their countries. They didn't act alone. The successful ones, at least, were part of a mosaic of interconnected groups which shared the same broad mission. While the youth acted as daredevil instigators, civil rights groups, independent media and election monitors had more sober, less telegenic but equally crucial roles to play, while the opposition was led by politicians, and brought politicians to power. But this is not a book about politicians; their stories will be told elsewhere. Neither does it set out to analyse the achievements, failures, crises and disappointments which followed these twenty-first century revolutions. This is the story of a remarkable group of young people who, against the odds, decided to stand up and fight for what they believed in. Being young, and full of innocent optimism, they could sometimes be naive, but there is no doubting their sincerity or their courage. Despite the threat of violence, imprisonment or worse, they dared to take action – whatever the personal cost – to change their own world.

CHAPTER ONE

LIVING THE RESISTANCE

SERBIA

Winter hadn't yet come to the capital of the country still known at that time as Yugoslavia, and the late autumn sun was breaking through when the first chords crashed down from the tower of speakers. An electric squall of guitars and drums shrieked and clattered across the concrete surfaces of the city's central square as an unknown group of youths moved through the afternoon crowd of downtown rockers and curious passers-by, passing out leaflets stamped with the sign of a clenched fist and a brief, poetic invocation. One of the organisers of the concert was intrigued by the message and read it out from the stage:

'Resistance is the answer! There is no other way. It will be too late when someone you know starves to death. When they start killing in the streets, when they put out all the lights and poison the last well, it will be too late. This is not a system, it is a disease. Bite the system. Get a grip. Live the Resistance!'

On the same day – 4 November 1998 – four students were arrested for spray painting anti-government slogans and the sign of the fist on the cracked stucco and grimy facades of buildings in central Belgrade. Like most vandals, they were questioned, processed and prosecuted.

Unlike most first-time offenders, who were routinely fined, they were sentenced to ten days in prison for 'disturbing public order'. After their release, one of the youths was asked if her short spell in jail would make her think again about causing mischief. 'Come on, you're kidding!' she replied. 'I'll just make sure they don't catch me next time… I am convinced that resistance to this fascist regime is my moral, political and patriotic obligation.'[1] They couldn't have known it at the time, but the insignificant acts of petty subversion which took place that day were the start of something which would resonate across the world, for years to come.

The cartoonish facsimile of the clenched fist had begun to appear on walls throughout the Yugoslav capital the previous month – often accompanied by a single word, *Otpor*, Serbian for 'Resistance' – although at first it wasn't clear exactly what it signified, who was doing it, or why. The fist was iconic: it had been the symbol of the pre-war Communist underground and the anti-Nazi partisan fighters of World War Two. But middle-aged officials of President Slobodan Milošević's Socialist Party of Serbia, which claimed the heritage of the partisans as its own, were hardly likely to be carrying out nocturnal graffiti campaigns.

This was a time of rising paranoia as Belgrade mobilised, once again, for war. The conflict in Bosnia had ended more than three years previously; Bosnia, Croatia, Macedonia and Slovenia had already seceded from Yugoslavia – a gutted union now composed only of Serbia and little Montenegro. But NATO was now threatening Milošević with an air attack if he didn't withdraw his forces from the southern province of Kosovo, where they had been waging a fierce campaign against separatist insurgents. The talk was of air-raid shelters and anti-aircraft guns, surveillance planes and radar defences, and the state media were gripped by an increasingly shrill patriotism as they turned on the 'fifth columists' of the political opposition who they said would embrace NATO's bombs as their own, the human-rights groups who were 'assisting terrorists', and the ideological perverts of the independent media who were 'spreading defeatism'.

It had been a bad year for the opposition to Milošević. Two

years earlier, at the end of 1996, hundreds of thousands of people had taken to the streets after the results of local elections in Serbia had been falsified. They had marched through the icy boulevards of Belgrade for three months in the most dramatic and imaginative mass protests the country had ever seen, and by February 1997, had forced the authorities to back down and concede defeat. Milošević had effectively lost the war in Bosnia, but this was the first time he had been beaten on his own territory, in Serbia itself. It was now clear that he was vulnerable.

There had been repeated outbreaks of urban protest since Milošević came to power in 1989, riding a wave of nationalist chauvinism which would help to destroy Yugoslavia. But those three months, that rapt feverish winter, made it feel as though the country was on the brink of a breakthrough. Yet less than two years afterwards, as 1998 drew to a close, such optimism began to seem naive, even foolish. The opposition coalition which had come together to fight the local elections as a united bloc rapidly dissolved into the kind of in-fighting and petty bickering which had so often paralysed it during the Milošević years. Many opposition supporters believed that their leaders had carelessly, incomprehensibly thrown away their advantage. The hope had been intoxicating; now the disillusionment was crushing. 'There was such a huge energy at those demonstrations, and what did we get out of it? It was a time of darkness for the democratic movement. It was horrible, we'd got nowhere and he was still in power, stronger than ever and getting ready to do Kosovo,' says Monika Lajhner, one of the young protesters.

While the opposition quarrelled, Milošević took the initiative. Students had made up the creative vanguard of the 1996–97 demonstrations, organising daily spectacles to keep the energy flowing, turning the marches into carnivals of joyous noise and colour. They had staged absurdist theatre performances, played satirical games in front of police cordons, lampooned the president and his family; they carried the most flamboyant banners, told the most ferocious jokes, invented the most sarcastic slogans. A year later, Milošević would exact his revenge, bringing in a new University Law which gave the government direct control over faculty appointments. Teaching staff were asked to sign a new contract, which many of them said was effectively an oath of loyalty to the authorities. Some refused to accept it and were dismissed.

The other catalyst for the 1996–97 protests had been the independent media. While state television had described the marchers as fascists and hooligans, independent newspapers and radio stations had boosted the demonstrations by simply reporting them. State media had helped bring Milošević to power and had spun the nationalist propaganda which had fuelled populist fervour during the wars which tore Yugoslavia apart. Now the president acted to tighten his grip. A new Information Law was introduced which allowed the authorities to impose huge fines on any media company whose troublesome journalism 'undermined the constitutional order of the country'. It was necessary, ministers said, at a time when the country had so many enemies, both outside and inside its borders.

It was in 1998, amidst this mood of encroaching gloom, that a group of around a dozen students from Belgrade University – veterans of the student rallies and members of various opposition parties, all of them in their early twenties – held a series of informal gatherings in city-centre cafés to discuss what they could do next. They met in a capital which looked and felt careworn and traumatised, raddled by international trade sanctions which were devastating the economy, where hawkers sold cans of petrol and packs of cigarettes by the roadside: a society which appeared to be in collapse. And yet they could still dream of something beyond it all, something vital that would break with the deadening failures, flawed strategies and petty politics of the past – something that would disrupt the pattern: a cadre of smart young guerrillas, but without guns. A Serbian resistance movement: so call it *Otpor*…

Among them was Ivan Andrić. 'Like some friends of mine who study film and so they're crazy about movies and spend all their time in the movies, we were crazy about revolution so we talked only about that all the time,' he remembers. 'We used to meet right after classes to talk about what we could do and how we could do it. That was our way of life.'

One of their early recruits was Ivan Marović, a baby-faced schemer who specialised in wisecracking satire and sardonic soundbites, and made a name for himself during the 1996–97 protests for unconventional, provocative actions carried out without the approval (and sometimes with the active disapproval) of the committee overseeing the demonstrations. One well-known press photograph from the time shows Marović's fellow radicals from Belgrade University's mechanical engineering faculty using him as a human battering ram as they tried to break into a university building. His headstrong adventurism won him the nickname 'Tupac Amarović', a reference to the Peruvian rebel group Tupac Amaru.

Simply winning the local elections hadn't been enough for Marović and his friends. 'We wanted more,' he says. 'We had a long tradition of guerrilla movements in this country, especially during the Second World War. We were not leftists in the style of the nineteen-thirties and nineteen-forties, but we were fighting for social justice. Some of the principles were the same – equality, and the belief that the government should not jeopardise people's liberties. So we tried to be what the resistance movement against the Nazis was, but against Milošević. That's why we picked that name and that logo.'

They all came from the generation that held cherished memories from the times before Milošević, when Yugoslavs had been relatively wealthy, unlike the eastern European countries directly under Moscow's control. They had grown up in a period when they had been free to travel and, with an economy partly funded by the Communist leader Josip Broz Tito's accumulation of loans from the West, they could afford to do so. 'The people born between the late sixties and the late seventies were old enough to remember the good times. We had a childhood with our beloved passport, and we could go to the seaside in summer and go skiing in the winter,' says another of Otpor's founders, Srdja Popović. But they had seen their country collapse into ethnic strife and poverty while other former Communist states – Poland, Hungary, the Czech Republic, places which had always been harsher, poorer and more restrictive – moved towards liberation.

Popović was a lanky young biologist with a sharp haircut and the zeal of a missionary, who had started his political career early and had already served on Belgrade city council as a member of the Democratic Party. He once called himself, jokingly, Otpor's 'ideological commissar', but for his contemporaries, this had some truth in it. More than one of them described him as a 'strategic genius'. Popović's generation was reaching adulthood when the free-wheeling reveries of relatively liberal Communism were extinguished by nationalist violence, as Yugoslavia began to break apart and the army started to call up young men to fight for the nation in Croatia and Bosnia. 'When I was 18, the hunt for recruits began, and we became military escapists because Milošević's wars had already started,' he says. 'So we remembered the good old times and could compare them to how we were living – and we were not old enough to surrender like our parents' generation.'

It was probably inevitable that the students would become the vanguard for change. They had less to lose, and much more to gain. They weren't old enough to be contaminated by collaboration. They had grown up on Western movies and music, and felt depressed by their country's increasing isolation. Dying for the poisoned fantasy of a 'Greater Serbia' held little appeal. They wanted, one of them said at the time, 'a life without fear; the fear of the future, the fear of facing the past'.[2]

Belgrade had always been fertile ground for student radicalism, dating back to the heady summer of 1968, the 'year of the barricades', when young people in eastern Europe, emulating their counterparts in the West, took to the streets and squares to demand free speech and the liberalisation of authoritarian Communism. Warsaw and Prague erupted first, and then Belgrade. A protest by students complaining about being excluded from a free concert was violently put down by police; the students then occupied parts of Belgrade University and began to hand out illegal newsletters contrasting the wealth of the privileged apparatchiks with the poverty of the Yugoslav population, attacking what they called the 'red princes' of the 'Communist bourgeoisie' and calling for the dismissal of senior ministers. After a week of sit-ins and sporadic unrest throughout Belgrade, as police began to encircle the university's dissident faculties, President Tito addressed the nation on television and unexpectedly endorsed the students' demands. However, victory proved brief; as soon as they returned to their studies, purges of 'extremists' began.

Three decades on, in the 1990s, as Serbian society became militarised and nationalism dominated public discourse, tens of thousands of young people were fleeing the country to search for a better life. They had simply lost all hope in Yugoslavia's future. The people who founded Otpor were those who thought they could – for the moment, at least – stay and change things. They had something else in common, too: they didn't have to worry much about money. 'None of us was poor,' says Milja Jovanović, the daughter of a writer and a professor, and the only woman in Otpor's inner circle. 'We were middle class, we had enough money to sustain ourselves, or our families supported us. We didn't need to go out to work to buy food or pay for electricity. I think that was really important because otherwise we couldn't have committed to Otpor 24 hours a day like we did. We could afford to do it.'

Otpor would be a new kind of movement; it would operate more like the fluid, highly mobile direct-action campaigns of Western environmentalists than a conventional political organisation. There would be no leaders, at least none who would be identifiable publicly, although the organisation would be controlled largely by the tight group of friends who founded it. Otpor would have a decentralised, cellular structure, like a genuine resistance movement, with each chapter carrying out autonomous actions, so if one was neutralised, others could carry on the mission. It was a strategy adopted partly out of fear that public faces could be targeted and eliminated, legally or otherwise. 'Any leader could have been arrested, put away or killed,' says Jovanović. 'In the situation at that time, there were no assurances that we would be physically safe. We just didn't know.'

The decision not to create a visible figurehead was also a result of what they had seen during the student protests of 1996–97. Some of the student leaders had become discredited when it was perceived that they had been co-opted by political parties – which was seen as a betrayal – while others were targeted by smear campaigns. They didn't want to be individually demonised, turned into symbolic ogres as the main opposition party leaders had been. 'Once [the Serbian Renewal Movement party leader] Vuk Drašković got stronger, he became a drug addict, a thief. When [the Democratic Party leader] Zoran Djindjić got there, then he became a criminal, a traitor, a mercenary,' explains Ivan Andrić. 'That was the way the regime settled accounts with people.'

Otpor's activists were smart, witty and media-literate. They were part of the rock 'n' roll generation which had grown up listening to the Belgrade-based independent radio station B92; its abrasive mixture of hard news, provocative comment and alternative rock was a vital influence. They understood the seductive appeal of advertising, and their immaculately stark, black-and-white graphics were designed for maximum visual impact. Unlike the politicians, they had style: they set out to make protest not just righteous, but fashionable. Ivan Marović would later say that Otpor worked like a slick Western marketing operation, selling resistance like Coca-Cola, running the movement like a corporate brand. But in its early days, it was just acting intuitively, inventing strategies on the run. 'A lot of things went on haphazardly and seemed to be coincidental,' says Andrić. The mythology would come later.

It was a former ally of the Milošević family who would bring them national notoriety in Serbia. Slavko Ćuruvija, the publisher of the *Dnevni Telegraf* newspaper, was an insider who had turned against the government and had just been fined around a quarter of a million dollars for publishing an open letter to Milošević, accusing him of establishing a criminal autocracy. After Otpor handed out its first manifesto – *Live the Resistance!* – at the concert in Republic Square in November 1998, Ćuruvija decided to republish it on his front cover, along with the sign of the clenched fist. Charges were immediately filed under the new Information Law, alleging that his newspaper had called for the overthrow of the government and endangered the citizens of Yugoslavia. This time the fine was over $100,000.

The students responded by taking their message directly to their enemies. At an official ceremony at Belgrade University in December, they unfurled an Otpor banner in front of a group of dignitaries including Vojislav Šešelj, the ultra-nationalist right-wing firebrand who would later be indicted for war crimes allegedly committed during the Bosnian war but at that time was a deputy prime minister in the Milošević government. It was a daring, even foolhardy act of calculated insolence, and they knew it: they made their point, and then they ran. But they had been noticed; the next day, Srdja Popović was arrested and beaten up in the cells. 'The officer told me that he would like to be in Iraq,' Popović said afterwards, 'because he could put a bullet in my head and no one would care.'[3]

At this stage, Otpor was hardly a sophisticated campaigning force. Its membership was small and most of its actions were centred on the university. 'We knew that Milošević was enemy number one and that if we didn't remove him, no change would happen, but at the same time we knew our capacity was limited,' says Ivan Marović. 'We were a few dozen people, we were just trying to stir up the university. I was pretty disappointed with our activities. I was radical, I thought that if we didn't move out of the university this would be just another false attempt. But I was wrong – those first months were useful in recruiting more people.'

After the signing of the Dayton Agreement which ended the Bosnian war in 1995, Milošević had been seen by Western governments as a man who could help to keep the peace; unsavoury, perhaps, but necessary. The students found this desperately frustrating. They thought the Americans and the Europeans, who were fearful of another outbreak of the Balkan conflict which had left some 200,000 dead, were propping up a dictator. 'I have to blame the international community,' says Slobodan Homen, another of Otpor's founders. 'Milošević was still the partner of the United States and the UK. The opposition was disunited and weak with no experience of how to rule the country. The international community thought Milošević was the only partner who could provide stability in the region. But if you look at what happened later in Kosovo, maybe it was better for them to support the opposition even in its weak position and to start new changes.'

In December 1998, a group of opposition figures, including Slavko Ćuruvija and the former mayor of Belgrade, Nebojsa Čović, went to Washington DC to testify before the US Congress and plead with the Americans to stop dealing with Milošević as if he was a legitimate leader. Čović stated that the last decade had been one of 'pure evil for all citizens of Serbia' and that people needed help to find their way out of the 'hypnotic dream' of Milošević's lies. Ćuruvija was full of fury at the Americans: 'Your government has weakened democratic forces in my country by strengthening Milošević's hand,' he declared. 'You have punished the population with rigorous economic sanctions and permitted him to use the Kosovo crisis as an excuse to crack down on any opposition to his regime.' Then an Otpor member, Boris Karajčić, stood up and argued that the US shouldn't just support opposition politicians, but the *entire process* of democratisation. He compared Serbia to Poland in the months before the rise of Solidarity, the independent trade union founded in the shipyards of Gdansk in 1980, which grew into a mass social movement and ultimately defeated the Polish Communist government nine years later. Solidarity was much larger than any political party, Karajčić said: this was the kind of movement that his country needed now.[4] A couple of weeks later, not long after his Congress speech was reported on Yugoslav television, Karajčić was hospitalised after being attacked by unknown assailants in Belgrade. The men gave him a message as they ran off: 'Say hello to your friends in Otpor.'[5]

As Ćuruvija had indicated, tension was rising in Kosovo, the province considered by many in Serbia to be the spiritual heartland of their civilisation, but where ethnic Albanians far outnumbered Serbs. As Milošević continued his campaign against the militants of the Kosovo Liberation Army, who wanted independence, villages burned again, and tens of thousands fled their homes for refugee camps. Western politicians saw it as another outbreak of the 'ethnic cleansing' which, to their shame and regret, they had failed to prevent in Bosnia. Military intervention seemed inevitable. The 'international community' which had propped up Milošević was now losing patience with him. Many Serbs began to fear that they would soon be bombed.

In this atmosphere of wild paranoia and nervous agitation,

ministers began to look for enemies within. Opposition leaders like Zoran Djindjić and Vuk Drašković had long been accused of disloyalty to the nation. But now the authorities had a new target – Otpor – even though at this stage it was no more than a few students with cans of spray paint and fertile imaginations. The deputy prime minister, Vojislav Šešelj, said Otpor's activists were being paid by the American intelligence services to help the United States occupy Serbia, overthrow the authorities and 'replace them with quislings'. He said the attack on Otpor's Boris Karajčić was justifiable retribution for his treachery: 'Maybe one of his neighbours recognised him as a foreign hireling and frowned at him while passing by; maybe he got a deserved slap or two somewhere. In any case there is no reason for official action, because our people cannot stand treason.'[6]

Dangerous subversives. Lovers of the enemy. Traitors who deserved to be beaten senseless by decent citizens. Otpor was out in the open now, and there was no way back…

A CERTAIN NUMBER OF PERSONS WITH ENDOCRINOLOGICAL ILLNESSES

On 24 March 1999, air-raid sirens wailed out across the Serbian capital. Radio Belgrade was playing patriotic songs. Diplomatic talks between American negotiators and the Yugoslav government to resolve the Kosovo conflict had broken down, and NATO planes were in the skies above Serbia. A state of war had been declared, and people rushed to bomb shelters. There was little reliable information on state television about what was happening in Belgrade, let alone in Kosovo, only constant attacks on the 'fascist aggressors' of the West, the murderous American president, Bill Clinton, and his British sidekick, Tony Blair. During the daytime, people gathered in squares and on bridges in defiance of the bombing. By night, when the sirens sounded, they hid in bunkers and basements, and waited. Energy supplies were intermittent because power stations had been bombed. There were queues for essential supplies. No public expressions of dissent were now possible.

Just before the bombing started, Otpor's leaders called a press conference and said they were suspending their activities until the war was over. They said they supported neither Milošević nor NATO: violence was not the answer to any conflict. A few days beforehand, Slavko Ćuruvija had contacted them to warn them that it was too dangerous to carry on campaigning once the country was at war. 'I remember Ćuruvija's quite rational explanation: in case of bombings, all parties would become patriotic, all media would be shut down and the students would remain the only opposition to the regime, which Milošević would not tolerate,' says Ivan Andrić. Ćuruvija also spoke of a 'hit list' of dissidents who could be liquidated if they spoke out; he thought that some of Otpor's main organisers might be on it.

Shortly afterwards, they received another warning, this time from someone with some inside knowledge of the West's strategy, the Austrian ambassador to Yugoslavia, Wolfgang Petritsch. 'I remember we were sitting together when Petritsch called to tell us the talks with Milošević were over and that the bombing was to start next day,' says Andrić. 'He told us, "Go away." That's when we realised how big a problem we had.'

Some of them immediately left Belgrade for Montenegro to sit the war out in safety by the coast; others remained in the capital but kept a low profile. 'We didn't do anything for those three months, just stayed in touch,' says Milja Jovanović. 'We knew if we did any actions during the war, it would be used against us. We all stayed undercover. Some were drafted to the army and it was terrible because somebody could have killed them and just said a bomb fell on them because a lot of the bodies of young soldiers never came back home. A lot of parents don't know where their sons are buried.

'We knew there was repression of Albanians in Kosovo, and of course they fought back. We were against NATO but we had the sense that NATO wasn't our business; there was something nearer that was our responsibility – the regime which let NATO bomb Serbia.'

Ćuruvija had been right. Severe restrictions were placed on the media, effectively turning it into a propaganda machine. The independent radio station B92 was taken over by government loyalists, who established a patriotic channel on its frequency under the same name. A few days later, Ćuruvija's darkest premonition came true: he was shot dead outside his apartment in central Belgrade by unidentified men in black; a mafia-style hit. Shortly beforehand he had been described as a 'national traitor' in the state media, which accused him of supporting the bombing campaign against his own country. During wartime, this was seen as a licence to kill. The government, it appeared, was using the cover of war to silence its enemies at home. Other independent journalists left the capital, and didn't return until the 78 days of bombing were over. The only people who dared to defy the government were a group of women who staged a demonstration demanding that their soldier sons be brought home.

The war ended when Milošević, faced with the crushing power of the world's most formidable military machine, capitulated and agreed to pull his forces out of Kosovo. The bombing had left hundreds dead but failed to resolve the conflict – now Serbs, rather than ethnic Albanians, began to flee the province. The opposition, too, was devastated; Milošević, the wartime leader, was the only figure left on the national stage. Defeated, yet again, but triumphant. State television declared a heroic victory.

But a few weeks after the bombing ended, Ivan Marović was on the road. Using contacts from the student protests of 1996–97, he was attempting to recruit activists who would set up new Otpor cells all across Serbia. The network already existed, it just needed reawakening from its long hibernation. This was the new plan – turn Otpor into a nationwide movement. 'We were looking for any pockets of resistance to Milošević,' says Marović. Because something strange had started to happen in provincial Serbia, where poverty was endemic, factories had been destroyed by the bombing and soldiers were returning, traumatised, from Kosovo. People were frustrated, depressed and angry, and Milošević's glorious triumph over the Western aggressors had brought them no relief. Thousands began to demonstrate in Čačak, Užice, Novi Sad; in the small southern town of Leskovac, a tape editor at a local television station interrupted the transmission of an international basketball game to air his own statement, listing the government's offences against the people and urging them to take to the streets. Twenty thousand responded – more than a quarter of the town's population. These were the kind of people that Marović was looking for.

Otpor moved into an apartment owned by one of the parents of its activists on Knez Mihailova, Belgrade's showpiece shopping thoroughfare, and embarked on a rolling programme of pranks and stunts. Activists 'celebrated' Milošević's birthday with a papier mâché cake made up of the pieces representing the countries which had once been part of united Yugoslavia; they marked the eclipse of the sun with an event predicting the eclipse of the president; they placed a barrel in the street with a picture of Milošević on it, offering anyone who dropped a coin into the barrel the right to batter away at their leader's face with a baseball bat. It was a pure energy release. 'In 15 minutes there were a hundred people in Knez Mihailova street, beating the barrel,' recalls Srdja Popović. 'They were so happy! The police didn't know what to do. They called the station once, twice… at the end, we left the barrel on the street, and they didn't know who to arrest – so they arrested the barrel! And they were photographed doing it and they were in the newspapers the next day. The whole country laughed.'

Milošević had launched a grand post-war reconstruction campaign, with medals for loyal citizens and military heroes. News broadcasts featured smiling workers laying bricks and digging foundations, overseen by beneficent officials who were building a new model country. It was a peculiar altered state of Serbia that few recognised. In the northern city of Novi Sad, where a vital bridge over the Danube had been destroyed by NATO's bombs, great show was made of the building of a new but somewhat makeshift pontoon. The Novi Sad branch of Otpor responded by building its own toy bridge in a city-centre park. If the authorities intervened to stop what was no more than a satirical joke, they would appear to be overreacting. If they didn't, they would show that it was possible to mock the president and get away with it. Either way, they lost. 'It all looks silly from this perspective,' says Ivan Marović, 'but at that time, just after the bombing, we needed something that would be easy enough for people not to be afraid, and to decrease the level of fear.'

There were more serious actions, too; a demonstration outside a military court which was hearing hundreds of cases against young men who had refused to be drafted into the army. 'We got our activists who had served in the army to go outside the court and protest because we thought that is the real message: we are not divided between who went to the army and who didn't, because we respect each other,' says Milja Jovanović. 'That slapped the face of the regime, because after the war they divided the nation between those who supported them and are patriots and those who did not support them and are traitors.'

Otpor reached far beyond politics for its inspiration. It drew influence from the English absurdism of *Monty Python's Flying Circus*, and from the language and attitude of rock music, using culture as a weapon. 'It gave us this huge freedom to express ourselves,' says Jovanović, a committed alternative rock fan who invariably dressed in black. The Otpor soundtrack, she says, was raucous agit-pop and rap, the serrated riffs of Rage Against The Machine, Body Count and Fear Factory – never the folk music which had become identified with the nationalist sentiments of the Milošević years.

There were concerts with Serbian rock bands like Darkwood Dub and Eyesburn – the sound of the dissident underground; musicians whose songs contained the same anger, disillusionment, thwarted hope and defiance which drove Otpor – while clenched-fist T-shirts started appearing on statues of famous Serbs, scientists like Nikola Tesla and writers like Vuk Karadzić. 'We were acting like a performance group, but with a political message,' says Jovanović. The authorities saw it differently. A statement issued by the United Yugoslav Left, the party led by Milošević's wife, described them as 'delinquents, neglected adolescents, a certain number of persons with endocrinological illnesses'. 'They do not enjoy the respect of the people, they fled the country during the bombing, their family reputation is disreputable, they are suspected of having a weakness towards the same sex,' the statement continued. 'They are known as the allies of the murderers of their own people.'[7]

The hysterical tone of the statement showed that Otpor was becoming increasingly influential. In November 1999, the movement organised its first major rally and stated its demands: free elections and a united opposition. At the time, neither seemed likely. A week later, Otpor rallied again. This time the police hit back with force, and running battles broke out on the streets of Belgrade. 'After that, we didn't organise another rally, even though after we clashed with the police, everyone was yelling, "Tomorrow, tomorrow!" But we said no, because we'd learned another lesson from 1996 – if we do it every day, people will get exhausted in a short while,' says Ivan Marović. 'Also, it's better to show up in a different place in a different way than to always give them the same thing so they know how to deal with you.'

NATO might have defeated Milošević, but he remained in power, with a stronger grip on the media, an opposition in disarray and an enemy upon which to blame all the country's troubles. But what he had lost was the belief amongst Western governments that he could ever be part of the answer to Yugoslavia's problems. 'The bombing in a way stopped the hypocrisy of the international community,' says Milja Jovanović. 'Afterwards it was more obvious than ever before that Milošević was isolated. There was nothing more to talk to him about. So the political stage had changed, the doors were more open to new ideas because they finally realised they should look for another solution. That's when serious talks with the opposition began, in terms of the West seeing them as the next partner.'

It was around this time that Otpor began to attract significant financial support from Western democracy foundations. They had already been helped by the Yugoslav branch of the Open Society Institute, the global democracy and human-rights campaign network founded by the billionaire financier George Soros. The head of Soros's Belgrade office, Sonja Licht – herself a veteran of the Yugoslav student movement of 1968 – believed that Otpor had a freshness and a passion which she hoped could transform the political scene. 'They appealed to people who didn't trust the political parties,' Licht says. 'They were a kind of catalyst, they created a framework which everyone who was against the regime could be part of. It was a new form of struggle which was much more genuine and focused.

'They were also ideologically very vague, so people of different beliefs could join, from monarchists to genuine leftists who understood that Milošević had made a mockery and a perversion of any left-wing idea. They were also advocating non-violence, which was very important because people were very sick of all the violent acts and violent speech here. Their timing was right, too.'

Slobodan Homen, who dealt with what he refers to as 'international relations' for Otpor, says that Western governments – the United States in particular – had finally decided that Milošević was a cancer which must be removed. They thought that Otpor could help them do the job. And yet many months earlier, when Otpor was founded, they had not been interested: 'We addressed the USA mission in Belgrade, asking them for some $200 to print some posters with Milošević's face on them, I don't know what the message was, but they told us they couldn't fund such a campaign that was directly involved with politics,' Homen recalls. 'One year later, they just asked us, "What do you need? We'll give you anything."'

The first American group to back them was the International Republican Institute, a Washington DC-based organisation linked to the Republican Party and funded by the US government, which describes itself as 'dedicated to advancing democracy worldwide' and 'guided by the fundamental American principles of individual liberty, the rule of law and the entrepreneurial spirit' – one of several US organisations which promote American values overseas by giving money to those whose causes they support.[8] The IRI also made contacts for Otpor within the US State Department. Homen spent a lot of time travelling – to Washington, Brussels, London and Budapest, where many of the Western embassies which had pulled out of Yugoslavia were based, explaining Otpor's mission and hustling up support. 'We started to receive international assistance, first from the United States and then from other countries in Europe,' says Homen. 'They were desperate for some kind of internal movement that was pro-democratic, that wanted changes and wasn't nationalistic. That was one of the greatest successes of Otpor, we showed the international community there are people here who want a normal life in a normal country.'

Some of the Americans initially expressed worries that the white clenched-fist logo resembled some kind of 'fascist' symbol. But the State Department's Special Balkans Envoy, James O'Brien, says US officials had no doubts about Otpor's potential: 'They made clear they wanted to be seen as a largely Serbian, Yugoslav institution, not as a tool of the West, and we respected that, we thought that was a smart judgement. So from the beginning we saw in Otpor a degree of enthusiasm and talent, just a kind of political sense that was really encouraging and deserved our support however we could offer it.'[9]

Otpor insisted that the international foundations which supported them didn't dictate their agenda, but simply enabled them to extend their reach deeper into Serbia: more propaganda material, more T-shirts and stickers with the sign of the fist, more spray paint to decorate the walls of police stations and governing party offices. Some of those who gave the money take the same line; Sonja Licht says the Open Society Institute had 'complete respect' for Otpor's independence: 'We didn't have any influence over their actions. I'm very firm about this.' Djordje Todorović, a Serb who worked for the Belgrade branch of the International Republican Institute at the time, says it was all a matter of logistics and back-up: 'What we did was support their creativity, so we gave them training, we connected them with the right people for advice to use in the field, but it was them who did the work and without them nothing would have happened.'

Ivan Marović says he is no great admirer of US foreign policy – his country had, after all, just felt the wrath of America's bombers – but on the subject of Milošević, Otpor's interests coincided with those of Washington. It was an alliance of necessity, for both sides; there was no way that the US was going to invade Yugoslavia and depose Milošević, nor would the opposition have wanted it. Otpor would later be accused of conspiring to undermine a sovereign government so its nationalised industries could be carved up by rapacious global corporations; of being covert agitators for free-market capitalism. But Marović, who has heard such theories many times over, laughs outright at suggestions that Otpor was dreamed up in some underground bunker by Uncle Sam's spooks. 'One thing that's certain is that we weren't created from outside,' he says. 'Anyone who knows what was going on in Serbia in 1996 [the year of the student protests] knows we were created then. That was our school – it wasn't Langley [CIA headquarters].'

Djordje Todorović of the International Republican Institute says that the country was facing a simple choice: progress or oblivion. They needed any allies they could find. 'What was our perspective? We were ruled by people who were getting richer and richer every day and had a very good relationship with Saddam Hussein's regime, with North Korea and with China. Excuse me, if I have to make a choice, my choice is Washington rather than these people,' he says. The IRI trained thousands of Serbian activists in campaign strategies, not just Otpor, as it tried to prepare the ground for a popular anti-Milošević movement, Todorović explains: 'Yes, the IRI supported these guys, and I am proud to have been a part of this effort to assist my country to become democratic and a member of the international community. But there was no conspiracy. There were some interests involved, the United States as well as European countries had an interest in ousting Milošević. But Milošević was a threat to the region and he was a threat to the Serbs. It was him or us, and whoever assisted was helpful.'

Otpor's leaders say they only had one goal: to get rid of Milošević and replace him with a genuine democracy. There was no plan for what would happen afterwards. Regime change aside, Otpor took no overt political positions, particularly on the highly-charged and divisive issue of Kosovo. Adopting any defined ideological stance could drive away potential recruits who didn't agree with it. Within the movement were conservatives, social democrats, even nationalists and anarchists. Anyone who supported the mission could participate. 'I'm a left-wing democrat, but in Otpor I could be friends and colleagues with a guy with different political beliefs,' explains one young activist. 'What we had in common was the idea that what was going on in the country – the NATO bombardment, the wars, the inflation, the devastated social climate – was wrong and it was Milošević's fault.'

But almost inevitably, there were divisions which turned some people away. A few prioritised their commitment to political parties while others despised them, says Milja Jovanović, and the left quarrelled with the right. 'The differences between left and right in Serbia mostly define what you think about things like Kosovo, women's rights, gay rights, Albanian rights. There were people who were extreme on both sides,' she says. There were also differences over religion, says Jovanović; some prized their Orthodox faith, others were agnostic, and those who were religious tended to espouse more 'traditional' social values: 'In the main body of us who were making decisions, there were such big differences that I don't know how it functioned at all.' But it did, somehow, and as 1999 ended, Otpor began to prepare for its ultimate challenge.

AN ODD COUPLE AND A TRADITIONAL INSULT

'At the beginning of 2000,' remembers Dejan Randjić, 'we said, *this is the year*.' It began with a cold, cruel shock of awakening. Otpor had advertised an event to celebrate Orthodox New Year's Eve in Belgrade's Republic Square. Thousands of people gathered in anticipation, expecting rabble-rousing rock 'n' roll and a wild party sprawling into the early hours: noise, drink, revelry... But at midnight, the loudspeakers fell quiet and a sombre film depicting the disasters and atrocities of the Milošević years began to play on a large screen, while a hidden narrator – a friendly politician called Boris Tadić – read out the names of those killed in Milošević's wars. Then he announced: You have no reason to celebrate the new millennium. Nothing has changed for the better, it is only getting worse. There is nothing to celebrate here. *Go home...*

...and then there was only darkness and silence. The crowd dispersed, stunned and confused.

'We could easily have organised a concert and let people have fun,' says Ivan Marović. 'But we wanted it to be really brutal, like the truth can be. It was the big turning point. Up to then we were doing these silly actions; New Year's Eve was the first serious thing. [Satirical rock singer] Rambo Amadeus is the craziest guy around, but when we told him what we going to do, he said, "My God, I thought I was nuts. You're even worse than me!"

'Up to that time we hadn't been noticed by Milošević. After New Year's Eve, he noticed us. Immediately after that, the first real attacks from state media started coming. We realised it had hit him hard. It had provoked something. This was when we became serious, and when he became serious. This was when the arrests started on a larger scale.'

Otpor began a series of audacious attempts to usurp the symbols of Milošević's power. It organised its first national congress on the same day as the governing Socialist Party held its own annual showpiece convention. The students were holding up a mirror to the authorities, daring them to react. The Otpor event was an impressive piece of political theatre; a parody of a totalitarian rally. The pre-war Yugoslav anthem played as Ivan Marović, with a severe military haircut and a heavy greatcoat, strode to the centre of the stage to address the congress, flanked by ranks of youths with their fists raised in unison, wearing identical black T-shirts bearing the words '*To Victory*'. A 'spider's web of resistance' was encircling Serbia, Marović announced. He listed the towns and cities where Otpor was now active – Niš, Pirot, Vranje, Pančevo, Smederevo, Novi Sad… from the north to the south, the east to the west, the list went on… This was no longer just a student group, he declared, but a *people's movement*.

On the first anniversary of the NATO bombing, while the government celebrated its momentous victory over the Western aggressors with triumphalist speeches and concerts of patriotic folk song, Otpor staged its first nationwide action. Thousands of posters went up in towns and cities across Serbia, as the 'spider's web' revealed itself. 'The NATO action was very important for Milošević in gathering the people around him, blaming the Americans and the opposition for everything, it was a huge pillar of his propaganda,' says Srdja Popović. 'We wanted to take it over from him, to withdraw that pillar and say, "We are celebrating this date, not you, this date is ours, this country was bombed because of you, and even after the bombing you never learned your lesson."'

The slogan was 'Resist the aggression'. 'It had a double meaning, you could read it however you wanted – resist NATO aggression, or resist the aggression towards the free media and students and people who want to speak out,' explains Popović. 'We put people on the streets and they took the bait; they arrested 67 people in 13 cities.'

Otpor then decided to target May Day, the traditional Communist show of strength, which for years had been a symbolic display of institutional celebration. Milošević's Socialist Party intended to mark the event in the industrial town of Kragujevac, the home of the Yugo car and the NATO-blasted Zastava manufacturing complex. Otpor was there too. They staged a rally in the town's main square, and in the place where Tito's portrait used to hang, they placed a giant clenched fist. 'People usually go to this May Day event whoever organises it, so lots came from nearby cities, towns and villages, and what they got was Otpor's rally,' says Popović. 'Again, we were taking over the symbols of state ideology.' Afterwards, this time, they gave the crowd some entertainment too; a music festival, a kind of provincial Serbian Woodstock which rocked the town into the night.

While Otpor had arrived intuitively at the idea of turning the government's strength against it, others had been studying the concept of 'political jiu-jitsu' for decades. Gene Sharp was an American academic who had been researching the techniques of non-violent resistance since the 1950s. He had seen his strategic advice at work – he advised people in the Baltic states of Estonia, Latvia and Lithuania during their fight for independence from the Soviet Union – and had witnessed what happened when a merciless state struck back: he was in Beijing in 1989 when Chinese soldiers opened fire on Tiananmen Square, killing hundreds of demonstrators.

Sharp's best-known work, From Dictatorship to Democracy, lists 198 methods of peaceful resistance to repressive governments, from pickets, strikes and sit-ins to 'protest disrobings' and 'rude gestures'. It was originally produced for activists working to subvert the military government in Burma, and has since been translated into more than 30 languages. Sharp, who looks more like an affable old professor than a revolutionary hothead, traces the ancestry of his ideas back to the beginning of the twentieth century, taking in the overthrow of Ferdinand Marcos in the Philippines, the American farmworkers' strikes and civil rights campaigns of the 1960s, resistance to Nazi occupation in Europe and Gandhi's struggle against British imperial rule in India. He counsels that in any campaign for democracy, there will be casualties, but if the resistance takes up weapons, the state arsenal is likely to prevail. 'If you have a ruthless dictatorship, you expect them at some point to do something catastrophic. That's the nature of those regimes,' he explains. 'But the casualties, catastrophic as they are, are not usually comparable to the casualties you get in a comparable violent uprising and the repression that attracts. Compare what happened in Estonia, Latvia and Lithuania to what's happened in Chechnya. It doesn't mean you say, "OK, we don't resist at all", because if people passively submit, they may also be slaughtered, just as an example to the rest of the population to behave themselves. You have to plan accordingly and continue the resistance.'

Otpor's leaders were introduced to Sharp's ideas in unusual circumstances. Some of their 'American friends' – the International Republican Institute – organised a series of seminars for Serbian opposition figures, across the Hungarian border in Budapest, in the sedate luxury of the Hilton Hotel; a bizarre venue for a revolutionary summit. 'It was funny because you had all these American tourists there, then a bunch of Otpor kids running around in punk T-shirts,' says one observer who was working for the IRI at the time.

Gene Sharp's leading acolyte, a retired US Army colonel called Robert Helvey, gave one of the keynote lectures. Helvey had served in Vietnam and later as an American defence attaché in Burma, where he had assisted the opposition to the trigger-happy military government. When he returned to the US, the army sent him to Harvard University, where he attended one of Sharp's lectures to find out what the 'troublemakers' had to say for themselves. He liked what he heard.

'Having been in combat myself, I wouldn't want my children or anybody else's children to go through it,' Helvey says. 'The collateral damage in warfare today makes you cringe, because an awful lot of civilians are being killed and there's no way you can get around that any more. So we have to have to find alternatives to reduce the number of deaths.

'I got a sense of that in Burma because I knew the military was in such tight control and they had such overwhelming superiority that an uprising in the traditional sense was going to be squashed. They showed no qualms in 1988 about killing thousands of people in one day. It was obvious that somebody needed to do some thinking about an alternative.'

Helvey went on to become the president of Sharp's Albert Einstein Institution, a small research and advisory group which promotes the tactics of non-violent resistance all over the world. He didn't, however, become a pacifist. 'Hell no,' he says. 'I think that there are realistic alternatives to armed struggle. And I think in many cases if people adopt a non-violent struggle, they won't suffer the humiliation of a military defeat which is almost certain when you have a dictatorship. Also the democracy they get is *theirs*, they fought for it, and I think they place an extra value on it.'

Ultimately, Helvey says, peaceful resistance *is* a form of warfare, but without firearms. 'It is a conflict for power, the same way armed conflicts are, but you're using different weapons systems. You're using the people, bringing them together to act collectively.'

At the Budapest Hilton, Helvey lectured the Otpor activists about the importance of strategic planning in undermining authoritarian governments. Their dynamism and thirst for knowledge impressed him – although at first he didn't think they were being entirely honest. 'They tried to bullshit me,' he recalls. 'I asked them about their leadership and they came up with this stuff, "Well, you know, we just don't have leaders." I said, "Wait a minute, guys, I didn't fall off the turnip truck yesterday, you know. You've got a nationwide movement, you're getting supplies in, you're getting material printed and distributed, and you tell me you don't know anything about it..."

'I could tell that what I was saying was what they were looking for. They already had a movement going but they had run into a wall and they couldn't move it forward any more than they had, and that wasn't going to be enough. So I was able to help them identify some of their problems. They needed to reassess the sources of power in the society, they had not focused enough on the legitimacy of the government and how to undermine it. They needed to identify the pillars of support – the military, the police, the education system and so on – and find out where they were most vulnerable, then design their propaganda and campaigns towards targeting them.'

None of this was, as it was sometimes portrayed later, covert intelligence-service instruction – Sharp and Helvey's ideas are out in the open, in commercially published books which are available for anyone to read. 'It wasn't spy training,' laughs Milja Jovanović. 'Some of the things that have been written about this are absurd, it sounds like some kind of military course, jumping over barbed wire or something.'

And yet a weird mystique has built up around this odd couple, the academic and the old soldier, travelling the world, fomenting unrest. 'That's nonsense, just nonsense,' says Sharp. Helvey is even more forthright: 'It's bullshit.' Neither, he says, is he a cheerleader for US government policy: 'I don't work for the government and I'm not affiliated with any right-wing group at all. I'm just a guy who thinks that people ought to have the opportunity to liberate themselves.' He is bemused at those who think he's some kind of postmodern spook. 'Maybe they've got this anti-military bias – "how in the world could a military guy even think about supporting pro-democracy groups?" Or maybe it's just a general anti-American attitude.'

For some of the Otpor activists, Sharp and Helvey's advice was all but irrelevant. 'They gave us some ideas that were useful, but *come on*, this was in 2000, we were more than active at that time. Of course, later their role was said to be very important, but that's not true,' says Slobodan Homen, dismissively. But for others, Helvey's cool analysis of state structures and how to bring them tumbling down made a powerful impact. These would be the tools of their trade – the heavy artillery of the non-violent revolutionary.

'It's an impressive feeling if you're working on something for years and then you find that knowledge condensed in one place,' says Srdja Popović.

For Popović, this was the moment of revelation; the key to something greater. Helvey and Sharp offered not only a practical framework, but a sense of Otpor's place in history, fixing the movement in a high moral lineage which stretched back through Vaclav Havel and Lech Walesa to Martin Luther King and Gandhi. Sharp's writing had already been published in a small-run Serbian edition. Now his methods were incorporated into Otpor's campaign manual, which was distributed to new recruits. His theories, says Popović, were probably repeated to newcomers 'three or four thousand times' (although some leading activists were equally happy to quote relevant phrases from the writings of Lenin when it suited them). One journalist pictured Popović scurrying around Belgrade with a heavily-underlined copy of Sharp's tract stuffed in his pocket; it was not such a far-fetched image.

But Otpor's contacts with the Americans came at a price, laying the young Serbs open to renewed accusations that they were working for foreign powers. The secretary-general of Milošević's Socialist Party, Gorica Gajević, declared that Otpor was spreading 'fear and chaos' on behalf of its masters abroad: 'They want to set Serbia on fire; they are attempting to topple the authorities with violence, to provoke street unrest, to incite a civil war.' The government would deal with the students 'just as it has dealt with every other evil', she promised.[10]

Yugoslav dissidents had long been denounced as tools of Western imperialist aggressors. 'It's an old thing, being accused of being a CIA agent, from Communist times,' says Ivan Marović. 'It's a traditional insult.' But now the authorities were on the offensive. Posters appeared on the walls of buildings in Belgrade, describing Otpor members as 'Madeleine Youth' – the regimented drones of Madeleine Albright, the US Secretary of State who had recently made it clear that she saw no future for President Milošević – and showing the Otpor fist grasping a bunch of dollar bills. 'We thought this was so stupid, you know – everyone here wanted to have a fistful of dollars,' says Milja Jovanović. 'They weren't doing themselves any favours.'

Nevertheless, Otpor took it seriously enough to attempt to counteract the propaganda with a new campaign slogan: *Resistance – Because I Love Serbia*. They were attempting to define another kind of patriotism based on democratic values rather than ethnic chauvinism. But while they were wary about discussing the help they received from their 'foreign friends' at the time, many of Otpor's leading activists were willing to admit later that they – just like the opposition parties and the independent media – couldn't have had the same impact without assistance from abroad.

'Cultivating foreign support is always important for non-violent movements, because if the foreign community supports your adversary, you have one enemy more,' says Srdja Popović. 'You need foreign support, whether it is in terms of sanctions or material support for your movement. It's a hypothetical question because the eye of the international community is already on every undemocratic regime in the world, even through the smallest United Nations attempts to protect the victims of torture. In the modern world it's impossible to have this theoretical situation where the people rise against the dictator alone. CNN is everywhere, Human Rights Watch is everywhere – you need to use those tools to help your struggle and harm your opponent.'

THE SHERIFF WIELDS THE CHAINSAW

Požarevac is a small, dusty town of around 50,000 people, an hour's drive south-east of Belgrade. Its tatty 1970s architecture, cracked pavements and potholed roads mark it out as a typically unremarkable Serbian provincial settlement. But Požarevac was also the home town of Slobodan Milošević and his wife, Mira Marković, although there were no grand statues of him here; no signs of a cult of personality. Unlike many authoritarian leaders, who often make ostentatious displays of loyalty to their heartland, there were no indications that he had diverted state wealth to beautify its drab municipal offices or parks. Even Milošević's relatively humble family compound, a squat building nestling behind metal gates in a nondescript side street, would hardly have been noticeable if it hadn't been for the guard dogs and closed-circuit television cameras.

The only monument to the Milošević family's roots in Požarevac was the Bambipark amusement complex, which was opened by their son, Marko, during the NATO bombardment. But Bambipark, with its skateboard ramps, little football pitches and climbing frames, was a rather tawdry and ramshackle attraction; hardly the 'Serbian Disneyland' of some descriptions. Nevertheless, Marko was the dominant force in Požarevac; unlike his parents, he made his presence felt. As a teenager, he had raced (and sometimes crashed) expensive sports cars around the town, before establishing a network of small businesses – a café, an internet company, a cellphone shop and the town's biggest dance club, Madona. He had also become one of the main players in Serbia's lucrative cigarette- and petrol-smuggling business while the country was under economic sanctions imposed by the United Nations during the Bosnian war. By this time, young Marko had styled himself in Formula One playboy image – designer clothes, bleached-blonde hair and expensive sunglasses – and had developed the swaggering arrogance of the wealthy small-town bully who knows that his father runs the country and that no law can restrain him. 'He was like the sheriff of the town – he controlled everything,' says Milorad Tadić, who ran the local independent radio station, Boom 93. Another Požarevac local puts it more starkly: 'He had absolute power here, and he liked to use it.'

Boom 93 was a constant irritant to young Marko, who believed that it insulted and slandered his beloved parents. Whenever there was a crackdown on the independent media, the Požarevac station, which never managed to get a licence to broadcast legally, was one of the first to be taken off the airwaves. During the protests of 1996–97, Marko had burst into the Boom 93 studios and threatened Tadić with a gun, saying he would kill him because of what the station was saying about his father.

In March 2000, Boom 93 was banned again. This time it would not return to broadcasting for many months. Some of its younger staff had started an Otpor cell, a far more risky enterprise in the claustrophobic environment of little Požarevac, where it was almost impossible to act anonymously, than in the capital. In direct challenge to the playboy sheriff, the first clenched-fist symbol was spray-painted on Marko's Cybernet shop. Marko's friends, showy young toughs, began asking around, trying to find out who was responsible. 'They went mad because they thought they had a cancer in their town,' says Tadić. 'They wanted to find anyone who was involved with Otpor. They would drive around town at night, trying to find guys spraying fists. It was not safe here.'

They decided that a young man called Zoran Milovanović was responsible, and coerced him into going to Marko's Madona club, where they demanded that he tell them who was running Otpor, and set about him with batons and pistols. Then, Milovanović told journalists, Marko brought out a chainsaw: 'He said, "What's up you traitor? You scumbag. You will not be the last one or the first one that I have cut up and thrown in the Morava river." Marko put the saw near my head and turned it on. It lasted for several seconds. Then he turned it off and put it on the bar. Marko told his guys to take me away and deal with me promptly. I started crying.'[11]

The day after Otpor's May Day stunt, Marko's Požarevac cronies enticed another Otpor activist to one of their cafés. When he arrived, he was told: 'You've come to the ninth circle of hell.' As two of his friends arrived to stage a rescue attempt, Marko drove up in a BMW, brandishing a gun and screaming, 'Kill the scum!' A fight broke out and the Otpor activists were ruthlessly battered. A photograph taken shortly afterwards shows one of them, Momčilo Veljković, with a deep head wound gaping red through his thick furze of dark hair. The others' faces were streaked with blood, their noses broken. 'After the hospital, the police took me straight to jail and my friends to the hospital of the central prison in Belgrade,' says Veljković. 'We were charged with attempted murder.' A police statement described them as fascist hooligans who had attacked a group of respectable citizens, and an opposition rally to protest against the arrests was blocked by officers who set up checkpoints to prevent busloads of demonstrators from reaching the town. But they could not prevent new posters going up all over the country, showing one of the Požarevac activists' wounded features and the words: 'The Face of Serbia.'

WE HAVE A WONDERFUL DENTIST HERE

During the war years, the connections between business, organised crime and politics – between arms dealers, militia leaders, gangland bosses, sanctions-busters and those whose political interests they served – had become so intimate that the line between the establishment and the underworld in Serbia was almost completely blurred. In the year after the NATO bombing, territorial battles and internecine disputes amongst Serbia's criminal elite led to a series of high-profile killings. Paramilitary commanders like Željko Ražnatović – the notorious Arkan – and politicians like the defence minister, Pavle Bulatović, were shot dead in what appeared to be ruthless contract hits. A few days after the events in Požarevac, the head of the provincial government in the northern Vojvodina region, Boško Perošević, was murdered at a trade fair in the city of Novi Sad. A suspect was detained, and police said they had found Otpor propaganda and 'brochures on terrorism' at his home, along with the phone number of a US official. 'This was not the work of a single maniac, but an organised murder with a deep political background,' announced the Serbian information minister, Goran Matić. He blamed Otpor for the killing: 'The time of their street actions is over,' he said.[12]

Although the 50-year-old gunman had no links to the students, a warrant was immediately issued for the arrest of Otpor's main organisers in Novi Sad, Miloš Gagić and Stanko Lazendić, in connection with the murder. But they couldn't be found. Both of them had left the country for neighbouring Bosnia a few weeks before the killing, after enduring an insidious campaign of harassment.

'Milošević's people knew who the leaders of Otpor were here,' says Gagić. 'They knew all the material was coming through us. So they started threatening our families, they told us they'd put us in underground cells and never let us out, or shoot us in the head.

There were calls in the middle of the night to my mother with voices saying that right at that moment I was being raped by two men in prison. We just couldn't take any more, so we decided to let other people take over for a month until it all blew over.'

After the murder of Perošević, news of the manhunt filtered through to Gagić in Bosnia. 'I'd never met the man and I hadn't been to the place where he was shot,' he says. 'The state television coverage was very stagey but very convincing at the same time. The satanisation of us was so strong in the media that even people who knew us started wondering whether we were guilty.'

Gagić and Lazendić returned to Serbia a few months later, proclaiming their innocence and their intention to carry on campaigning. They were arrested, but most of the questions they were asked related to Otpor rather than the murder of Perosević, and the charges were ultimately dropped. Nevertheless, it was a warning that even provincial agitators could expect the harshest of treatment.

While attacks on Otpor increased, the authorities moved to destroy another stronghold of the opposition – the independent media. Independent newspapers had been hit with mounting fines under the Information Law introduced the previous year, and on 17 May, under cover of darkness, armed police burst into the offices of Studio B television, confiscated equipment, and threw their staff out on to the street. Studio B was accused of stirring up violent insurrection, and its broadcasts were replaced by pro-government programming. There were angry protests in central Belgrade, but with the opposition parties still in disarray, the energy soon dissipated.

With the state media full of talk of spy cells and clandestine groups of heavily-armed traitors plotting new assassinations, the authorities announced that a new anti-terrorism law would be introduced – one that appeared to be directed at the opposition in general and Otpor in particular. At a televised press conference, the information minister declared that Otpor was a vicious criminal organisation in the tradition of the Red Brigades, the ultra-leftist Italian militant group which carried out a lengthy bombing campaign and murdered a number of Italian politicians. Such terrorists would be dealt with, the minister promised.

'At first we were being portrayed as we were in 1996 – as drug addicts who don't attend classes and get low grades,' says Ivan Marović. 'After New Year, the whole idea that we were "NATO infantry" started; they said NATO was continuing the same war by other means, using the youth. Then they started saying Otpor would use terrorist methods to destabilise the political and social system in Serbia, killing politicians and blowing up buildings.' Marović genuinely expected that they would soon be banned and jailed. 'We organised it so nobody went home alone,' he says. 'We were afraid.'

Slobodan Homen believes that it could have been worse. Homen looks like what he is, a soberly-suited, bespectacled, polite young lawyer, not a wild-eyed insurrectionary, although he says his family has a long tradition of dissent. But he believes that the government considered him and his friends so dangerous that they placed them on a list of troublemakers to be considered for elimination. While this cannot be proved, the fact that Homen thought it to be true is an indication of how tense and paranoid the situation had become.

At this point in the summer of 2000, Milošević still appeared to be unassailable, and anyone who questioned his power seemed certain to be crushed. In July, he moved to secure his rule deep into the future. The country's constitution was changed, allowing him to stand for another term as Yugoslav president. Shortly afterwards, he announced new presidential elections for 24 September, believing that, with the opposition on the run and the media emasculated, he was now virtually unchallengeable.

The United States had been urging the Serbian opposition to unite around a single presidential candidate for months. Opinion polls and focus groups had shown that of all the opposition leaders, only one had the mass appeal to beat Milošević in a presidential election race: Vojislav Koštunica, the leader of the Democratic Party of Serbia. Koštunica was a conservative nationalist with a measured, legalistic manner, who directed as much anger at the US and the international community as he did at the Milošević government. Many within the opposition disliked his views, and knew that serious difficulties lay ahead if he ever came to power. But he was the only candidate with the chance of winning; all the other party leaders were tainted by image problems accumulated over a decade of grubby Yugoslav politics.

Otpor had also been haranguing the 18 opposition parties which made up the fractious Democratic Opposition of Serbia coalition to work together. At a rally in April, Otpor's Vlada Pavlov had urged all the party leaders on the stage to hold up an Otpor flag and raise their fists. While some of them grasped it enthusiastically, others looked distinctly uncomfortable. Pavlov threatened that thousands of youths would demonstrate under the window of any one of them who betrayed the public by perpetuating their long-running internecine squabbles. He encouraged the crowd to chant Otpor's most profane slogan: 'Whoever betrays the unity is a cunt!'

'Thinking about it now, I'm not surprised they didn't really like us much because we were really cheeky towards them,' says Milja Jovanović. But for Ivan Marović, the relentless hectoring was justified by past experience: 'We had to pressure them to remain unified because we knew if we relied on their reason and common sense, nothing would happen, because they didn't have any reason and common sense.'

Some of Otpor's inner circle had close links with liberal opposition leaders like Zoran Djindjić and Goran Svilanović, who understood that any movement for change needed its rebel vanguard. But the more right-wing Koštunica was suspicious of the young upstarts, saying they relied on 'dubious funding' from the West. Most Otpor activists had little time for Koštunica either, but they recognised his candidacy was necessary for victory: this time, anyone but Slobo. Under pressure, the opposition parties finally announced that Koštunica would be the joint candidate.

Everything was starting to fall into place. By the end of the summer of 2000, Otpor would claim to have around 70,000 members in 80 towns. 'It's spreading,' one of its slogans asserted confidently. And the repression had begun to backfire; each new arrest, each fresh beating brought in new recruits, disgusted at what was happening to their college friends or schoolmates. They felt that their generation was under attack, and had decided that it was time to fight back. Some security service officials are believed to have been aware of this, and cautioned their superiors that Otpor was using the crackdown as a recruiting tool. They were ignored.

18-year-old indie rock fan and comic book aficionado Gavrilo Petrović joined up after he heard how Marko Milošević had menaced the Otpor activists in Požarevac. He walked into Otpor's Belgrade headquarters and was given a few hours of training: the message, the strategy of non-violence, the cellular structure, the use of humour as a weapon. Then he was sent out into the streets to distribute propaganda; a footsoldier of the resistance, one of many. 'I was at the office at 10 a.m. sharp, I would spend my whole day there, go home and maybe read a couple of pages before I passed out, then do it again,' he recalls. 'All of us flunked a year of whatever we were studying.

'We were the drones, we were the ones writing out press releases, handing out leaflets, we were the driving force, and none of us are known today. We are anonymous. We didn't know who was funding us and we didn't care. Was it Washington? Was it the [Serbian] Democratic Party? Whose concept was Otpor? We didn't care, we just knew it was something we could get involved in and help to bring down this beast.'

From the start, he saw Otpor as much more than a traditional political campaign: 'People in Otpor wanted Slobo out, sure. They wanted no more wars, no more death, an open state and a democratic system. But that also involves wanting to have a good band coming to play over here and not having to be ashamed of this country, or not having to go into the army if you don't want to.'

Petrović and his colleagues hung out together, drank beer together, smoked dope, listened to music, watched movies. They were comrades on a mission, bonded fast by youthful enthusiasm and an overwhelming sense of moral righteousness. 'It was a special thing,' he says. 'There was a sort of collective identity which always springs up in such groups and dissolves when the cause is over. There was so much kindness and camaraderie. If a person you held dear got arrested, you immediately stepped up to the officer and said,

"I'm an activist too, you should arrest me too." There was that kind of solidarity, and I have never seen anything like it before or after.'

They were younger than Otpor's founders, and had entered their teenage years when Yugoslavia was already beginning to disintegrate. 'We were too young to remember when different nations lived together [in Yugoslavia] and there was no problem between them,' he says. 'None of us was ever in the States or Britain or France. We knew about Europe from music and films. At this time, Yugoslavia was so isolated. But we considered ourselves citizens of the world – the *real* Serbs, what Serbs *should* be. We felt enlightened, liberated, we felt we could actually change things, we felt that every one of us as an individual mattered.'

Otpor had become a political youth cult, something that the smartest kids wanted to be part of; every day, keen-eyed teenagers in jeans and trainers – schoolchildren now, as well as students – would arrive at the office, demanding stickers and badges, anything with the clenched-fist logo on it. It had become a way of life for a generation which felt it was breaking with the past forever. 'We were a positive example to other countries, which was something Serbia hadn't created in a long time,' says Siniša Šikman. 'People all over the world thought we Serbs were people with beards and guns, with blood on our hands and knives between our teeth. I think we changed some of that thinking.'

The public face of the movement, for many people, was Branko Ilić. He was, says Gavrilo Petrović, 'the poster boy of Otpor'. Ilić looked like the consummate rebel with a cause, and the young activists saw him as their hero. The other Otpor leaders were from the class of 1996–97, they were mostly older and straighter, they had links to traditional politics, while Ilić was… the real thing. More than anyone else, it seemed, he *lived the resistance*. 'He represented all of us; he *was* one of us,' says Petrović. Ilić was effectively an outlaw; he'd been on the run from the police since he was accused of bombing a café in his home village. He moved from apartment to apartment, never staying anywhere too long for fear of capture. Back in the village, the police harassed his family, detained his father. He could do little to help them.

But Otpor was also recruiting other public figures who some civil rights campaigners found distasteful. Otpor activists insisted that anyone who wanted to remove Milošević was welcome. But some worried that they were collaborating with people who were part of the problem, not the solution; people who bore part of the responsibility for what had happened in Serbia over the past decade. The author and former Yugoslav president, Dobrica Ćosić – who many say was the intellectual force behind Milošević's dream of a 'Greater Serbia', the seedling of Yugoslavia's disintegration – was among those questionable figures who signed up. 'I hate Dobrica Ćosić but we wanted to use every possible situation to get some debate going,' explains Milja Jovanović. 'We wanted people to focus on the main thing, which is to be anti-Milošević. We knew Dobrica Ćosić meant a lot to a lot of people. It was just something we did to make them understand we were not traitors. We were just plainly using him.'

It wasn't to be the last incongruous connection during the summer of 2000. One day, Jovanović spotted the former Bosnian Serb commander and war crimes suspect, General Ratko Mladić, in the street outside Otpor's Belgrade office. She went up to him immediately. 'He was with a group of bodyguards, we really wanted to provoke him, we tried to give him a T-shirt but he wouldn't take it,' she says. 'He was trying to be nice, you know, he said, "I like all Serbian children."' Mladić had already demonstrated his feelings about the children of other ethnic backgrounds at Sarajevo and at Srebrenica.

Sensing that Otpor was gaining ground, the authorities stepped up the arrests, trying to shock the students into submission. By September 2000, more than a thousand Otpor activists had been taken in for what were called 'informative talks'; some of them were offered incentives to become informers. Of course, such heavy-handed policing was also to their advantage. Ivan Marović says that Otpor 'deliberately provoked the repression' – it was the best publicity that the movement could get. Once parents saw that children like theirs were being busted for wearing a T-shirt with a fist logo, and noticed that these neighbourhood youths were probably not clandestine agents of the CIA, they began to question Milošević, then turn against him. It was a sign of the president's growing insecurity, not his strength, says Marija Baralić: 'When he started pushing us hard, we knew he was already losing. Because why would he bother with us? We were just funny little students doing funny little things.' But, says Baralić, the arrests paid off: 'We were in the newspapers every day.'

It was all part of the plan – the Sharp-Helvey strategy: *use the media.* Otpor was a revolutionary movement with a press office and a website. Arrests were written up on huge sheets of paper on the wall of the Belgrade headquarters, press releases were hastily put together and sent off to the news agencies, and activists were summoned by mobile phone to demonstrate outside the police stations where the detainees were being interrogated. While the authorities made increasingly outrageous accusations, Otpor played a smart media game. Daily actions created a constant drip-feed of stories, complete with dramatic pictures of clean-cut teenagers being dragged off by burly officers: allegorical images of brutish insensitivity. All part of the plan: *show their ugly faces to the world.* Detained activists were told to repeat the same phrase upon their release, the words of the writer Jorge Luis Borges: 'Force is the last refuge of the weak.'

Otpor's leadership was now under constant surveillance. From files later released by the security services, it's clear that their mobile phone conversations and movements were monitored. They had already banished certain people from their inner circle, believing they could be police informers, although they could never be completely certain. 'Maybe we excluded the wrong people, we will never know,' says Nenad Konstantinović.

Those who remained simply had to believe in each other, and face the consequences. They had no other choice. 'In our circle, we had this deal that we should trust each other, no questions asked,' says Milja Jovanović. 'When somebody said he was going somewhere, I would never ask where, because I didn't need to know. He would just come back afterwards and say what the meeting was about and whether Otpor would benefit or not. Everything was on a need-to-know basis in case we were arrested at a critical point. But I knew that nobody was really co-operating with the police because the things that we did that were really risky – like going to meetings with officials in Budapest, or going to Montenegro for meetings with Americans and Europeans and donors – the police were never there.'

If Otpor's central core was detained, the engine of the movement could have been shut down. Once they had to escape through the window of a restaurant where they were meeting, with moments to spare before the police cars arrived. But it wasn't the regular force that they feared – many ordinary serving officers, by this time, had also had enough of the government – but Milošević's secret police, for whom there were few rules and fewer qualms, and who had more to lose if their leader was driven from office. 'Every now and then one of us would be kidnapped by the secret police,' says Ivan Marović. 'I was kidnapped three times. They would drive me somewhere in a car, then interrogate me. They would ask who were our leaders and who financed us. There were threats. Once I was told, "We have a wonderful dentist here, a real master who's going to pull out all your teeth."'

This was a very different game to the sophomore pranksterism of 1998 and 1999. Like Branko Ilić, some of the other leading activists only went home infrequently now, preferring to stay with friends, moving around, dodging the state's intrusive gaze. When they collected funds from donors, they went in rented cars. Their propaganda material, the stickers and posters, were hidden in various different places around Belgrade, in people's houses, in the offices of sympathetic political parties; only one person knew where of all of it was being kept. This wasn't paranoia, they told themselves, it was merely a sensible precaution. A group of football fans from Red Star Belgrade gave them devices to monitor police radio transmissions. There were other offers, too, from shadier characters, says Milja Jovanović: 'Every once in a while you would meet somebody and you wouldn't know who it was – CIA or [US] National Security – offering some kind of practical help like something to jam television signals. We always said no, thank you. We weren't that kind of people, that wasn't something we would do.'

HOW BRAVE ARE YOU?

As the summer of 2000 drew to an end, the election campaign was entering its final phase. Milošević said that a victory for the opposition – the running dogs of NATO imperalism – would lead to the destruction of Serbia's national identity. He promised freedom, reconstruction, higher living standards – the opposite of what he had brought to the country in recent years.

However, he was now facing the most powerful and sophisticated peaceful campaign for change ever mounted in the Balkans. The opposition parties, civil rights groups, independent media and trade unions were united as never before, and determined that, this time, they would not lose. Opinion polls showed the public were dissatisfied and wanted change. But they were also apathetic; many believed that whatever happened, Milošević would remain in power. If he didn't win, he would simply steal victory for himself, as he had in 1996. And so the campaign set out not just to motivate them, but convince them that what seemed impossible was now within reach.

A coalition of civil rights and campaign groups launched a joint programme called Exit 2000; although it remained unstated, it was clear whose exit was desired. It focused on those who felt utterly disconnected from the political process, who believed that voting was futile: youth, women, people living in rural villages. The country was flooded with propaganda; hundreds of thousands of leaflets, posters, T-shirts and baseball caps bearing slogans like 'Choose to change things' and 'There are more of us'. It was meticulous, relentless; the material was spread deep into the country by car, by bus, even by bicycle. The Centre for Free Elections and Democracy began a rigorous programme of training for thousands of election monitors to ensure that any fraud at the polls would be detected and exposed.

A nationwide rock 'n' roll tour brought a travelling festival of the resistance to the central squares and urban parks of 25 cities and towns across Serbia – the biggest musical roadshow of its kind in the country's history, featuring the most gifted players of the protest generation. Its slogan was 'Come to the line' – meaning 'Get out and vote'. 'That's the literal translation, but it's also city slang which says something like "How brave are you?"' says Dragan Ambrozić of Radio B92, who organised the tour alongside Otpor and the national independent media network, ANEM. 'We wanted to help people understand they could change the situation in which they lived, to make them believe that it was their responsibility to change things. That was the message in what the bands were singing. The authorities couldn't ban rock shows because there were no political parties or political messages involved, but they didn't understand the power of the messages coming from the bands.'

The overall slogan of the voter-mobilisation drive was 'Vreme je': *It's Time*. Its bright, urgent pop graphics looked more like adverts for Nike or MTV than political messages, and its logo showed a ticking clock: five minutes to midnight. Vreme je relied heavily on the work of polling research agencies and focus groups, but it was also influenced by a campaign to defeat the hardline right-wing prime minister of Slovakia, Vladimir Mečiar, two years previously. The Slovaks had also realised that the youth, if motivated, could be a decisive force. As part of a wider campaign called OK98, they had toured the country by bus, giving out T-shirts and spraying graffiti, staging street performances, rock gigs and raves under the banner *Rock Volieb*: 'Rock the Vote'. 'We did not try to appeal to young people with messages of responsibility or participation,' says one of its organisers, Marek Kapusta. 'Our goal was rather to appeal to the natural rebellious attitude of youth. We wanted to make voting cool, it was a way to "rock" the system.' It worked: 80 per cent of people under the age of 21 turned out to vote, and Mečiar was beaten.

In 2000, Kapusta brought what he had learned to Serbia, travelling the country with Otpor and helping to train its young activists in the run-up to the election. He says that one of the most important things was making them believe they were part of a dynamic movement which was gaining unstoppable momentum – creating a self-fulfilling myth. 'We were trying to spread optimism and hope that they could "make it" without spilling blood,' Kapusta recalls. 'This was one of their biggest fears.'

Now OK98 and Rock Volieb – in the form of Exit 2000 and Vreme je – would become the blueprints for the Serbs. This was a non-partisan campaign; it didn't mention Milošević or urge people to vote for the opposition parties. What was implicitly understood by everyone, however, was that if young people did come out to vote, most of them would not be backing Slobo for president.

It is difficult to estimate exactly how influential Otpor was; its limitless supply of photogenic images gave it a profile that less visually seductive campaign groups couldn't hope to equal. But was it a driving force, or did it simply supply the naive energy that the resistance needed? 'There is this optical illusion that Otpor was *the* campaign, but it was just one part,' says Pavol Demeš, who worked for a democracy foundation called the German Marshall Fund of the United States, and was involved as an adviser to both OK98 in Slovakia and Exit 2000 in Serbia. 'All the other NGOs which did other work are usually overlooked because of the oversimplification of the situation.'

The exact amount of money that the US, European governments and a whole range of pro-democracy and free-media foundations spent on direct and indirect activities to destabilise Milošević in 2000 is also unknown, but it certainly amounted to many millions of dollars. There were reports of nervous Serbs making frequent tourist trips to Hungary and returning with unusually heavy suitcases. The US pumped in money through USAID, the American government agency which promotes both democracy and US foreign policy objectives; through the National Endowment for Democracy, an independent but government-backed democracy-promotion organisation, and through the International Republican Institute. The *New York Times*, quoting officials from all three organisations, estimated that 'several million' dollars went to Otpor.[13]

The US established an office in neighbouring Hungary which supplied training and financial assistance to the Serbian opposition, civil rights groups and the independent media. Deposing Milošević, America's former regional partner, had now become a 'foreign policy objective'. 'Milošević was personal for [US secretary of state] Madeleine Albright,' said William Montgomery, who ran the operation from the Hungarian capital. 'She wanted him gone, and Otpor was ready to stand up to the regime with a vigour and in a way that others were not. Seldom has so much fire, energy, enthusiasm, money – everything – gone into anything as into Serbia in the months before Milošević went.'[14] What war had failed to accomplish would now be attempted using peaceful means. The resistance might have been Serbian, but unlike Milošević, it was not acting in isolation.

The countdown to the election was already under way in the city of Novi Sad, with a hundred-day free festival, also called Exit. On some nights there was live rock 'n' roll, on others there were plays, lectures, film screenings, DJs playing techno and house music. 'We wanted to take our underground culture which was connected with the student movement and the independent media, and put it on the front line,' says one of the organisers, an Otpor member called Dušan Kovačević. 'Their official culture was promoted by the state media and supported Milošević. It was turbo-folk singers like Ceca [the pop star wife of the paramilitary leader Arkan] who ran side by side with war politics. It was a lifestyle which embraced war criminals as heroes. It's hard to imagine the psychology of that era now. We felt we were in prison, we felt that any day there could be a new war. It was hard to predict anything. In those days, it was a political battle to the finish.'

Exit brought together the political dissidents and campus agitators with the non-aligned night-trippers of the subterranean club scene. It would, in years to come, become the most important rock festival in the Balkans; Serbia's answer to Glastonbury. 'Everyone gathered there to charge themselves up with positive energy,' Miloš Gagić remembers. 'It represented the true meaning of the word "exit" – an escape from the dark state of Milošević.'

It was Otpor, not the politicians, which would come up with the slogan that defined the election campaign. It emerged spontaneously; a group of activists were sitting around a café table, chatting, when one of them simply blurted it out: 'Gotov je.' *He's finished*. It was perfect. The defeat of Milošević was not just desirable – it was destined to happen. This time, they were an irresistible force. As day followed night, the just would prevail.

Otpor was involved in the Vreme je campaign, but it ran the parallel Gotov je offensive on its own. This was black propaganda; targeted negativity, hardcore political jiu-jitsu – turning the darkness against itself. Posters depicted an image of Milošević walking away into oblivion, with the date of the election and the slogan: *He's finished*. Milošević's own campaign posters were easily transformed into advertisements for the opposition; just slap on a cheap black-and-white sticker, right up next to the man's face: *He's finished*. On bridges and underpasses, lamp posts and bus stops, the words were repeated, over and again: *He's finished*. The opposition candidate, Koštunica – unloved by most activists – was never mentioned. 'There was only one candidate for us,' says Ivan Andrić. 'That was Slobodan Milošević, and he had to lose.'

Like the opposition, Otpor had also begun cultivating support amongst state institutions – what Gene Sharp would call the 'pillars of the regime' – giving flowers to policemen and sending packages of food and cigarettes to soldiers. Its activists were in no doubt about what they had to do. The analysis was in place: how many votes Milošević would win, how many he could falsify or steal, and how many were necessary to defeat him. The numbers were written up on a board at their Knez Mihailova headquarters, memorised and repeated constantly.

It seemed that Serbia was truly on the brink, and that Milošević was playing his final cards. As the campaign frenzy reached its peak, civil rights organisations were raided, independent journalists were harassed, and yet more Otpor youths were hauled in for yet more 'informative talks' with the police. In the southern town of Vladičin Han, two activists were hung upside down by their feet while drunken officers set about them with unrestrained savagery. The former president, Ivan Stambolić, went missing while jogging in a park in Belgrade. Onlookers reported that he was pushed into a white van by a group of unidentified men; his dead body would not be discovered for years. Stambolić had once been Milošević's mentor, but had been ousted during Milošević's rise to power in the late 1980s. He had recently returned to the political scene with scalding criticism of his former friend.

Police burst into Otpor's headquarters and seized all its files and computers – everything but the overflowing ashtrays. Activists gathered outside the office the following day and mocked the raid by walking around, groaning under the weight of what appeared to be heavy boxes of files and papers. The police rushed to seize the boxes, believing they were making another haul of vital intelligence – but found them to be completely empty. The Vreme je campaign offices were also raided and four leading activists were detained; one of them was chained to a radiator for eight hours and physically abused. 'They wanted to deliver a message that they were serious, that they could kill us all,' says Ivan Andrić, who was among those arrested. The insults were familiar: mercenaries, terrorists, traitors. But the questioning was mostly for show, says Andrić. The months of surveillance had already revealed Otpor's secrets: 'They more or less knew everything, they just wanted to scare us and show us they knew.'

By this time, the opposition was confident that it would win, but it was also certain that Milošević would rig the results to remain in power. Its strategy was to get the exit poll results – the *real* results, they believed – out quickly, then get people on to the streets to defend the victory. Branko Ilić spoke excitedly to journalists about what he called a 'war plan': a mass outbreak of civil disobedience. He promised chaos in Belgrade, a general strike, a boycott of state institutions, and then... *revolution!*

Not everyone was so optimistic. The prevailing worry was that the police and the army – or Milošević's special forces, the ones who did the worst of the killing in Bosnia and Kosovo – would move in to crush the uprising. 'The fear was there would be shooting and people would be killed,' says Milja Jovanović. 'But I think the message was really clear to the police. There was a very powerful article in [the news magazine] *Vreme*, aimed at the police. It said, "You did a lot of things, you arrested us, you harassed us, you were involved in political repression and war and the destruction of this country, you were involved with the mafia. But if you shoot people who're protecting their lawful votes, this will not be forgotten. Everything you've done fades compared to the choice you now have to make." It said what everyone was thinking.'

The results, when they came, were no surprise. The day after the election, the opposition announced the findings from its exit polls: Koštunica had won, taking 52 per cent of the votes. The turn-out was estimated to be the highest in recent Yugoslav history – particularly amongst young people. The campaign had worked, decisively. Thousands took to the streets of Belgrade in a mood of high excitement; mobile phones flashed text messages across the city, spreading the news. Supporters of Milošević organised a morale-boosting concert in the city centre, but only a hundred or so turned up.

But the electoral commission declared that Koštunica had only reached 48 per cent – two per cent short of the amount needed to win outright – meaning that there had to be a run-off poll with Milošević. It was a blatant falsfication, and as Branko Ilić had predicted, the strikes and the civil disobedience began. Miners at the huge Kolubara colliery complex walked out, threatening the possibility of power cuts. Cities were paralysed by blockades and demonstrations, while the opposition leaders toured the provinces, urging people to come to the capital for the final push. 'You could sense a community building in the days after the election, this common feeling building up,' says Milja Jovanović. 'The streets were stopped, the police were going out of their minds. You could feel the tension rising.' As some of his faithful supporters in the state media began to desert him, Milošević was under increasing pressure to step down, but it was unclear how he would react: would he go quietly, or would he try one last stand, backed by the physical force of whoever within the military establishment still supported him? Many still remembered the tanks on the streets back in 1991, when a previous mass demonstration had been put down.

The fading autocrat made a rare television appearance, warning that if he was desposed, foreign powers would dominate the country. The opposition leaders responded with a simple demand:

admit defeat by 3 p.m. on 5 October, or suffer the consequences. They had set the scene for the last act. If Milošević did not give in, they would force him out and seize power – by whatever means necessary.

Amongst Otpor's leaders, there was both excitement and apprehension. Although they hadn't been fully involved in the preparations for what would happen next – the opposition parties were now in total strategic control – they knew what they had to do. Some weren't certain that they would prevail; a few made preparations to flee the country if the day went against them. 'I had a flat rented that nobody knew about,' says Ivan Andrić. 'I had a passport there, a new mobile phone with a new phone card and the phone numbers of my contacts. I was supposed to go to Zaječar [in eastern Serbia], where a man would wait for me and take me to Bulgaria or Romania. I was supposed to go to western Europe afterwards. I had a visa, I had everything.' Others, like Miloš Gagić, simply trusted that Milošević would be ousted. 'If it didn't work, the only contingency plan was "meet you in the forest near Belgrade",' he laughs.

At dawn on 5 October, convoys of buses, cars and trucks from all over Serbia began heading for Belgrade, moving in five long columns. Some of the protesters had armed themselves with petrol bombs, clubs and stones, and leaders of the opposition coalition, DOS, had assembled 'task forces' of former policemen and soldiers. They had a plan, but it would run out of control in the hours ahead.

Miloš Gagić and his Otpor comrades were at the head of a line of vehicles heading south from Novi Sad. When they reached the edge of the city, they were halted by a police roadblock. Unknown to them, the police had been ordered to fire on the convoys; an order which was to be disobeyed. The protesters got out of their buses and simply pushed the policemen out of the road. The convoy rolled onwards towards Belgrade. 'If we'd stopped, we'd have deserved it if Slobo ruled the rest of our lives,' says Gagić. Other convoys also ran into roadblocks; here too the police simply withdrew in the face of greater numbers, or were forced aside, their vehicles heaved into ditches by the highway.

Thousands of Otpor activists converged on Belgrade University's philosophy faculty. Flags were handed out, along with handkerchiefs to protect against tear gas and buckets of water to douse fuming gas canisters. Urgent electronic beats blasted out from speakers mounted on a big truck; Branko Ilić yelled instructions through a megaphone. The swelling crowd of demonstrators – one at the wheel of a bulldozer – streamed towards parliament. 'Save Serbia – kill yourself, Slobodan,' they chanted. 'Gotov je!' Now there were to be no more pranks or play-acting, just grim determination. 'For me, personally, I went out to finish the job,' says one Otpor activist. Half a million other people in Belgrade that day had the same idea. This time they were organised, this time they were ready. It was now or never. *Milošević must fall.*

Riot police stationed around the parliament building on Revolution Boulevard fired tear-gas, but the protesters burst through the cordon and into the building, throwing petrol bombs and setting it ablaze. The police inside surrendered. The crowd then began to aim their Molotov cocktails at the headquarters of Radio-Television Serbia. The police responded with more tear gas, rubber bullets and a few live rounds, but they made little impact; the bulldozer crashed through the doors of the station and the staff fled in panic. The riot police began switching sides, deserting, or ripping off their uniforms and running for their lives. Milošević ordered the army to intervene; the order was ignored.

The mood became jubilant; after all these years, they were winning... 'It was like a movie – the parliament on fire, the sound system playing techno, people dancing in the streets, not knowing whether the army would move in... I think it was one of the craziest parties in the history of the world,' says Dušan Kovačević. The headquarters of the Socialist Party was ransacked; a perfume shop owned by Marko Milošević was trashed; a city-centre police station was gutted. The symbols of the past decade were being taken over, burned down, destroyed... by that evening, the Milošević government had effectively ceased to exist. The next day, he admitted defeat. Within a year, he was in a secure cell in The Hague, awaiting trial on war crimes charges. He would ultimately die there.

WE ARE WATCHING YOU

Otpor had one goal: the overthrow of Milošević. Its mission was accomplished. What next? For many activists, the answer was simple enough: go back to university and try to catch up on all those lost months of study. It had been the most exciting time of their young lives. Now it was finished. 'I felt deflated,' says Gavrilo Petrović. 'We had been struggling so much for this cause, then when it finally happened it was, "Great, we did it, but what are we going to do now?" We started to feel disorientated. The only thing we were fighting for was done.' A few days after the revolution, he decided it was time to leave. 'I just handed in the cellphone which they gave me, and said goodbye.'

The differences which had been submerged beneath the unity of the mission began to bubble to the surface. Some of Otpor's leaders prepared to return to their political parties. Now the opposition was in power, they wanted to be part of the project to build a new Serbia; this was where the action was now, they reasoned. Others thought that since its struggle had been won, Otpor should shut down forever. Most controversially, a few argued that Otpor should become a political party and campaign in the forthcoming parliamentary elections. The movement had repeated again and again that it would never do this; to some, it sounded like heresy.

Huge posters went up around Belgrade, with a picture of the bulldozer which had become the icon of 5 October, and the words: 'We are watching you.' It was a message from Otpor to the opposition coalition which now held power – on behalf of the people, they said: don't betray the ideals of the revolution. After an internal poll showed that the majority of activists were against founding an Otpor party, it decided to become a kind of watchdog organisation, to push the new government to fulfil its promises, and, in the absence of a democratic opposition, to act as a tough but friendly critic when necessary. It was a compromise, partly because many who had been energised by the frenetic highs of the past year felt they could not simply give up and move on.

'A lot of people became so addicted to the fact that they had some stature just by being an important person in Otpor,' says

Milja Jovanović. 'They just needed to continue that. If we decided to go into the political arena and become a party, it would mean a completely new game. I think there was a strong feeling for a lot of people that just by continuing to be Otpor they would still have an influence. When you're young, you want to do things the easy way, not the hard way. Also, we really hated the politicians. A lot of people, me included, couldn't see ourselves as political party officials. We couldn't imagine that. So a lot of these factors contributed to making that wrong decision of becoming a watchdog of democracy, which I don't think anyone could have been in Serbia.

'I think it was the worst decision we ever made. Now it seems that the best thing we could have done was to call it a day: die young and leave a good-looking corpse.'

But Nenad Konstantinović argues that, in the chaotic post-revolutionary situation, they had little other choice. The new government wasn't moving quickly enough to reform the state apparatus, too few people from the Milošević era were being punished for their misdeeds; indeed, some continued to wield their malign influence. 'The overthrow of Milošević was just the first step to democracy, just the first step towards becoming a modern civilised country,' he says. 'People didn't vote for the opposition because they liked them; they voted against Milošević. The political parties didn't have any kind of experience. Their leaders had been in opposition since 1990 and they weren't capable of overthrowing Milošević until 2000. It took them ten years! Why should we believe that now they were in power, they would be fantastic? And we were right. In DOS you also had former Communists – one of them was later even [at the international war crimes tribunal] in The Hague. Was he a guy you could trust to introduce modern European democracy? There needed to be someone with credibility who could criticise the government to keep them on the right path in the transition period. That was Otpor. I think we did the right thing.'

These simmering internal disputes boiled over at Otpor's second congress, early in 2001. Some argued for a move into traditional politics, others that Otpor should be dissolved immediately. Eventually, a strategy was announced, based on the idea of a 'new patriotism'; they would promote a new model for Serbian democracy, based on fighting organised crime and corruption and campaigning to join the European Union – a goal that still seemed many years away. The clenched-fist logo would be 'retired'.

But some provincial activists weren't happy. They thought that the Belgrade elite was imposing its own views on something which had been – nominally, at least – a decentralised, leaderless movement. Some of them angrily declared that they would split from Belgrade and continue as autonomous Otpor cells, and publicly attacked the leadership in the media. Aleksandar Marić, an activist from Novi Sad, thinks the arguments were inevitable: 'We were an organisation created by Milošević. He was the "founder" of Otpor; without him there would be no Otpor. So with Milošević out of the picture, we experienced an identity crisis.'

Otpor continued campaigning for three years after the revolution, but although many of its ideas were taken up by Zoran Djindjić's Democratic Party, its impact increasingly diminished. Some of the Belgrade tabloids began to run lurid exposés alleging that Otpor was no more than an American puppet show – a theory which had also begun to percolate through websites run by left-wing commentators who saw any kind of alliance with the United States as poisonous.

'There were stories that nothing was our idea, that we were trained by the CIA and given a lot of money and instructions about what to do,' says Milja Jovanović, who was deeply hurt and saddened by the allegations. 'It seemed so improbable to us that people would believe that, but then it became an accepted truth. It's because people were so disappointed with what happened [after the revolution]. Because we were a symbolic organisation, we became symbolic of the failure as well. It was a disappointment for me but more for ordinary people who had so much hope. Maybe it was unrealistic hope, but I can't blame them, I blame every single person who was in power.' They had helped to overthrow a president, but they could do little to set the course for Serbia's future.

'The euphoria lasted less than a year,' says Ivan Marović. 'It just disappeared after the first split in DOS. It went away, like it never happened. Everything was back to normal – agony and disappointment and apathy. All that stuff. People knew rationally that it would take years to improve, but we were so deep in the gutter that the hopes were so high that everything would be much better.'

For a few of those who had immersed themselves in the Otpor lifestyle, who had truly *lived the resistance*, it was even worse. They had soared through the extremes of emotion during the battles of 2000 and found it hard to deal with the aftermath, when none of it seemed to matter any more. They had lost the thing that meant most to them, the moment which had defined their lives. 'The problem is that if a young man reaches the top before he is 30, then for his entire life he is trying to reach the same success,' says Ivan Andrić. 'At least five people that spoke on behalf of Otpor have had terrible psychological problems.'

Within three years, the political landscape had changed completely. Yugoslavia had ceased to exist, replaced by a fragile, short-lived union called Serbia and Montenegro. The energetic prime minister, Zoran Djindjić, the driving force of Serbian reform and the man who sent Milošević to The Hague, had been assassinated by a shady cabal of gangsters and state security operatives. New elections were approaching in December 2003 and Otpor, finally, decided it would run its own candidates in the poll. Otpor would be a social democratic, left-of-centre party – to 'counter disillusionment with the reform process', Ivan Marović wrote at the time.[15] He said that the opposition had failed to break with the Milošević era and confront the criminal structures which were embedded within the state apparatus. Otpor, he promised, represented a new generation, untainted by the mistakes and misdeeds of the past.

It proved to be a spectacular failure. Perhaps they had left it too long; perhaps the tabloid accusations had tarnished Otpor's image; perhaps people admired them as idealistic young campaigners but didn't think they had the experience or the political skills to be members of parliament. Some Otpor activists had believed that their local popularity would translate into support at the polls. 'That,' says Nenad Konstantinović, with a large measure of understatement, 'was an incorrect estimation.' Otpor won just 1.6 per cent of the vote.

'It was too late, it was over. The momentum had been lost,' says Ivan Marović. 'For three years, it was a long slow death. I stayed a member to the very end, even though it wasn't the organisation I wanted it to be.'

In 2004, the new Serbian president, Boris Tadić – the man who had read out the names of those killed in Milošević's wars during Otpor's cathartic New Year's Eve performance four years earlier – invited them to join the Democratic Party. They accepted. Six years after the movement was founded by a small group of students with high ideals and crazy dreams, it was time to admit that it could go no further. 'It was sad,' says Milja Jovanović, 'but to tell you the truth, it was more than that – it was a huge relief.'

Otpor was finished. Or at least, that's how it seemed…

CHAPTER TWO

A RED ROSE (WITH THORNS)

GEORGIA

Giorgi Sanaia was already dead when they found him in his apartment, lying on his back in a pool of blood. At some point in the early hours of the morning, a bullet had entered his head at close range. Although he was only in his mid-twenties, Sanaia was already one of Georgia's most popular television journalists, the anchorman of an incisive talk show which was known for raising uncomfortable questions and pursuing allegations of official corruption. The circumstances surrounding his death in July 2001 were not clear – and, indeed, would never convincingly be explained – but many believed this was a political murder. Sanaia, they thought, had offended one too many of the powerful, interconnected cliques which ran Georgian politics, business and organised crime; he had crossed the line, become a target. There was a mood of brooding sadness as tens of thousands of people gathered for his funeral in the capital, Tbilisi. Some of the mourners tied a long black ribbon around the parliament building in a gesture of remembrance and accusation. 'It didn't just feel like Sanaia had been killed,' says one of them. 'It felt like something in the country itself had died.'

Sanaia had worked for Rustavi-2, a television station which had become increasingly critical of the Georgian president, Eduard Shevardnadze, covering stories which other stations ignored.

Rustavi-2 was a commercial operation which had seen a market for liberal values and had allied itself with the political opposition. Around three months after the killing, police raided the station, saying they needed to investigate its finances. This, after Sanaia, was too much. The sadness turned to anger. Thousands rushed to the station and assembled outside, saying they would defend it from what appeared to be impending closure. Shevardnadze pledged to protect free speech and ordered an inquiry, but as the crowd grew, the protesters' demands escalated. Initially they wanted the security minister and the hard-line minister of internal affairs to resign; then the resignation of Shevardnadze and his entire government. As some began to speak of revolution, Shevardnadze sacked his cabinet, although he insisted it would be 'irresponsible' to resign himself.

There was no real leader yet, and no coherent movement – both would come later – but the protests felt like a kind of awakening. They had delivered a wholly unexpected victory for people power, and connections had been made, between political activists, journalists and discontented students, which would re-emerge with renewed vigour in fewer than two years.

ROLLS-ROYCE IN THE HOUR OF CHAOS

Eduard Shevardnadze was a colossus of the late Soviet era, and the dominant figure in Georgia for three decades. He had been the top Communist official when the country was still part of the USSR, before moving to Moscow to become Soviet foreign minister under Mikhail Gorbachev, where he was instrumental in ending the Cold War and helping to push through the reforms known as *perestroika*, which eventually led to the demise of Communism. When he was invited to return to post-Soviet Georgia as head of state in 1992, the newly independent country was in chaos. A military council of warlords was running the state. Paramilitaries – like the notorious *Mkhedrioni*, the 'Horsemen' – stalked the country, treating it, one observer recalls, 'like a massive protection racket'. There had been firefights in Tbilisi, political killings were commonplace, and there was civil war in two regions, Abkhazia and South Ossetia, which wanted to break away from central government control.

Shevardnadze slowly managed to lead Georgia away from anarchy, surviving several assassination attempts in the process, although he effectively lost the breakaway regions. He jailed some of the leading paramilitaries, introduced a new national currency, and made steps to establish the rule of law. But at some time towards the end of the nineties, his appetite for change ran out. He had brought Georgia stability, but he wasn't able to bring its people prosperity. As his popularity began to diminish, he resorted to increasingly primitive measures, keeping himself in power through ballot-rigging and shady alliances with unsavoury characters.

By 2001, according to the opposition, Georgia had become a 'liberal autocracy'. Free speech, political parties and elections were allowed, as long as they didn't do too much to displace the ruling elites. Beneath the formal state structures lay a web of personal and family allegiances, some of them linked to organised crime. Nevertheless, grey-haired Shevardnadze was a wily political survivor and a supreme deal-maker, full of pragmatic cunning – the 'Silver Fox', some called him. He had powerful friends in Washington from the last days of the Soviet Union, and managed to make Georgia one of the leading recipients of American aid, bringing in around a billion dollars in the years since independence. The US had its own strategic reasons for supporting Georgia; one of its main concerns was ensuring stability to enable the construction of an oil pipeline from the Caspian sea to Turkey's Mediterranean coast, feeding Western markets while bypassing Russia. Washington wanted reliable political partners in the 'great game' for black gold, and Shevardnadze was thought to be their man. In return, he would unconditionally support the US-led war in Iraq, even offering the use of Georgia's military bases. His backing from the US put him in a powerful position. He portrayed himself as the only person who could hold the country together and prevent it sliding back into the savagery of the early nineties.

As the twenty-first century began, Shevardnadze's Georgia

was visibly decaying. The ramshackle beauty of the capital was pockmarked and potholed by neglect; the wild rambling glory of the provinces disfigured by deprivation. Census figures showed that Georgia's population had fallen by a million in the 13 years since independence. As in Serbia during the Milošević years, many had left in search of opportunity and prosperity; they had simply run out of patience. Regular power cuts threw the country into darkness; despite all the American money, Shevardnadze couldn't keep the lights on. And while the poorest waited for their meagre salaries and pensions, the nouveau riche – some of them members of Shevardnadze's family – flaunted their wealth, building opulent mansions and buying expensive foreign cars. There were reports of one flamboyant relative cruising through the crumbling streets of Tbilisi in a Rolls-Royce. Georgia looked like it was being eaten alive by greedy men.

'Corruption manifested itself everywhere, from the policeman standing on a street corner collecting two *lari* [around one dollar] from drivers for no reason, to every state agency which people had contact with – passports, IDs, health, the registry of births, weddings or deaths, the judiciary, the prosecutor's office,' says Tinatin Khidasheli, a profoundly committed, serious young woman who founded the Georgian Young Lawyers Association. 'Any contact with a state official was associated with the paying of bribes. It could have been a symbolic two *lari* or it could have been tens of thousands of dollars.'

There were fine spoils to be had in smuggling and counterfeiting; bootleg versions of some of the country's best-loved products – effervescent Borjomi mineral water and hearty Georgian wine – could be found in Tbilisi's markets, where inspectors were bought off with kickbacks. In the east of the country, an illicit plant was discovered producing fake Coca-Cola and Fanta. The police said the confiscated drinks were very tasty.

The universities had gone rotten too. Instead of places of learning, they had been transformed into illicit money-making rackets. Students could buy their way past the extrance examinations: the price list ranged from a few hundred dollars to thousands, depending on how prestigious the department was. The curriculum and teaching methods, like some of the buildings, were decrepit. Many of the university authorities were old Soviet placemen whose only interest was in topping up their wallets. All that many students learned was that it paid to be corrupt. One observer sketched a dismal picture of the country's top college, Tbilisi State University: 'It had old people who called themselves professors, there were occasional encounters which had the appearance of classes, but actually there was no education going on there at all. The professors knew nothing and the students bought their diplomas. It *looked* like a university, but it wasn't a university.'

Giorgi Kandelaki had gone to Tbilisi State University to study political science. A bright and ambitious young man, he was disgusted at what he found; he believed his future was being stolen from him by immoral old men, while his fellow freshers didn't want or need to open their books. But Kandelaki and his friends were not typical Georgian students; they thought, perhaps naively, that they could change things. In 2000, they set up an independent student council, an alternative to the official students' union. They surveyed their classmates, published a list of the most corrupt figures at the university and even took the university authorities to court.

But they remained a minority; since many students had bought their way in, they had no interest in changing the system. 'It became obvious that the whole issue of higher education was political, and it wouldn't be possible to change it without changing the government,' Kandelaki remembers. He had been involved in the Rustavi-2 protests of 2001; they were proof, he says, that non-violent resistance could work in Georgia, where any social unrest raised fears of a return to anarchy: 'They showed that civil protest wouldn't lead to civil war, which was what the government was saying. But they also showed that to make a breakthrough you needed structure, and there was no structure at that time, no organisation. It was spontaneous and uncontrolled.'

Kandelaki and his friends had started hanging out at the Liberty Institute, a think tank and research group which campaigned for civil rights and democratic reforms. For them, these light and airy offices, up a steep wooden staircase in central Tbilisi, were a kind of intellectual resource centre. They were joined by another close-knit set of young people, leaders of the Georgian Students Movement, which had also come together during the protests outside Rustavi-2. Together, they trawled the internet for ideas, strategies, inspirations, avidly consuming articles about Gandhi, Martin Luther King… and Otpor. 'We saw our country was going down and down, and there was no light at the end of the tunnel,' says Ako Minashvili, then a law student at Tbilisi State University. 'We needed to do something, but we didn't know what.'

The Liberty Institute had been launched in the mid-1990s, after an earlier incident in which Rustavi-2 was temporarily shut down. Its founders, Levan Ramishvili and Giga Bokeria, were former journalists at the TV station who gradually became two of the country's most dynamic democracy activists. They took on issues that many others thought too sensitive to touch, like the freedom of religious minorities, a highly controversial subject in their conservative Orthodox Christian country. This had attracted the thuggish attentions of a group of unidentified black-clad heavies – religious extremists or their hired bruisers, it wasn't quite clear – who attacked their offices, smashing up anything and anyone in sight.

Ramishvili had grown up listening to the BBC World Service and Voice of America, picking up slivers of information amidst the crackle and hiss of short wave, learning about books which were banned in the Soviet Union. He had been campaigning for civil liberties since his days at university during the collapse of Communism. Those were desperate, dangerous times; in 1989, Soviet troops had massacred around twenty Georgians during a protest for independence from Moscow. Some accounts say they used poison gas and then finished the demonstrators off with sharpened shovels. Ramishvili's appearance was somewhat deceptive; he was softly-spoken, bespectacled, studiously intellectual. The fast-mouthed, keen-witted Bokeria, on the other hand, had a kind of dark Caucasian charisma, with his heavy-lidded eyes hidden behind blue-tinted sunglasses as he chain-smoked his way through packs of cigarettes.

Ramishvili and Bokeria were deeply worried about what was

happening in Georgia. They thought it was on the verge of becoming a failed state; politically and socially bankrupt. They were searching for a new direction, and found it in late 2002 when a delegation of democracy campaigners from Serbia came to visit Tbilisi. Among them were Slobodan Djinović from Otpor, Marko Blagojević from the Centre for Free Elections and Democracy, and the head of the Belgrade branch of George Soros's Open Society Institute, Sonja Licht.

Licht says she was shocked by what she saw: 'I was in Georgia in 1996, and six years later, nothing had moved anywhere – I had the feeling that society had simply stopped. It was clear that something must happen. The situation was already ripe for change.'

'People were very apathetic, like in Serbia in 1998,' recalls Djinović. He was looking for some sparks of imagination, and was disappointed that there appeared to be no youth movement in Tbilisi. 'I asked one guy from an NGO, do you have any young people involved? He said, "Oh yes, but they are troublemakers." But when I went to see these troublemakers, the people around the Liberty Institute, they were great guys, they had great energy. Giga Bokeria, Levan Ramishvili, these were brilliant people, they were extremely intelligent – they were visionaries. When we spoke about possible strategies, they understood perfectly well how to proceed and what steps to take.' In the months to come, Djinović and other Otpor veterans would become regular visitors to Tbilisi; they had discovered kindred spirits who were thirsty for knowledge.

The next step was a return trip to the Serbian capital. Bokeria and his colleagues met student activists from Otpor as well as the prime minister, Zoran Djindjić, and many of the key players involved in the Exit 2000 voter mobilisation drive. Bokeria was captivated by Otpor. What struck him deeply was how the young Serbs had managed to achieve total moral superiority over the Milošević government – and how well-organised they had been. 'We knew a little bit, but they told us about their tactics, their mistakes, about how structure and organisation mattered so much,' he says. The Georgians then travelled on to the Slovakian capital, Bratislava, to learn more about the OK98 campaign.

The idea of a youth movement was already in the air, but Bokeria and the others returned with a more audacious plan: nothing less than a repeat performance of the Serbian drama. Even at the Liberty Institute, some believed it was a dream too far – it couldn't happen here, they insisted… 'Levan Ramishvili was the guy who was really advocating it,' remembers Giorgi Kandelaki. 'Some people were saying, "No, it's different here, it's not possible." But Levan insisted it was.'

Finally, the decision was made. There would be a new youth movement, and it would be called *Kmara* – Georgian for 'Enough'. Its aims would be free elections and, ultimately, the end of the Shevardnadze era. The group of inquisitive students who had been drinking tea, chatting, and surfing the net would be its hard core, alongside the older, more experienced activists from the Liberty Institute, Alexander 'Kakha' Lomaia from the Georgian branch of the Open Society Institute, Tinatin Khidasheli from the Georgian Young Lawyers Association and Gigi Ugulava from the Association for Legal and Public Education. Ugulava says he had become exasperated with the passive neutrality of 'non-governmental organisations'; while Georgia fell apart, they were sitting at their desks, compiling statistics and writing reports, and being ignored. 'Many NGOs said they didn't want to be perceived as taking part in politics, they wanted to be seen as neutral. That was legitimate, but it wasn't enough. It was about which direction the country was going in,' he says. 'We decided we didn't want to be neutral, we wanted to mobilise people against the government. We'd had experience of being neutral, of just observing elections and making reports, but we thought this was over, it was not enough any more.'

While Otpor found its allies over a two-year period, Kmara emerged almost fully-formed. It would be the feisty vanguard of a more complex and ambitious campaign of opposition activism, voter mobilisation and election monitoring designed to establish a new order in Georgia. Nini Gogiberidze, a law graduate in her early twenties who had been part of the delegation to Belgrade and Bratislava, drafted a wide-ranging proposal which closely reflected the Serbian Exit 2000 strategy. This was not an incendiary manifesto; it was intended to secure funding from potential donors who might be troubled by radical rants. 'The 2003 campaign for free and fair elections in Georgia will be divided into two essential parts; in order to increase the voters' turnout on the elections, the civic movement "Kmara" will be launched, to conduct strong Get-Out-To-Vote,' it read. 'Jointly with this action, the International Society for Fair Elections and Democracy, which has a tradition of wide-scale election monitoring at all levels, will carry out voters' education campaign and monitoring campaign.'[1] However, anyone who was familiar with the Serbian revolution could have read between the lines: it was a blueprint for mass action. 'We wanted to involve everyone in a movement which was not partisan,' says Gogiberidze.

The important matter of a suitably dynamic logo took a little longer to settle. They knew they needed one, they just couldn't decide what it should be. In the end, Kmara decided simply to copy the clenched-fist graphic from Otpor. 'For us it was important to stress the connection, to say this was the same concept as Otpor,' says Giorgi Kandelaki. 'Not least because we wanted to frighten the government.'

The way Kandelaki tells it, revolution was not on the immediate agenda; as in Serbia, this was to be a long game – it would take years, not months: 'There were parliamentary elections coming up in November and the common understanding was that the elections were of course going to be rigged, and this time there was the momentum to fight for our rights. But we thought these elections would be a step forward, they would serve as a base for the main battle which we thought would take place in 2005, when Shevardnadze's term in office expired. That was the vision.'

Nor did they think that their situation was comparable to what the young Serbs had been through. Georgia was poorer than Serbia – far poorer; the only electricity cuts in Serbia were caused by NATO's bombs – but Shevardnadze was a peacemaker rather than a warmonger; and he was not a genuine authoritarian. 'They had a real dictator in Serbia, a real tough guy – the "butcher of the Balkans", as they called him,' says Kandelaki. 'Also they were the first, although we were the first in the post-Soviet space. We had less Western support, too. Much less.'

For a canny strategic operator like Giga Bokeria, Kmara was a part of a wider coalition which also involved the political opposition and the media. 'Kmara's main goal was to be a detonator – to create a chain reaction, which would leave less space for bad compromise,' he says. 'The main message of Shevardnadze's regime was, "We know your life is bad, but if you try to challenge us it will be worse, so be quiet and don't interfere and we won't go too far."

'The regime was saying, "Relax, nothing's going to change and if you do speak out, there will be bloodshed and chaos here again – do you want chaos, don't you remember what happened here in the past?" They were not trying to win the hearts and souls of the people, or make out that they were good – no, they knew that was pointless. They were just saying that it's all the same shit and it doesn't matter, it's just better to accept the way it is. Our job was to challenge that manufacturing of apathy; to show the government's real face and say that we couldn't just sit back and watch.'

If Kmara had an ideology, it was vague and implicit – although strongly pro-Western. 'There was no time to think about ideology, it was an action-oriented resistance campaign,' says Giorgi Meladze, another founding member. 'People had different ideas about how things should be in the future. It was about building democratic institutions, basic human rights, trying to get rid of the Soviet past. Basic liberal democratic principles.' Beyond that was a complex jigsaw of intertwined concerns and grievances. 'For me and most of my friends who graduated from the international law faculty, we knew about international rights but we saw every single day how those rights were violated and how nothing was done about it,' says Nini Gogiberidze. 'It was about addressing how religious minorities were treated in Georgia, addressing how police were beating and torturing people. That was us, but every single person had a different reason to be in Kmara, everyone saw it in the way they wanted to see it.'

In April 2003, they began, as Otpor had almost five years earlier, with a graffiti campaign. They pooled what money they had, bought some tins of blue, pink and yellow paint, and spent a night driving around the city, daubing the roads with their name: *Enough!* When the city awoke, Kmara had arrived. This confusing development was big news, even more so because it was anonymous: at first, nobody claimed responsibility. Even Shevardnadze commented on it, saying he had seen the graffiti during his drive to work. In a small country, it was easy to get noticed quickly, particularly when there was guaranteed television coverage from Rustavi-2. 'The graffiti gave the impression that Kmara was massive, which wasn't so at that time – it was only a few people,' says Giga Bokeria. 'But the reaction was enormous, which contributed to our recruiting. It was easy and it was cheap – *very* cheap. All it needed was courage and the regime to show its stupidity in its reaction.'

For those who had been waiting for something new, it was an alarm call. 'I know people who joined us later, and they said that "Enough" was the word they'd been searching for, for such a long time,' says Keto Kobiashvili. 'It was a kind of signal, it awakened something in their brains.'

Later that month, they marched on the State Chancellory – the presidential administration building – carrying old Soviet flags with the faces of Shevardnadze's allies attached to them. The message was clear: these are men from the past. The date, 14 April, was significant. It was 25 years after students marched from Tbilisi State University to the centre of the city in protest against a Soviet plan to reduce the status of the Georgian language in the republic; Kmara was adopting the heroic legacy of the young patriots as its own. However, they could only count on a few dozen activists at this point, so they had to improvise, calling in friends from the youth wings of opposition parties to raise numbers into the hundreds. It was a cunning deception, says Giorgi Kandelaki: 'Bluff was a very serious weapon, especially in the early stages. There are many ways in which you can pretend you are much more powerful than you are. That was important not only for frightening the government but for inspiring our activists, to make them feel it was possible.' One of them got a little overexcited and set fire to one Soviet flag; they threw the others into the bushes and swiftly left, leaving onlookers bemused. Kmara was still a somewhat mysterious phenomenon in a country where street demonstrations were viewed with some suspicion.

While Otpor had been called agents of NATO and Washington, the Georgian authorities had their own insults, intended to strike a chord with a public which saw Moscow as a malign entity, constantly seeking to undermine and subjugate their country: the old imperial oppressor. A spokeswoman for Shevardnadze's political bloc, For a New Georgia, revealed the disturbing news that Kmara was a front for the Kremlin's spymasters: 'Russian special services are planning a large-scale, tried and tested operation under the name Enough,' she declared.[2] Others played on traditional Georgian conservatism, saying that the students promoted gay rights. 'The things to blame here are Russians and homosexuals, so of course we were called both,' says Kandelaki.

Dressed in black, white and orange T-shirts bearing the sign of the fist and the slogan *Kmara – Because I Love Georgia* – another echo of Belgrade – they launched a rolling programme of actions, targeting the symbols of Georgia's decline. They held simultaneous nationwide pickets of police stations to highlight the use of torture and the planting of evidence; they symbolically swept up rubbish in litter-strewn suburbs, organised rock concerts and football matches, collected books for school libraries and invited election candidates from all sides to public debates. When Georgia played Russia in a qualifying match for the Euro 2004 football tournament, they gave out flags in the stadium and spray-painted graffiti: *Enough of losing – it's time to win.* Unexpectedly, against a stronger Russian team, Georgia won the game 1–0.

'We wanted some action every day,' says Gigi Ugulava. 'When you don't have action, you have stagnation. We had to keep the motivation going. As soon as you stop, you fail. Action, always action.' They would wait at corners where police were known to stop cars and demand bribes – for an ill-paid policeman who might have handed over a bribe himself to join the force, extortion was seen as a legitimate salary supplement. When a driver was pulled up, the Kmara activists would spring forward and offer them a booklet detailing their rights. However, unlike in Serbia, they weren't often arrested. The Georgian police preferred to settle such matters informally, with their fists.

In the beginning, they were a close-knit cell working out of one dilapidated room, its walls decorated with naive hippy drawings and a few revolutionary slogans. 'It was friends, friends of friends, friends of friends of friends, and so on,' says Nini Gogiberidze. 'Imagine you and your friends doing something crazy that the government doesn't like, something slightly deviant... you feel good about yourself. It's a good cause, yes, but it's *fun*. We were making things like headbands and small flags ourselves, everyone was using their printers and copying machines at work to print things out. It was creative.'

But when the summer came, it was time to widen the network. Kmara arranged a camp in a village in the mountains outside Tbilisi to train hundreds of potential activists in civil disobedience tactics, using material from files they had downloaded from the internet and documents translated from Otpor's Serbian originals. 'It was like an army camp, because we thought we were some kind of army – a freedom army, you know,' says Ako Minashvili. 'It was in the countryside, in an old-fashioned Soviet campsite which was totally neglected and ruined; no comforts, no running water. We had to go down to a stream to get water.' The Serbs offered practical advice on how to mobilise, a journalist from Rustavi-2 advised on communication techniques, and veterans of the campaign for independence from the Soviet Union spoke of their experiences. But although the Georgians knew Gene Sharp's work on the theories of non-violent struggle, they didn't think it was worth passing on to the new recruits in its raw form. 'Gene Sharp's book is very academic; it doesn't get you hot-blooded,' says Giorgi Kandelaki. 'Only a couple of people read it.'

It was Otpor that most people wanted to know about. The Serbs had lived the dream, achieved the impossible. They were heroes of the resistance. 'There have always been Americans around this place,' says an American who worked with the National Democratic Institute and advised Kmara from its early stages. 'Every day there's some foreigner here doing some training for someone who doesn't need it or doesn't care. But actual, real-life Serbs – everybody wanted to talk to them. They were big stars here.' More than anything, though, the camp brought them closer together, bonded them tighter into the collective mission: *Enough!*

By the time it was announced that the parliamentary election would be held on 2 November 2003, Kmara already knew what its role in the opposition coalition would be: get people out to vote – and then inspire them to take to the streets to defend their rights. President Shevardnadze's popularity had fallen to new lows, and he was under strong pressure from Western governments to ensure the vote was honest. The former American secretary of state, James Baker – an old friend of Shevardnadze's from the twilight days of the Soviet Union – visited Georgia with a blueprint for fair elections, which all sides accepted. But the government quickly went back on the plan, ensuring that it would maintain control of the process. Shortly afterwards, the US cut its aid to Georgia, citing its inability to deal with corruption.

A few months later, another high-level US delegation arrived in Tbilisi, with similar aims. But few thought Shevardnadze would take much notice. 'Despite the strong signals about fair elections, we thought Shevardnadze would say, "Oh, these Westerners will shout and complain about all this, but they'll shut up in the end." That was his approach,' says Giorgi Kandelaki. The problems were symbolised by the list of registered voters. Some people who had died before World War Two were deemed free to cast their ballots, but a significant number of the living were excluded. Even the speaker of parliament discovered that her name was not on the list. 'By this time, although we were still talking about conciliation and hope, we already knew the elections would be a disaster and we were preparing ourselves for every possible scenario,' says Tinatin Khidasheli.

Shevardnadze, now aged 75, had announced his intention to step down at the next presidential elections two years later, in 2005. But some feared he would attempt to maintain control beyond that by arranging for a pliant crony to assume the role. If Shevardnadze's bloc, For a New Georgia, was victorious in November, this would be much easier to achieve.

However, the opposition was stronger than it had been for years, led by influential figures who had served under Shevardnadze. Foremost among them was Mikheil Saakashvili, an American-educated lawyer who was still just 35 years old. He had been the justice minister in the Shevardnadze government, but resigned in 2001, saying it would be immoral to remain part of a corrupt cabinet of ministers. One observer recalls him causing outrage at a cabinet meeting when he brandished documents which he said showed ministers had bought themselves luxury villas with the proceeds of crooked business deals. Saakashvili formed his own National Movement party and became Shevardnadze's most outspoken critic, calling him a tragic figure, a 'trivial semi-dictator hated and despised by his own people'.[3] He said oligarch clans with criminal connections were taking over the country. Saakashvili had genuine presence; he was a captivating orator with a profound taste for populist rhetoric who could harness and ride the emotions of a crowd. As the head of Tbilisi city council, he had a high profile and wasn't too modest to use it. He, too, had studied the Serbian experience and consulted the vetarans of the Belgrade revolution.

The links between the Liberty Institute, Kmara and Saakashvili's National Movement ran deep. Kmara used the opposition party's greater resources when it organised demonstrations, while the party consulted the activists on its media campaigns. 'We co-ordinated our actions quite closely, it's not a secret,' says Giga Bokeria, who would later become one of the National Movement's most influential members of parliament. 'Our goal was to have co-operation with most of the opposition parties who were considered more or less liberal democratic. The National Movement was closer to us because they had the same vision, that there should be no bargaining with the regime; they were the most radical, so that brought us closer. But we were not the same, we never overlapped totally.' Nevertheless, Kmara was sometimes accused of being the covert radical wing of Mikheil Saakashvili's party, however often they denied it.

The other main opposition leaders were more sober figures. Zurab Zhvania had also been close to Shevardnadze – he had created the president's political party and at one point was even seen as the Soviet veteran's natural heir, but broke with him in 2001 after the attempted shutdown of Rustavi-2 and went into opposition, damning the government as a 'corrupt swamp'. Nino Burjanadze was the speaker of parliament, another former Shevardnadze ally, and an admirer of Margaret Thatcher; like the former British prime minister, Burjanadze was nicknamed the 'Iron Lady'. She formed a coalition bloc with Zhvania's Democratic Party: the 'Burjanadze-Democrats'. One of their slogans reflected their cooler tempers: 'Revolutionary Changes without a Revolution'. As part of the image which Shevardnadze had sought to build of Georgia as a liberal, Western-style democracy, he had promoted 'young reformers' like Saakashvili and Zhvania, and allowed civil society groups and independent media to flourish. All had now turned against him. 'Some of the credit for what happened must go to Shevardnadze,' says Giorgi Kandelaki. 'He made it possible.'

I'LL KICK HIM IN THE ASS

The momentum was building as the election approached. By the autumn of 2003, Kmara claimed to have recruited around 3,000 activists. They had also learned from Otpor that motivating the liberal elite in the capital was not enough, and headed out into the regions in an attempt to put together a nationwide network, establishing chapters in provincial cities, towns and villages. There they found ready recruits amongst bored teenagers because they provided entertainment and activity as well as a political vision, organising discos and sports tournaments, cleaning up riverbanks and planting trees.

Unlike in most political campaigns, many of the new recruits were female. A lot of young men, suggests Keto Kobiashvili, were simply not interested. 'You can see such boys on the streets, just hanging around and smoking cigarettes, they have no motivation and they think anyone who does something is politically extreme,' she says. 'In most Georgian families, the woman organises everything. We have a saying, "The man is the head of the family, but the woman is the neck", because the neck moves the head. Georgian women are not passive.' It was also testament to the indomitability and organisational verve of Kmara leaders like Kobiashvili, whose mother had been part of the anti-Soviet resistance, and Tea Tutberidze, a tiny woman driven by a fierce dynamism; 'a tough, gutsy broad with a lot of lead in her pencil – a great people-mover', one observer called her. Tutberidze and her colleagues drove hundreds of miles around the regions, maintaining personal contacts with the activists; inspiring, cajoling, motivating. 'All the time, we were telling them that this was their last chance,' she says.

But there was another reason why Kmara targeted the regions: they had not managed to transform their own university, Tbilisi State, into a stronghold of the resistance. The institutionalised culture of bribery meant that few students cared much about corruption, while others were simply ashamed of themselves; this was the system that they had literally bought into. 'A guy from Otpor was here, Aleksandar Marić, and when we told him what was happening, he said, "Take me to this university"', recalls Giorgi Kandelaki. 'We took him, he walked around during the day, and thousands of students were just standing around outside, talking and smoking, doing nothing. Almost none of them had books with them. They weren't there to study. Marić just said, "Forget this place".'

They didn't neglect the capital, however. When a Georgian energy company was sold off to a Russian state firm, they hauled a coffin to parliament, inscribed with the words: 'Georgia's Energy Industry'. Whether they knew it or not, it summoned up images of the civil rights movement in 1960s America, when black activists carried a coffin representing racial segregation laws through the streets of Washington. It also appealed to widespread suspicions in Georgia about Moscow's desire to maintain its 'sphere of influence' in the former Soviet region.

Kmara perfected the art of making a big impact with limited resources. When the head of Russia's electricity monopoly, Anatoly

Chubais, arrived in Tbilisi after the power deal was done, Kmara activists met him at the airport and harangued him to get back on the plane to Moscow. 'We had banners but there were only seven of us,' remembers Kandelaki. 'There was one policeman at the fence in front of the VIP area. He said, "Give me $1,000 now and I'll kick him in the ass and leave my job." We called about 20 people but all we could get together was $500, so he didn't do it. But it was televised everywhere that Kmara was there. In one report it said that crowds of angry students met Chubais at the airport – but we were only seven people. It was an example of this mythology we succeeded in creating around ourselves, which portrayed us as far more dangerous than we actually were.'

Some people seemed to be taking that mythology very seriously indeed. Kmara's office near the downtown Tbilisi branch of McDonald's was attacked, windows were broken and equipment damaged. Threatening letters were left as a kind of calling card. A spokeswoman for Shevardnadze's bloc said the students had caused the damage themselves in order to pin the blame on pro-government forces. New rumours spread: no longer were they gay KGB operatives, now they worked for some kind of unholy alliance between the CIA and the international financier George Soros, and were paid $500 a month to sow chaos and unease across Georgia. Kandelaki says that the rumours were so widespread that even his mother was almost convinced they were true. 'We wouldn't have minded if the US government gave us money, but it simply didn't happen. We don't consider it something to hide, but it didn't take place,' he insists. 'They always used to say we were financed by George Soros, but they had received hundreds of millions from the US and the energy system was still collapsing.'

The majority of the funding did come from Soros's Open Society Institute, says Nini Gogiberidze. But the British Council and USAID – the American agency which says it provides 'economic, development and humanitarian assistance around the world in support of the foreign policy goals of the United States', and was a long-term supporter of the Liberty Institute – also contributed money for cultural events and election monitoring, while staff of the

National Democratic Institute, the democracy foundation linked to the American Democratic Party, acted as advisers. But, like Otpor, Kmara denied that those who paid the bills controlled the agenda. Indeed, says Gogiberidze, some of them may not have fully understood what kind of campaign they were backing: 'When you put together a proposal, you don't write that you're recruiting Kmara members. You say, "We want to build a coalition network." But what does that mean? Trying to find people to support you: recruiting Kmara members.'

Despite intense scrutiny from the local media, they tried to evade questions about where the money was coming from. A film shot at the time shows Giga Bokeria and Levan Ramishvili instructing activists to deflect such inquiries, telling them to say that the people supplying the cash don't want to be named in case of reprisals. 'You can just say generally that there are people who are concerned with democracy issues in Georgia and they are helping us and we will announce the names of those people when democracy wins in this country,' Ramishvili tells the younger recruits.[4] Some say now that they would have liked a little more financial support than they actually received. Speaking anonymously, one Georgian MP says that many of their potential foreign donors thought that this scrappy gaggle of kids was more than a little crazy.

Indeed, Kmara members were resolutely impertinent – blowing whistles to drown out the speeches at an official ceremony hosted by Shevardnadze; insulting police chiefs to their faces; shouting at politicians: 'You are the plague!' – and so it wasn't surprising that they became controversial. They had their critics within the opposition, too. Bakar Berekashvili was a political science student at Tbilisi State University who had joined Kmara and trained at their summer camp, but left a couple of months afterwards, saying the movement was too pro-American, and that it was no more than a strategic tool of the opposition leader Mikheil Saakashvili. 'It was like in Communist times when all students thought the best country in the world was the Soviet Union; Kmara thought it was the United States,' he says. 'I never supported Saakashvili, I just wanted democracy in Georgia, but the senior activists of Kmara were controlled by the Liberty Institute, by Saakashvili's party and so on. They were just pretending to be independent. It was all to provide power for Saakashvili.'

Even some opposition politicians thought Kmara was a nuisance, or even downright distasteful. Nino Burjanadze said she thought the movement's methods were effective but unacceptable. Pavement stunts inspired by seaside photo booths, where passers-by could stick their head through a hole in a huge canvas and be photographed pretending to be the driver of a van taking Shevardnadze to prison, or posters of the president and his allies being flushed down a toilet, were seen as somewhat crude and disrespectful, even among some of those who had little love for Shevardnadze.

'Many people disliked Kmara,' says Tinatin Khidasheli. 'There was this audience-participation show on TV, and most people who sent in a message hated them. But that was the strategy when we were planning Kmara. We didn't need them to be nice and talk this civilised, high-culture language. We needed something that would shock people and make them angry. No political party could do what they did. They were young, they were naive, they could convince the average person much better than politicians, because in Georgia, when politicians come to talk to you, you always wonder what they want for themselves.' Giorgi Kandelaki puts it more simply: 'Politicians wear ties. We didn't.'

Rustavi-2 was also intensifying its attacks on Shevardnadze. Unlike in Serbia, where all the major television channels were controlled by Milošević loyalists, the Georgian opposition had substantial access to the mass media. 'This was their great advantage,' says Otpor's Slobodan Djinović, 'as well as the fact that Shevardnadze was not as repressive as Milošević.' Rustavi-2 had been screening a satirical cartoon featuring a duplicitous, white-haired old man who stumbled and bungled his way from crisis to catastrophe; a caricature which would have been unthinkable on Serbian state television. Now it showed a series of Kmara propaganda clips, for which it was fined thousands of dollars. One satirised a campaign advertisement produced by Shevardnadze's party, which featured picturesque images of old Georgian houses. The Kmara clip showed the quaint buildings, and then snapped: 'These are not their houses – *these are...*' – and flashed up pictures of government officials' opulent mansions.

Rustavi-2 also broadcast an American film about Otpor called *Bringing Down a Dictator*, which Kmara had been using as an induction video for new activists. There onscreen was US Colonel Robert Helvey, coolly outlining how to undermine a government: 'You've got to think of it in terms of a war... You've got to get your forces together at the decisive point... You've got to take the offensive...' And then Srdja Popović, urging them onwards to victory: 'Now you face the greatest task of your lives. You must lead the protests. It is now up to you...'[5]

Less than two weeks before the Georgian election in November 2003, disputed polls in neighbouring Azerbaijan provoked riots during which hundreds of opposition members and journalists were detained. The Georgian opposition was dismayed that there was little condemnation of the Azeri election from the West; it was a bad omen, but also a reminder that they had to keep any resistance peaceful if they were to maintain international support. Shevardnadze praised the conduct of the Azeri polls, and went on to promise 'strict order' during the polls in Georgia. 'What forced the Azeri president to jail about 200 individuals? He just took the measures envisaged by their laws,' he said. 'I am not threatening anyone, but I will stop at nothing to ensure the elections are held properly.'[6]

To the opposition, the promise certainly sounded like a threat. Shevardnadze confirmed his position in a televised interview a few days later. 'The state has the necessary force to prevent any illegal street action, be it a rally, demonstration or anything else,' he warned. 'If they are illegal and unauthorised, of course the state will do what it has to do and prove its worth.'[7]

It wasn't clear exactly what would happen after the election, but some kind of upheaval seemed to be inevitable. It was time to take sides. The kind of rhetoric heard all around Serbia just before the elections which led to the fall of Milošević was now being heard in Georgia: 'At that moment, if you were not with us, you were against us,' says Keto Kobiashvili. 'That was the choice. It was all or nothing.'

THE LIGHTS GO OUT (AGAIN)

Tinatin Khidasheli wasn't surprised by what happened on 2 November 2003. She wasn't surprised by the empty ballot boxes that suddenly disappeared, then reappeared some time later, stuffed to bursting. She wasn't surprised by the men who drove from polling station to polling station, voting again and again. She wasn't surprised by the unidentified goons who turned up to menace and bully election observers. She wasn't surprised by the death threats or the police intimidation. There was, she says, only one trick that she hadn't seen in Georgia before. 'In one place, the lights would go off in the polling station, you would hear some noises, and then after ten minutes the lights would go back on again and you would see this full ballot box. It was' – she laughs – '*quite innovative.*'

The Central Election Commission immediately announced that Shevardnadze's bloc, For a New Georgia, had taken an early lead. But an American-funded parallel vote count carried out by the Georgian monitoring group, the International Society for Fair Elections and Democracy, and an exit poll conducted by a US firm, the Global Strategy Group, both suggested that Mikheil Saakashvili's National Movement had won the most votes. The strategy developed earlier in the year by the opposition was being set in motion. The news went out immediately on Rustavi-2, and Kmara activists drove around Tbilisi on a lorry bedecked with flags, handing out thousands of leaflets contrasting the parallel vote count with the official one. Shevardnadze admitted there had been some flaws in the voter lists, but he said this had nothing to do with fraud. He said that the country was about to enter a 'new phase of democracy'.[8] He was more right than he could have imagined.

The two main opposition factions, the National Movement and the Burjanadze-Democrats, decided it was time to set their differences aside and unite to oppose the results together, their supporters merged into one. But even they were stunned by the size of the crowd that turned out for their first joint rally at the Philharmonic Hall in central Tbilisi. The protests then moved to Freedom Square – which had, in Soviet times, been known as Lenin Square – and demonstrators started to arrive from the regions as they gathered strength. 'I knew that the parties had lots of support, but I was honestly quite surprised to see so many people coming out, especially people from the villages with their old cars and buses, trying to come to Tbilisi even though the ministry of the interior tried to block the roads,' says Nini Gogiberidze. 'I was coming back to town the day the protests started and my car was in the middle of this traffic jam, thousands of people going to Tbilisi. What was impressive was that it was people you wouldn't really expect to get involved in such things.'

Loudspeakers and a big video screen with a feed from Rustavi-2 were set up right in front of the arched portico of the parliament building on Tbilisi's main street, Rustaveli Avenue. The National Movement's symbol – the flag of St George, with five red crosses on a white background – fluttered above the crowd, alongside the flags and fists of Kmara. Some of the country's best musicians drove in a truck in the middle of the night, set up an improvised stage, and began to play: folk-rock, traditional dance tunes, indie pop, even the Causasian skank of Georgian reggae. Young activists handed out flowers and sandwiches to policemen. Artists, writers and motley players began to tour the country, stirring up dissent – the 'Artcom', they called them, this caravan of literati and rockers – while Kmara set up civil disobedience committees in the universities, encouraging yet more people to head for Tbilisi.

A few days later, early in the morning, a black armoured limousine drew up near the parliament building. A grey-haired man stepped out and looked around him. It's not clear what Shevardnadze thought he could achieve by confronting his opponents face to face, although he had always considered himself a brave man, but he didn't get the reception he might have hoped for. When he tried to speak to people, thousands began to jeer and whistle, the rising clamour of abuse obliterating his words. The great artist of the deal could find nobody willing to make one last compromise. He looked sadly at the mocking crowd, got back into his car, and left.

As the first week of protests ended and the election results continued to trickle in, rain started to pour down and the temperature dropped. Winter was coming on fast. The protesters lit up braziers and huddled under plastic sheeting, but everyone was shivering, wet and dirty. They slept where they could, some of them dossing down in buses or dozing fitfully, in shifts; in Kmara's headquarters, there were crumpled bodies in every corner. Some fell ill through cold and exhaustion. The downpour continued but the bands kept right on playing, locked into the groove. 'We called them the "rain musicians", because they just didn't stop, despite the weather. One night at 3 a.m. their equipment exploded in the rain, but they played on,' says Giorgi Kandelaki. Some of the tunes which were adopted as revolutionary anthems seemed to capture the feelings of longing for a new kind of unity which had spilled out onto the streets. 'If we sing the same song together,' one urged, 'we can build a house...' The crowd immediately identified another popular song, about people selling rotten apples, with the Shevardnadze government. The hypnotic one-word chorus of a third song seemed to transport people into a communal trance, as the Georgian name for Georgia – 'Sa-kart-ve-lo, Sa-kart-ve-lo' – was endlessly repeated.

Soldiers and armed police in flak jackets and helmets filled the streets of Tbilisi and prevented opposition supporters from entering the capital. Mikheil Saakashvili told the demonstrators that Shevardnadze must recognise that his governing bloc had been defeated, or he must resign. 'Resign! Resign!' echoed the chanting crowd. He demanded the arrest of the ballot-rigging 'bandits' in the administration, and said that if Shevardnadze didn't quit, he would share the fate of Slobodan Milošević. 'There is a 12-square-metre cell waiting for him,' he warned.[9] This was incendiary talk, and the crowd loved it. But Saakashvili's allies, Zurab Zhvania and Nino Burjanadze, weren't going quite so far, at least not yet. They merely demanded a re-run of the dubious polls. Indeed, most people in the opposition still believed that this was a dress rehearsal for the presidential elections in 2005. 'At this point, I couldn't imagine Shevardnadze resigning,' recalls Gigi Ugulava.

Events were accelerating by the hour; few could foresee what would happen next; predictions became obsolete almost as soon as they were made; 50,000 people were on the streets now, and the protest was fast becoming a revolt. Shevardnadze warned of civil war, again invoking the demons of anarchy which devastated Georgia in the 1990s. He said the elections had been democratic and transparent, and that his future shouldn't be decided by the baying of the mob: 'I do not intend to resign at the demand of individual politicians and a few dozen young people waving flags.'[10]

Saakashvili called a temporary halt to the round-the-clock demonstrations and headed out into the provinces to speak at a series of public meetings. It was then, with the streets empty, that Shevardnadze made a disastrous mistake. He asked the ruler of the semi-autonomous Georgian region of Adjara, Aslan Abasidze, to send his supporters to Tbilisi and occupy the space outside parliament where the opposition rallies had been. Critics had called Shevardnadze a feudal lord, but Abashidze was closer to the real thing. He ran Adjara like a medieval estate, taking little notice of the government in Tbilisi and refusing to hand over tax revenues. His party, Revival, never won less than 95 per cent of the votes in any election, and no dissent was tolerated. Abashidze had quarrelled with Shevardnadze many times, but the president now decided to use the Adjaran leader's hired muscle to maintain his hold on power. People in Tbilisi were astonished, furious. 'I couldn't believe it, it was so stupid,' says Gigi Ugulava. 'But it was a sign that Shevardnadze was ready to go all the way.' Several thousand Adjarans, many of them promised money or threatened with the loss of their jobs, set up camp outside parliament. Moving among them were Adjaran special forces: Abashidze's heavy mob.

Some feared that physical clashes were now inevitable. 'I thought the most likely outcome was a bloodbath,' says one observer. But for Nini Gogiberidze, who knew some of the Adjarans through family connections, the situation was not as ominous as it seemed. 'It was stupid but it was not scary,' she says. 'Most of them were told at their work to come to Tbilisi and participate in the demonstration, and they had no option of saying no. They were just regular people; of course some of them were a bit crazy, fans of Abashidze, but most of them were just regular guys who were obliged to stand there because of the regime in Adjara. At the end of the evening, some of them were coming to the other side, they were getting money from Abashidze's guys and just going drinking with friends they had in Tbilisi.'

Two days later, the official results were finally declared: Shevardnadze's bloc in first place, Abashidze's Revival party second, and the National Movement third. The US State Department said it was 'deeply disappointed' in the results and in Georgia's leadership, speaking of 'massive vote fraud'. But Shevardnadze pressed ahead regardless, calling the first session of the new parliament for 22 November 2003, setting himself on a clear collision course with the opposition. Mikheil Saakashvili said he would not allow the new parliament to start work. If it did, it would become legitimate and difficult to dislodge without open conflict.

Tension was rising; there were fears of civil war, rumours that Abashidze would be appointed as the speaker of parliament, effectively second in line to the presidency. A number of pro-Shevardnadze officials resigned; his support was starting to crack. The chairman of the state television and radio company quit his job, saying the president had pressurised his channels for more overt support. He accused Shevardnadze of living in a vacuum, surrounded by reactionaries who weren't giving him a clear picture of what was really going on in the country.

Mikheil Saakashvili had been touring Georgia's western provinces, staging rallies where no opposition party had before, sometimes as many as five a day. The day before parliament was due to convene, dramatic television pictures showed a long column of vehicles crawling through the night, closing in on Tbilisi, carrying thousands of people: battered old buses, Ladas, Mercedes, minibuses, flying the flag of the National Movement and sounding their horns in unison; a cacophony of defiance. Saakashvili was perched in the front seat of a grimy red-and-white bus, his face set hard in determination.

The images were breathtaking; as the convoy moved through the darkness, headlights shining, it looked like a stream of fire coursing through the hills… It's said that it was the Liberty Institute's Levan Ramishvili who had recalled the freedom ride to Belgrade three years earlier, which brought the provincial footsoldiers of the revolution to the capital. If it worked in Serbia, he thought, why not here too?

This was the signal that it was time for the final push. 'When the convoy entered Tbilisi, we started to feel that it was nearing the end of the time of Shevardnadze,' says Keto Kobiashvili. 'We were just waiting for the command to go in.'

The opposition leaders met late into the night, finalising their battle plans. By dawn, it was decided; they would storm the Georgian parliament and prevent the new government from sitting. It would be revolution. 'Some people argued no, we shouldn't do it, but by the morning it was finally accepted,' says Giga Bokeria, who attended the marathon session. 'Time was not our friend by that point. It had to be done before they legitimised the parliament, and it had to be done because the people were demanding it.'

PEOPLE DESERVE WHAT THEY CHOOSE

On 22 November the heavy weather had lifted and the sun had begun to shine as around 100,000 people gathered in Tbilisi's Freedom Square. A truck pulled in carrying an effigy of President Shevardnadze; it was set upon and smashed. Among the flags and banners, one bore a message in Serbian: 'Gotov je' – *'He's finished'* – the slogan of the Belgrade revolution. This was the biggest demonstration that the Georgian capital had seen since the protests for independence from the Soviet Union; it wasn't just the political activists and the Kmara students, it was also the poor and the fed up, the ones sick of waiting for wages and electricity and justice and all the other things that President Shevardnadze had promised. For them, Shevardnadze embodied everything that was wrong with Georgia. He had failed, and he was taking the country down with him. It was time for him to go.

From his headquarters at the City Hall, Mikheil Saakashvili ordered the crowd to start moving. But thousands of policemen and soldiers had sealed off roads leading to the presidential administration building and the Georgian parliament, barricading the way with buses. In front of the parliament building, the Abashidze followers still stood, waiting. Saakashvili's supporters began to heave the buses out of their way and the crowd surged forward into the lines of riot police – which parted, allowing them to go through. 'I had no idea what was planned that day,' says Nini Gogiberidze. 'But when we started to move towards the presidential administration building, the police were not doing anything, they were just allowing us to go, and then I knew how it was going to be.'

It seemed amazing, in the moment, but it was the culmination of weeks of informal conversations on the street and secret negotiations behind the scenes, encouraging Shevardnadze's forces to defect, disobey orders, or at least not to attack the protesters. 'They all had to know that they were losing, they were doomed,' says Giga Bokeria. 'We were telling them that if they used violence it would be a very risky terrain for everyone.' According to one Georgian journalist's account, the message had hit home. She recalls being trapped between a crowd of protesters and a line of policemen in black masks, when a protest leader started shouting through his megaphone, 'Shevardnadze must resign!' The masked officer right in front of her responded with a single word: '*Amen.*'

Then the final call came to march on parliament. Another line of defence was breached. It seemed that nothing could stop them. 'We had critical mass, we had complete superiority,' says Giorgi Kandelaki. 'When we confronted the troops we all raised our hands to show we had no weapons. Some people were carrying flowers in their hands – roses.'

The parliamentary session was due to start at 4 p.m. The national anthem had ended and Shevardnadze had started his speech when Mikheil Saakashvili rushed into the parliamentary chamber, shouting at the president, 'Resign! Resign!' There was a brief scuffle and Saakashvili was forced out again through the doors, but he quickly burst back in, waving a long-stemmed red rose above his head. Tea

Tutberidze and a group of Kmara activists shouted for others to follow him in. People rushed through the doors, and fist fights broke out as Shevardnadze's supporters were driven back. Shevardnadze was quickly bundled away by his bodyguards, looking startled and bewildered, his white hair dishevelled, the pages of his speech flapping in his hand. The former Soviet potentate, the man who had helped to end the Cold War, Washington's long-time buddy, was on the run. The protesters jeered at his undignified retreat. They controlled the parliament; they controlled the city; they controlled Georgia.

Flanked by a group of youths, some of them wearing orange Kmara T-shirts, Saakashvili strode up to the podium, picked up Shevardnadze's unfinished glass of tea, drained it insouciantly, and called on Nino Burjanadze to take up the role of acting president. He was still clutching the rose, although its bloom had been decapitated somewhere in the melee. Shevardnadze was hustled into his limousine and driven away, amidst a clamour of derisive whistling from the crowd. 'When I saw how Shevardnadze left, I really felt our victory. He was humiliated and frightened,' says Tinatin Khidasheli. 'He could have left as a hero. But that was his choice, and people deserve what they choose.'

Meanwhile, protesters had dragged Shevardnadze's chair out of his office and were busily smashing it to bits – apart from that, the only damage was a couple of broken windows. There had been no beatings, no killings. Over the past few weeks, the opposition had been telling people again and again that violence would only provoke a crackdown; they had restrained people from fighting with the police or attacking Abashidze's Adjarans. Now they felt relief, and a sweet surge of pride. Tea Tutberidze and a couple of her friends raced through the labyrinthine corridors of the presidential administration building, right up to the roof, where they raised the Kmara flag alongside that of the National Movement.

Outside parliament, people danced, drank and sang folk songs; some of the Adjarans disappeared, while others joined the celebrations. Activists set up an all-night vigil to protect the building from looters and vandals. There were rumours of a backlash, of an army crackdown, of the arrival of Russian special forces. They never came.

The mood was charged with euphoria and disbelief. As one Tbilisi blogger wrote shortly afterwards: 'Everybody's still reeling. The idea of Georgia without Shevardnadze is simply too big to grasp. For all practical purposes, this guy was Georgia, and he was such a major international figure for so many years that it was simply assumed that he'd always be around; much as the sun rises every day, Eddie would just always be there. What was maybe most amazing about last night was how peaceful it was... A major political upheaval in the Caucasus with no bloodshed? Come on, nobody does anything here the non-violent way. A year ago, or hell, a month ago, if you'd have asked me where the next bloodless, popular revolution would take place, Georgia would've been pretty low down on my list. Like, after Haiti. It's just amazing.'[11]

Mikheil Saakashvili was triumphant: 'A velvet revolution has taken place in Georgia,' he declared.[12] But one Rustavi-2 presenter had been watching young women handing out flowers to policemen, and coined her own phrase, one that would stick: this was the 'Rose Revolution'.

The next day was a national holiday, but Shevardnadze was not celebrating. He had retreated to his official residence on the outskirts of Tbilisi, accusing the opposition of an 'attempted coup d'etat' and saying he wouldn't resign.

Rustavi-2 showed units of troops changing sides and joining the demonstrators; one special forces commander phoned the studio to announce that he would not support Shevardnadze any more. The president declared a state of emergency – but it wasn't clear who, exactly, would enforce it. 'It was so funny – this guy who's already a nobody is announcing a state of emergency and calling troops to control things,' recalls Tinatin Khidasheli. 'It was like, who are you? Yesterday's man!' Saakashvili claimed that Shevardnadze commanded the military to attack the protesters and assassinate him, although Shevardnadze strongly denied this.

Saakashvili asked his supporters to march on the presidential residence if Shevardnadze didn't resign. When he and his allies arrived there for the final negotiations, an angry mob had already formed, determined to storm the compound. 'There was a huge crowd and I was having real problems stopping them going up this narrow road to Shevardnadze's residence,' says Giga Bokeria. 'Some people even attacked us because we were not allowing them to go up there, they were saying, "Who are you to stop us?" If they had gone up, they would have been unstoppable. It would have been really bad. He could have been killed.'

That evening, Shevardnadze resigned. The country's new rulers promised to guarantee his security; unlike for Milošević, there would be no cell for old Eddie. Looking tired and subdued, he gave a farewell interview to reporters. 'Mr Shevardnadze, where are you going now?' one journalist inquired. 'Home,' he replied, and said no more.[13]

As the news came through, there was an outburst of jubilation on Rustaveli Avenue. People set off firecrackers, opened up bottles of wine, ran to the shops to buy champagne. Cars raced around the city honking their horns. It had all happened so fast, faster than even those who had wished for it had expected. 'I felt happy, but I also felt sad because it was so good being in Kmara – taking risks, doing these actions – but now it was back to the quiet life,' says Keto Kobiashvili. 'I was sad that the most exciting experience of my life was over.'

A LOYAL BEAST'S LAST FAREWELL

In the weeks that followed, intense debate continued over what, exactly, had happened during those days on the streets of Tbilisi. Had there really been a revolution? Or was it simply a coup which installed Mikheil Saakashvili and his allies in place of Eduard Shevardnadze? After all, these had been parliamentary elections; Georgia hadn't been due to change its president for months. The Georgian political analyst Ghia Nodia called it a 'revolt in defence of the constitution': an uprising to enforce the law. But one British commentator insisted that it was just a 'changing of the guard within an unchanged power structure', a putsch 'stage-managed' by the Americans in order to ensure the safe flow of oil through the

Caucasus pipeline to the greedy, gas-guzzling West.[14] Shevardnadze accused both the Russians and the Americans – the US embassy in Tbilisi and the National Democratic Institute, as well as George Soros – of having been involved in a plot to overthrow him.

Some have pointed to the role played by the US ambassador to Georgia, Richard Miles, who had also served as the US ambassador to Yugoslavia in the run-up to the NATO attack on the country. Was he employing the dark arts of regime change in Georgia? American funding helped to prepare the environment in which the revolution became possible – training politicians, lawyers, journalists and civil rights campaigners, creating a network of democracy advocates. But although the Americans had lost faith in Shevardnadze to secure their interests in the country, Miles says it would be wrong to suggest that the US supported the act of insurrection, although he admits that American unhappiness over the manipulation of the election may have given some encouragement to Saakashvili. The Americans, he says, had been worried about the volatility of the protests, fearing a total meltdown. 'It could have gotten extraordinarily messy extraordinarily fast,' says Miles. 'It was quite a dangerous situation.'[15]

Some Kmara activists say that the US clearly supported them, but all of them reject the idea that the American ambassador somehow orchestrated the revolution. 'This whole story of him being the mastermind is nonsense,' says Giorgi Kandelaki. 'He was not only *not* contributing, but also at times calling for everything to stop.' Some suggest that the Americans were both slow to realise exactly how unpopular Shevardnadze had become and suspicious about the radicalism of Saakashvili, despite his strong pro-Western, free-market stance.

'Serbia was much different, the United States had declared an open interest in getting rid of Milošević. But in many circles, particularly in the US, one day before the revolution, Shevardnadze was still the man,' says Kandelaki. 'Western assistance specifically for this revolution was very small. They were sceptical, they were saying, "In five minutes, civil war will start." It was only Soros who knew directly what he was giving money for.'

Nevertheless, the US quickly wrapped Mikheil Saakashvili in a fervent embrace. He was now their man. Fewer than two months after the revolution, Saakashvili won a landslide victory in a new presidential election, gaining an almost unbelievable 96 per cent of the vote. Shortly after that, his party and its former opposition allies swept the board at parliamentary polls. They now had almost total power to shape the country's future, with unequivocal Western support and no significant internal opposition. Symbolically, the red-and-white emblem used by Saakashvili's National Movement party was adopted as Georgia's new national flag.

But there was still some unfinished business in the west of the country. Directly after the revolution, Aslan Abashidze had broken off relations between his region of Adjara and the government in Tbilisi, saying that Saakashvili had desposed a legitimate president. 'Revolutions have never brought any benefit to any country,' he stated. 'They can only destroy, and such movements are usually led by people who have not brought any good to the nation and use all methods to get into power.'[16]

For Saakashvili, and so for Kmara, there was only one logical response. The opposition had unseated Shevardnadze; the next target had to be Abashidze. But this was a far more tricky game. Abashidze appeared all-powerful; a strongman with few qualms about flexing his muscles. In Adjara, Kmara was forced to operate as a genuine underground resistance movement; some of its cells didn't even know of each other's existence. They worked cautiously, stealthily, often under cover of darkness. 'They would throw their leaflets off the roofs of buildings or just leave them on the pavement then run away, because if they were arrested they would be severely beaten,' says Keto Kobiashvili. 'Some of them would have to come to Tbilisi to be taken to hospital because they were beaten so badly. Once when they were putting up posters, police caught them and made them drink the glue. They had no protection.'

Kmara activists smuggled propaganda across the border into the province, travelling separately on public buses to reduce the likelihood of capture. 'They really were remarkably crazy guys, really hot-headed people,' says Giorgi Kandelaki, admiringly. Abashidze's security forces were searching vehicles for subversive material, collecting passport numbers and registration details. Nevertheless, posters, leaflets and graffiti began appearing, accusing the Adjaran leader of being a dictator. Nothing like them had ever been seen in Adjara before.

Small groups of students then began to protest openly. They were quickly detained, and when police searched their apartments, they claimed to have found arms caches and drugs. 'They "found" so many weapons that we started joking that we were surprised they hadn't found ballistic missiles yet,' says Kandelaki. Opposition party offices were ransacked and burned; gangs of toughs in black leather jackets swaggered through the streets, looking for rebel youths and dealing out summary justice.

By April 2004, the storm was close to breaking. Georgian troops were deployed close to the border with the province, and Abashidze responded by declaring a state of emergency, imposing a curfew, mobilising army reservists, and distributing weapons amongst his supporters. He said Saakashvili was plotting a coup and Georgian officials were planning to assassinate him, and called on Russia – which had a military base in Adjara – to send in peacekeeping troops. All the signs suggested he was preparing for war.

A few days later, Abashidze's forces blew up the bridges connecting the region to the rest of Georgia, sealing off the borders, saying an invasion was imminent. Schools and universities were shut. On 4 May students and teachers took to the streets of the Adjaran capital, Batumi, but they were drenched by water cannon and beaten back by police units armed with iron rods and batons; dozens were hospitalised. The province was on a high state of alert; houses were raided and opposition activists taken away. Saakashvili had given Abashidze an ultimatum: disarm his militias and submit to Georgian government control, or resign. Abashidze refused. His militiamen patrolled the streets, firing their machine guns into the air in warning.

But, as in Tbilisi, police and senior officials started to switch sides, realising that Abashidze's power was crumbling, panicking that they might be dragged down with him. 'We had done a lot of work on defections,' says Giga Bokeria. 'We knew all the regime structures, all the criminal structures, we knew who was soft, who was hard. One by one, the defectors came out: military, police, his criminals. It was unpleasant but it had to be done.'

The next day, the protesters were back, but now there were thousands more of them. 'We were angry, we didn't want them to demonstrate again because we didn't want them to be beaten again,' Bokeria recalls. 'Abashidze's message was, "Back off, I will shoot, I will kill the kids – do you want to be responsible for that? No? So go home." But when we saw they were gathering again, we signalled for all our people to come out – *everybody*.' The main routes into Batumi were sealed off but people streamed towards the city on foot. As the demonstrations grew, Abashidze's militias began to melt away. Within hours, all the mechanisms which had kept him in power for more than a decade had begun to collapse. People crowded around television screens to watch Saakashvili announce that the Abashidze era had ended. In the early hours of the morning, the Adjaran leader handed in his resignation and fled into exile in Moscow. Fireworks lit up the night sky above Batumi as the celebrations raged into the night.

Gigi Ugulava, by now a deputy minister in the Saakashvili government, showed journalists around Abashidze's opulent residence in Batumi. Abashidze had amassed a huge hoard of antique furniture, expensive foreign cars, speedboats and a kennel filled with scores of pedigree dogs – part of a wider portfolio of properties, businesses and bank accounts which Georgian officials valued at tens of millions of dollars. All of this, declared Ugulava, was now owned by the people. But one prized item would escape appropriation: Basmach, a prize-winning Caucasian shepherd dog who had been refusing to eat for days, pining for the departed autocrat. The touching saga of the loyal hound gripped the public imagination, and Georgian officials took pity on him. Basmach, too, was allowed to leave, and was put on a plane to Moscow to comfort his master in exile.

The opposition had achieved its goal: not just one revolution, but two, and far more quickly than even the most fervent believer could have predicted. The main players who shaped Kmara began to disperse; some back to their studies, some into business, some into politics. Giga Bokeria went into parliament; Gigi Ugulava would move through a series of high-profile posts, becoming the head of the presidential administration and then the mayor of Tbilisi; Alexander Lomaia was appointed education minister. The revolutionaries sat down to work in the same buildings they had once blockaded. Unlike in Serbia, there was no discussion about forming a Kmara political party. With the National Movement in power, it wasn't seen as necessary. The movement simply dissolved.

'We just returned to normal life,' says Giorgi Kandelaki. 'The Serbian experience showed that if we had founded a political party, it was very doubtful that it would have succeeded. One of the reasons we achieved what we did is because we told everybody that we were not a party. Because in this typical post-Soviet society, all people – especially young people – were completely apathetic about participation in any kind of politics. They thought that if you were in a party, your aim was to come to power and be able to steal. So it wouldn't really have worked if we had come up with some political ambitions afterwards.' Other Kmara activists took jobs at the Liberty Institute, which now had a significant influence on government policy.

Some of those who had helped to inspire the revolution were concerned by the extent of the control that Mikheil Saakashvili now had over Georgia – particularly after the subsequent death of his more moderate and less populist ally, Zurab Zhvania, in a mysterious gas-heater accident. Tinatin Khidasheli, who rapidly split with the 'rose revolutionaries' and went into opposition, suggests that when Saakashvili changed the constitution to give the presidency more power, he seized the power to behave like an 'absolute monarch', espousing democratic principles but ignoring them if they prevented him from getting his own way. Many, however, were willing to give the new president the benefit of the doubt as he vowed to bring prosperity to Georgia. 'Before the revolution, Georgia had no chance of becoming a normal country,' says Keto Kobiashvili. 'Now we have the chance. It will all depend on how we use it.'

The fact that a youth movement had helped to spark the second bloodless, popular revolution of the twenty-first century had not gone unnoticed. Once was unusual, but twice… for authoritarian leaders all over the former Communist bloc, this was an alarming development. The *Washington Post* reported that President Putin of Russia approached Nino Burjanadze at a state funeral in neighbouring Azerbaijan and told her: 'All the leaders of the CIS [the union of former Soviet states] are [expletive] in their pants.'[17] The newspaper spared its readers the exact details of Putin's profanity, but the underlying sentiment was unmistakeable: the Rose Revolution had them rattled.

The phone at the Liberty Institute's office in Tbilisi began to ring; democracy activists from abroad wanted to offer their congratulations – and to find out how, exactly, they had done it. One of the calls would come from Ukraine.

CHAPTER THREE

THE YELLOW AND THE BLACK

UKRAINE

The clocks went forward in Ukraine on the last Sunday of March 2004, signalling the dawn of springtime. In the depths of that night, in cities right across the wide expanse of the former Soviet republic, thousands of black-and-white stickers appeared on walls, lamp posts and bus stops. They posed one enigmatic question: *What is Kuchmism?* Next to the question was the image of a rising sun, a website address, and the word 'Pora' – *It's Time*.

Yaryna Yasynevych, a student from the grand western city of Lviv, was one of the hundreds of young people who went out that night to cover the country in stickers. There was a sense of rising excitement as she and her friends stepped into the darkness; it felt, she says, like setting out on a fantastic journey, its destination as yet uncharted: 'The clocks were changing and it was like a new beginning for us, the start of a new time...'

Andriy Ignatov from Kiev was also out that night: 'People were shocked: "How could they have done this, they must have a big secret network." No such thing had been done before, so it immediately caught the attention: "Who are these people? It's time...? Time for *what?*"'

A few weeks later, more leaflets appeared bearing the same word: *Pora*. A logo showed a clock ticking down: fifteen minutes to midnight. They directed people to another website, and a manifesto: 'Time to give birth to a wave of freedom that will wash away the dirt, that will purify the soul of Ukraine... We say – we cannot wait any more... Time to stand up or fall... Time to fight for ideals, not politicians... Time to act, time to struggle, time to win!'

And then there was a prediction, made more in hope, it seemed, than anything else: 'Slovak Republic 1998, Serbia 2000, Georgia 2003... and Ukraine 2004.'[1]

A BODY IN THE FOREST

Just as in Serbia and Georgia, the roots of this new youth movement lay deep in bitter and seemingly futile years of thwarted struggles for democratic change, and had been nurtured by a sense of righteous fury about attacks on the independent media. Three and a half years earlier, in November 2000, the mutilated body of a young journalist had been discovered in woodlands outside the capital; 31-year-old Georgiy Gongadze was the founder of a website called *Ukrainska Pravda* – 'Ukrainian Truth' – which specialised in muck-raking investigations into the murky business practices of Ukraine's oligarchs and political elite. Before Gongadze disappeared, he had been complaining for some time that he was being followed by the secret services. His corpse was eventually found buried in a shallow grave – or, rather, his body was found there. The killers had cut his head off.

The investigation at first seemed to be going nowhere. This was a journalist writing for a relatively obscure website – hardly a nationally recognised figure – and the police couldn't seem to find much enthusiasm for tracing his murderers. But then the Socialist opposition leader Olexander Moroz released transcripts from a set of remarkable audio tapes which he said had been made secretly by one of President Leonid Kuchma's bodyguards. The extracts, taken from hundreds of hours of recordings, seemed to suggest that President Kuchma himself had been involved in ordering the killing of Gongadze. The conversation on the tapes, a torrent of ranting and cursing, was almost unbelievable. Using what more sensitive media outlets referred to as 'colourful language', Kuchma appeared to demand that Gongadze be deported and handed over to Chechen rebels for punishment. His interior minister responded by boasting about a special unit of 'eagles' under his command which was ready to fulfil even the most unconventional of orders. He promised Kuchma: 'Everything you want, they'll do.'[2]

While Kuchma admitted that it was his voice on the tapes, he said that they had been electronically manipulated to incriminate him and denied that he had any role in Gongadze's death. 'Why should a president who had just won an election seek to murder an unknown journalist?' he asked.[3]

Kuchma had become Ukraine's second post-Soviet president in 1994. He had overseen the defeat of hyperinflation and the slow recovery of the Ukrainian economy from post-Communist ruin. But he had allowed the country to become dominated by powerful business clans, who came to control not only the economy but the media and politics; as the tapes also revealed, they believed themselves to be above the law. The Gongadze affair – the grisly killing of a young man who had attempted to expose what he saw as the sordid realities behind the façade of Ukrainian democracy – would become the greatest scandal of Kuchma's presidency, even more damaging than revelations of alleged plans to sell military equipment to Saddam Hussein.

Mykhailo Svystovych was a veteran of the struggles for independence from the Soviet Union. In 1990, Ukrainian students who were inspired by the velvet revolutions in Prague, Berlin and Warsaw had blockaded buildings, set up a tent camp in the centre of the capital, Kiev, and staged mass protests until they achieved major concessions from the Communist government. Svystovych – a garrulous, erudite, slightly scruffy figure who describes himself as a conservative and lives in a small town on the outskirts of Kiev – had been among them. He had absorbed at first hand the tales told by the Ukrainian political prisoners who had been released from the Soviet gulag in the late 1980s, spread the word at clandestine meetings in student dormitories, joined the hunger strike when students took to the streets demanding independence – 'I had the simplest role in those protests, I just lay down and didn't eat anything' – and later helped pull down the statue of Lenin in central Kiev after Communism fell. He was also an old friend of Georgiy Gongadze. Like everyone else, he was astonished by the covert recordings.

'Many people were amazed by Kuchma swearing, but that meant nothing to me; what struck me were his actions,' he says. 'Why did he pick on this particular journalist? It's simple. Ukraine had no proper opposition then and Kuchma felt he was a kind of king. Very few people could say anything against him. His character is very particular, he always goes after little things and he always gets revenge. He takes any criticism with a great deal of pain. You could see it in the election campaign in 1999 when Georgiy was posing questions to Kuchma. His reaction was close to hysterical, even though the questions were absolutely normal.

'Georgiy had many friends abroad, he knew many people in the foreign media. Georgiy was trusted. His words had weight because everyone knew he would not lie. That was the reason he was killed.'

Before the tapes were made public, Svystovych had been putting up posters asking, rather forlornly, 'Where is Giorgiy Gongadze?' There was a suspicion, even then, that the authorities were somehow involved in his disappearance. Afterwards, Svystovych wasn't clear what he could or should do next. 'A friend of mine called me and said he wanted to come over. He said to me, "You are just sitting here and doing nothing – why? Georgiy was your friend." I said we were putting up leaflets and writing articles in small newspapers. I understood it was not enough. He said we needed to go to the streets. I said, "Yes, but with who? There's no political support for this." He said, "Let's just go and stand there, the two of us."'

Their first demonstration in December attracted a few hundred people; by the end of the month, thousands more had joined them. Some of them, their faces hidden behind masks, pitched a few tents along Kiev's opulent shopping boulevard, Kreshchatyk – the same place where students had also set up camp during their hunger-strike for independence a decade earlier – and vowed to stay there until justice was done. The 'Ukraine without Kuchma' campaign wasn't just about Gongadze, but about the whole rotten morass they believed the state had become, with its political and moral decadence symbolised by one brutal act. The president dismissed the demonstrations as the work of troublemakers and fascists.

With most of the mainstream media in the hands of presidential allies, the protesters needed their own outlet. Svystovych and his friends decided to set up a website where people could post news, views and rumours, plot direct action and break through what he calls the 'information blockade'. 'At that moment, I'd only been familiar with the internet for about three days,' he says. Their alternative news service, called Maidan, took its name from the Ukrainian words for Independence Square – Maidan Nezalezhnosti – the huge plaza which lies at the heart of Kreshchatyk.

'Unexpectedly for us, within a month the site became hugely popular,' says Svystovych. 'We started getting messages from government employees, from inside the police and the security services, giving us information. Then we started organising these affinity groups and helped them co-ordinate their activities. For them it was easier to be in touch through the website. So there was this whole community of people all around Ukraine that somehow grew around the website, and they started getting acquainted with each other in real life.'

The tent camp held out through the winter, but the Ukraine without Kuchma campaign never reached critical mass. In this country of 47 million people, they needed hundreds of thousands to make any real impact. At the start of March 2001, police evicted the demonstrators from the camp and swept it away like so much litter. Yuri Lutsenko, one of the leaders of Ukraine without Kuchma, declared that the campers would return: 'I can't say now how quickly, but we'll be back.'[4] It would be a long time before his promise would be fulfilled.

Just over a week afterwards, on 9 March, thousands of demonstrators converged on the presidential administration building. Fights broke out with police and some 200 people were arrested – clashes which effectively ended the movement. Some of its leaders simply froze in shock; others were frightened or demoralised. Ordinary Ukrainians had not rallied to their cause. 'We were ready but the people were not, and we couldn't mobilise them,' says Andriy Gusak, another veteran of the 1990 independence movement and a member of Za Pravdu – *For Truth* – a youth group which grew out of the Gongadze protests. 'People were criticising the regime, but only in their kitchens. We couldn't find the key to their hearts.'

They had lost the moral advantage amidst the flying bottles and flailing truncheons. Kuchma had not fallen, and they were no nearer to solving the mystery of what had happened to Giorgiy Gongadze. Za Pravdu imploded. But its leaders – young people who were ready to sacrifice everything for a chance of change – were to keep in touch over the coming years. Among them, Mykhailo Svystovych believed that despite their failure, they had set a kind of example; this was not the end, but a new beginning. 'Before, the left was fighting the right and the authorities were using both sides whenever it suited them,' he says. 'We showed that things could work differently – that you could have honest people against dishonest people. The message we sent was that we first need to get rid of the criminals, and then when we have democracy, people will be able to choose between the right and the left. Before that, we need to forget about political differences, religious differences, language differences, regional differences – all that must be forgotten.'

BANDITS AT LARGE!

Three years later, Leonid Kuchma's time was running out. He had served two terms as president, and wasn't eligible to stand for another. Whoever succeeded him after the presidential election of 2004, his rule would soon be over. He would leave a country which was both utterly corrupt and, in many places, desperately poor. The watchdog organisation Transparency International rated Ukraine among the 15 most corrupt countries in the world. Bribery had become a way of life; doctors, policemen, judges and university administrators regularly elicited kickbacks. State industries were sold off cheaply to relatives and cronies of those in power. Counterfeiting was widespread, with pirated compact discs and computer software openly available everywhere. While neighbouring Poland, Hungary and Slovakia were getting ready to join the European Union, Ukraine's progress had stalled; indeed, it seemed to many that the country had been carved up by profiteering cabals and was becoming an amoral kleptocracy, like the governments of Slobodan Milošević in Serbia and Eduard Shevardnadze in Georgia. The oligarchs and their clans ran innumerable complex and devious schemes and scams designed to filch from the public purse. They took up seats in parliament to bolster their commercial interests and attain immunity from prosecution, set up their own political parties to ensure their economic dominance went unchecked, and funded other 'opposition' parties – some supposedly socialist, some supposedly nationalist – to bleed votes and credibility from the genuine opposition. 'The authorities had no real ideology,' suggests Mykhailo Svystovych. 'The same people would change their views depending on the situation, they could be left-wing one day and right-wing the next day. They were only acting in the interest of their own pockets, like a gang of bandits.'

With its glittering, golden church domes and stately boulevards lined with chestnut trees, Kiev appeared to be an affluent European capital. Cheery Euro-pop blared from rows of chic boutiques, expensive restaurants served up the ubiquitous 'byznes lanch', sportswear shops sold imported Nike and Adidas, and entrepreneurs in Italian suits and dark sunglasses cruised the streets in Jeeps and Mercedes. But even here, in the city centre, pensioners begged for spare coins and scavenged for scraps in skips, while a survey in a Ukrainian business magazine suggested that more than half of the country's young people were thinking about emigrating to find wealth or happiness elsewhere.

As Kuchma's days in office drew closer to their end, his government had become increasingly intolerant of criticism. All but one of the major television channels were virtual mouthpieces for the president and his administration, which instructed editors how to report the news through a system of secret guidelines called *temnyky* ('themes'). Investigative journalists were routinely threatened and attacked; a few, like Gongadze, had died in suspicious circumstances. As the presidential election approached, there was growing pressure on the few remaining independent media outlets. Radio stations rebroadcasting Ukrainian-language news bulletins from the BBC and Radio Liberty were driven off the airwaves.

The opposition believed that the 2004 election could be the most important moment in Ukraine's history since independence: a turning point for the nation. They were determined to be ready. But they also had to overcome what was seen as the traditional easy-going passivity of the Ukrainian public and the fact that young people were utterly disaffected – a phenomenon ingrained by years of Soviet rule and encouraged by the post-Soviet authorities and mass media.

In the year before the election, training seminars for potential opposition activists were held all over Ukraine. Some of them were backed by the Westminster Foundation for Democracy, an organisation funded by the British Foreign Office which aids democratic institutions overseas; others by the US-based Freedom House and other democracy foundations from the Netherlands and Poland. They brought in trainers from Serbia, and later from Belarus and Georgia, to teach the techniques of non-violent resistance – the Gene Sharp doctrines – which had helped to topple the government in Belgrade, but had yet to achieve much in the Belarussian capital, Minsk. The young activists would also learn a little of their own history: about the hunger strikes and tent camps in Kiev in 1990. 'First was usually the Serbian guys, they shared their experiences, told us how they did things, showed us pictures and videos,' says Tetyana Boyko, then a student in Lviv. 'The next day was the guys from [the Belarussian youth movement] Zubr telling us about their experiences, and the third day there was a discussion analysing which of those experiences we could use here in Ukraine, and what we should do. A bit later, through those seminars we held, we started collecting people – colleagues, friends, relatives – who then got acquainted and decided to work together.'

Aleksandar Marić and Siniša Šikman from Otpor were among the trainers who offered their advice, first in Ukraine and later on a field trip to the Serbian city of Novi Sad, Marić's home town. They explained the importance of using the media, of clear messages and strong images – and, above all, the power of *organisation, organisation, organisation*… As they talked and drank late into the evening, a collective spirit began to emerge. The Serbs saw in the young Ukrainians the same creativity and passion they had experienced back in Belgrade during the Milošević years. 'The only difference between Serbs and Ukrainians was that the Ukrainians were harder to motivate,' says Šikman. 'They were more afraid than we had been.'[5] But there were other differences; the Ukrainians didn't have the same umbilical links to the rock 'n' roll counterculture as their Serbian counterparts… and while the Serbs had rejected the folk music which had become so identified with the Milošević government and its warped nationalism, the Ukrainians embraced traditional iconography as part of their patriotic vision.

As they had already shown in Georgia, the Otpor veterans had a certain outlaw glamour, and a big advantage over the 'democracy-builders' from Western foundations: 'One of the reasons why Serbs were so popular as trainers is because no movement in the world would like it to be perceived that they were trained by the Americans,' says Srdja Popović. 'But Serbs, that's something else, we're not Americans, we were even in a war with the Americans.'

They were already becoming experienced in what would later be described as 'exporting revolution'. They didn't see it that way; there was no magic spell which could summon up a resistance movement, they insisted. Each country had to find its own way. And revolution had to be the last resort, not the immediate goal. 'There must be elections and your candidate has to win them,' explains Aleksandar Marić. 'Only if that victory is not recognised, you start organising demonstrations. A takeover of power must absolutely be legal in terms of elections. Then you have a full moral and legal right to protect the electoral will of the citizens through a non-violent revolution. Otherwise you are no different from the dictator you are fighting against.'

In November 2003, during one of the training sessions, the Rose Revolution erupted in Georgia. The young Ukrainians gathered around to watch a CNN report from Tbilisi, awestruck, as Mikheil Saakashvili and his followers stormed the parliament and drove President Shevardnadze out. A peaceful uprising, live on television, and in a former Soviet republic… just like theirs. It had a huge psychological impact, says Mykhailo Svystovych: 'It gave us faith. The conditions in Georgia were much worse for a revolution to start, and still they did it. They had less experience than us, and still they did it. We thought, if a revolution was possible there, it would definitely be possible here.'

Possible… but achievable? Ukraine's population was far, far larger – ten times that of Georgia. There were other differences too; in the industrial east of Ukraine, the majority spoke Russian and many felt a comradely affinity with their old masters in Moscow. In the west, which had become part of the Soviet Union much later than the rest of the country, and where nationalist guerrillas had held out against the Soviets until the early 1950s, people mainly spoke Ukrainian and looked to Europe for their political inspiration – although on the ground, it was far more complex than that, with regional variations of culture, religion, history and politics making easy definitions hard to pin down. A national youth movement would be a spectacularly difficult project to put together. But by the end of 2003, the collective mood was coalescing fast. They had to try. *It's time*, they thought.

The decision was made by a group of veterans of Za Pravdu and Ukraine without Kuchma. Many of the thousand or so young initiates who had been through the training seminars were ready to follow them. They had saved some of the money which the Western foundations had provided for the seminars and used it to print up their first stickers. The movement would be called *Pora* – conveniently, it meant the same in both Ukrainian and Russian, and was instantly familiar to many Ukrainians from a verse by the nineteenth-century poet Ivano Franko, who had urged his people to unite against oppression and had gone to jail for his beliefs. Like Otpor and Kmara, Pora would have no leaders and no political ambitions beyond obliterating all traces of the current government.

On 28 March 2004, the night of the changing clocks, they announced their presence with the nationwide sticker operation. The website address led people to the answer to the question posed by the stickers: 'What is Kuchmism?' It was, they said, poverty, unemployment, organised crime and hopelessness. The only solution was to get together and act against it, before it was too late for Ukraine.

NIGHT OF THE BLACK LEATHER JACKETS

Mukachevo is a quaint little town beyond the Carpathian mountains, in the far west of Ukraine, just a few miles from its borders with Slovakia and Hungary. Its dainty cobbled streets, pastel-painted buildings and Austro-Hungarian architecture survived the central planning of the Soviet era. It's a multicultural place, where Slovakian, Hungarian and Polish words litter the local dialect; this penultimate Ukrainian stop on the express train from Kiev to Budapest had, over the centuries, been ruled by many nations, and they left their traces behind in its narrow, atmospheric lanes. It was here that the newly-founded Pora would face its public test.

At a mayoral election in Mukachevo in April 2004, an opposition candidate appeared to be heading for victory – until polling day, when supporters of the candidate who was loyal to President Kuchma launched an all-out assault on some of the polling stations. 'It was very frightening,' says Maryana Savytska, a 20-year-old who lived in Mukachevo and was one of Pora's earliest recruits. 'After voting ended at about 8 p.m., the attacks started. They attacked the polling station where I was twice. Their main aim was to steal the ballot papers.

'They were big strong guys dressed in black, with leather jackets, sunglasses and skinhead haircuts. They looked like mafia. They knocked down the doors and kicked people and smashed up two buildings. There was a terrible situation when these gangs were kicking election observers, and a hundred or so metres away was a police car, and the police didn't go and help, they just sat there and watched.'

Another young election observer called it 'theatre of the absurd'. She saw MPs, journalists and Pora activists thrown out of polling stations – one sent sprawling headlong down the stairs – and then a group of what she called 'unknown persons' breaking in to try to steal the voting papers. '"Unknown persons", she noted, 'seem to play an unusually significant role in Ukrainian elections.'[6]

The Kuchma loyalist was, unsurprisingly, declared the winner, despite exit polls suggesting that he had been roundly defeated. But Pora set up a small tent camp outside Mukachevo's pastel-green town hall, and as the scandal resonated beyond the borders of Ukraine, the forged results were eventually reversed. It was only a lowly mayoral contest in a relatively obscure provincial town, but for many, it pointed to what lay ahead, and how far those around President Kuchma would be prepared to go to retain their power. 'Since 2001, both government and opposition had been getting ready for the elections in 2004, because both sides realised that their future depended on the outcome. Both were preparing for the showdown,' says Yaryna Yasynevych, who had travelled from Lviv to help set up the Pora camp. 'Mukachevo was like the start of the presidential election campaign, because there was not only fraud and incorrect counting of the votes, but also the use of force. It was like the government was practising for what it would do later. They wanted to frighten people, to make them afraid to react in a way the government didn't like. But it was also like a practice session for us.'

Mukachevo was also the place where the deep complications which would characterise the next few months of Pora's existence first became clear – at least to those who were controlling the movement in its early stages. Outsiders and rank-and-file activists would remain largely unaware of what was really going on until the height of the 2004 presidential election campaign. It even came as a surprise to some of those inside its inner circle: there were two similar but separate youth organisations, both called Pora.

The first Pora – what would become known as 'black' Pora because of its black-and-white graphics – was the one which had staged the overnight sticker operation. The second – nicknamed 'yellow' Pora because of its yellow leaflets with the ticking clock logo which strongly resembled the one used in the anti-Milošević campaign in Serbia – appeared in public at Mukachevo for the first time.

'Yellow' Pora had held its inaugural meeting in the western city of Uzhgorod, not far from Mukachevo, just before the disputed mayoral elections. 'We were preparing people to eat bad meals and work with tents and sleeping bags instead of notebooks and manuals,' recalls Olexander Solontai, who would become one of its spokespeople. On the very first day, the meeting was raided by police – a sign of times to come.

The 'Yellow' Pora website was vague about the movement's origins, stating – in somewhat bureaucratic language – that it had been created by 'representatives of numerous civic organisations' to campaign for a democratic Ukraine with a 'Euro-Atlantic' outlook: pro-Western, eager to become part of the European Union and NATO. The website said Pora would try to attract the public towards 'progressive forces in society' and mobilise protests if the elections were falsified. It was, it said, completely independent and non-partisan.[7]

However, 'Yellow' Pora was originally intended to be just one part of a complex election project organised by a pro-democracy organisation called the Freedom of Choice Coalition. It would use the Freedom of Choice Coalition's premises in central Kiev, and would be able to tap into the nationwide network of youth groups which the Coalition had already built up with backing from its international supporters – some of the same groups which had also been involved in Serbia and Georgia, including USAID, the National Democratic Institute, Freedom House and the American, British and Canadian embassies.

Some of the main players in yellow Pora had also worked for the Freedom of Choice Coalition. Vladyslav Kaskiv had been the Coalition's coordinator and would emerge as the central figure in yellow Pora – the closest thing it had to a leader. Kaskiv was tall, swarthy and earnest, although he would occasionally allow himself a burst of shy laughter. He had grown up in western Ukraine where, as he put it, 'the air is steeped with the idea of freedom'. It was the student strikes of 1990 which had turned him into a career democracy activist. 'Those times completely changed the situation in the country,' he explained. 'Everything you were taught in childhood began to disintegrate in front of your eyes.'[8]

As well as the Freedom of Choice Coalition, Kaskiv had worked for one of George Soros's international network of democracy organisations and had been involved in the Gongadze protests as a member of Za Pravdu. By 2004 he was 30 years old; a smart operator with all the right connections, and a logical figure to motivate the next generation. 'There was something about the personality of Vlad Kaskiv that suggested he could make things happen,' says Marek Kapusta of the Slovakian OK98 campaign, who had advised the Freedom of Choice Coalition. Kaskiv says that he never wanted to be a revolutionary or a politician, although eventually he would become both. 'Revolution was never our goal,' he insists. 'Pora was created to bring the truth to ordinary people. Revolution was just Plan B.'

Iryna Chupryna, a young woman who worked as Kaskiv's assistant at the Freedom of Choice Coalition and at Pora, says the emergence of two youth organisations with the same name was just a remarkable coincidence. 'Two different groups were thinking about this idea independently. Simultaneously, or very close to each other in time, they came to the idea that Pora would be the best name for it. It's a curious fact but it's true,' she says. 'Maybe you can sometimes hear that one wing stole the name from the other, but it's not true: two different groups came to the same idea. Black Pora was a much more aggressive campaign against Kuchma. Ours was more positive and educational.'

This was a tricky problem for the fledgling 'black' Pora group. It had to decide whether to go on the offensive, complain about the parallel youth group and begin the election campaign with a divided public image, or to remain silent in the cause of unity. Many were angry and wanted to hit back; Mykhailo Svystovych counselled them to remain calm. 'Some of our people were appalled that another organisation used our name,' he says. 'But I used whatever authority I had as an older person not to raise this issue. My motivation was that people didn't know much about us, we'd just started, and it would be very difficult to explain this to people, they would see this as fighting over a brand name. What was most important for us was fighting the regime, not fighting for a brand. So we didn't raise the issue. We were trying to establish some kind of relations with those guys; we knew them all personally.'

Olexander Solontai of 'yellow' Pora says he initially thought that the existence of a parallel movement was some kind of security service plot to discredit them. But eventually he came to the conclusion that the 'black' Pora had been first. 'We stole the name,' Solontai says. 'Although it's basically a name that was stolen twice, because it comes from the Serbian campaign, *Vreme je* [It's Time].'

None of this really mattered much – at least, not for many months. From Mukachevo onwards, the two groups worked closely together. They posted each other's campaign information on their separate websites. Activists were members of one or both without even realising that two Poras existed. Only insiders knew the whole truth. Those who saw the fresh-faced young men and women in the television pictures coming out of Mukachevo simply realised that there was a new force within Ukrainian society; a force for justice which was mobilising for action. 'The disgrace of Mukachevo has awakened us, and we will awaken the Ukrainian nation,' the yellow Pora site declared.[9] The country, it stated, was at a crossroads, facing a critical choice between two possible futures: European integration or authoritarian regression. The emails began arriving instantly. Many young Ukrainians liked what they saw, and were ready to sign up for the mission ahead.

THE EGG PROCLAIMS ITS INNOCENCE

The leading opposition contender in the 2004 presidential race was a cautious, mild-mannered technocrat called Viktor Yushchenko, who had been prime minister in President Kuchma's government in the late 1990s. During his relatively brief time in office, Yushchenko, who was also a former head of the national bank, became a favourite in Washington, where he was seen as the 'great liberal hope'. He attempted to put an end to some of the oligarchs' scams and tax dodges, but as the economy improved, those who stood to lose their lucrative perks helped to get him dismissed, and he went on to set up his own party, Our Ukraine.

Yushchenko had originally trained as an accountant and he was hardly an incendiary orator. Although he promised to end the corrupt rule of the 'bandits', he was, as one commentator pointed out, no street-fighting man, but an insider with broad appeal and backing from other Kuchma defectors. To his supporters, he appeared principled and trustworthy. His detractors considered him a slick hustler for Western capitalism.

In stark contrast to the placid temperament of Yushchenko was the leader of the other main opposition bloc, Yulia Tymoshenko. Tymoshenko was a strange creature – a billionaire businesswomen turned radical firebrand. With her hair plaited in Ukrainian peasant style, the glamorous tycoon was as tough and strong-willed as she was beautiful and charming. Here, her supporters believed, was a woman who would never compromise, never capitulate. Tymoshenko had made her fortune by cornering the gas market during the economic chaos of the wild post-Soviet years. The 'gas princess', as she was known, had also been close to Kuchma's circle and had served as deputy prime minister in Yushchenko's reformist government. She became a vital force on the streets during the Ukraine without Kuchma protests, and was briefly imprisoned over allegations of corruption, although the charges were soon dropped. The gas princess – once hated, like the other oligarchs and profiteers – had become the militant warrior queen. A Tymoshenko speech could make people believe that anything was possible.

Although Kuchma was soon to leave the presidential building forever, he was determined that his system would continue intact. The candidate chosen to succeed him was his prime minister, a bulky figure with a blunt demeanour called Viktor Yanukovych; a former head of the regional administration in Donetsk, the coal-mining hub of industrial, Russian-speaking eastern Ukraine. Yanukovych would fight his campaign on a populist platform, saying he would boost public spending, increase wages and cut prices. In one of his last acts as prime minister, he had doubled the state pension. To his enemies, Yanukovych was a thuggish menace, one who would perpetuate the worst excesses of the Kuchma years. But to his ordinary supporters, this was a man who was articulating very real fears: that the state industries which still employed so many people would be privatised or shut down, and the working-class communities of the east would be devastated as capitalism ran unchecked, ripping apart both livelihoods and the welfare system.

Yushchenko had the support of millionaires like the 'chocolate king', confectionery magnate Petro Poroshenko, but Yanukovych's backers were richer still: Ukraine's billionaires. Among them were Rinat Akhmetov, the country's wealthiest businessman and the owner of the Shakhtar Donetsk football club, Viktor Pinchuk, Kuchma's son-in-law and a television magnate, and Grigoriy Surkis, the owner of Dynamo Kiev. Yanukovych also had the backing of the Russian president, Vladimir Putin, who visited Ukraine to praise and endorse him. Russia, which feared it might lose one more battle in the great game for influence in the former Soviet zone, provided millions of dollars in financial support for Yanukovych's campaign. It still saw Ukraine – as it had Georgia – as part of its legitimate sphere of influence, its little brother in the 'near abroad'. Yanukovych was the man who would ensure that influence held strong, whereas Yushchenko spoke of looking West, towards Europe. Yushchenko's election posters were folksy and a little sentimental, portraying him as the home-loving keeper of traditional Ukrainian family values. But in the negative campaign against him, he was depicted as the agent of Washington – 'Bushchenko'.

Even in the early stages of the campaign, it was widely believed that the results would be faked if Yanukovych didn't win. The mood was one of resigned fatalism; Kuchma's man would simply roll into power. Even when Yushchenko led the opinion polls, the majority still said they believed that however they voted, Yanukovych would become the next president. Ukrainians had become accustomed to dubious elections and few had reasons to believe this one would be different – or that they could do much to prevent it. 'We had this joke,' says one Pora member. 'One of Yanukovych's staff comes to him and says, "I have bad news and good news for you. The bad news is, Yushchenko won the election. The good news is, you are the new president." We knew what was going to happen.'

Pora's task was to make people believe that it didn't have to be that way. The young activists focused on Yanukovych's greatest image problem: his past. As a young man, the prime minister had been jailed twice, for armed robbery and assault, something which turned many voters against him and provided a fertile source of black propaganda for the opposition. A criminal – a *zek*, they called him, using the slang for a convict – should never lead the country, Pora insisted. They marched around the centre of Kiev, wearing striped prison uniforms and chained together in a long, straggling column, urging people to vote for a criminal future and praising the virtues of life behind the bars of a renegade state where the top dog in the jailhouse could make up his own rules.

They had absorbed the lessons taught by Otpor and Kmara: cheeky humour with a surreal twist was a relatively non-confrontational way to undermine people's trust in the authorities. 'We didn't do rallies with speakers, we did theatrical events,' says Mykhailo Svystovych. 'We were trying to get across that in every problem people encountered in their lives, "Kuchmism" was to blame. That when you dealt with a cheating tax inspector, a bureaucrat who was trying to kick you out of your apartment or a dishonest judge, that was falling victim to Kuchmism.' What is striking about Pora's early protests is how blithe and guileless its activists appear, with their faded denim and college rucksacks, home-made banners daubed with little smiley faces and shining suns, chatting and joking cheerfully as if they were on a university field trip rather than a political demonstration.

Just as in Serbia and Georgia, the movement brought together young people with widely differing beliefs. There were nationalists and liberals, social democrats and conservatives. Svystovych says that around three-quarters of 'black' Pora members were politically right-wing – 'maybe like the British Conservatives or the German Christian Democrats; not like [the French extreme-right Front National party leader] Le Pen' – and a quarter were from the left, although his estimates are impossible to quantify. Many of them, however, were completely new to politics.

Nelly Verner was one of them; a 23-year-old graduate who had seen Pora's leaflets and got in contact by emailing the 'yellow' Pora website. She was soon in command of a platoon of some 20 youths who roamed the subways and metro stations of Kiev, covering any bare surface with stickers. 'I was never interested in politics before, but when I saw what was happening and I realised one of the presidential candidates had a criminal past, I felt I had to join in and do something,' she says. 'If he was elected, no civilised country would want to communicate with us.'

She found herself part of a network of friends she never thought she would have. 'Never before had I met such clever young people,' she says. 'They were already capable of organising such big actions even though they were only in their early twenties. I was so impressed by their patriotism.'

But Pora also drew in people with years of experience. Yevgen Dykiy, a jolly, bearded, bear-like man, had been a biology student before the collapse of Communism. He had grown up listening to Western rock music and the 'voices of the enemy' on the BBC World Service, and had helped to set up one of the first independent youth groups in the country while it was still a Soviet republic. He was arrested for the first time in 1989, for waving the blue-and-yellow Ukrainian flag, which at the time was seen as a dangerous nationalist provocation, although it would later become the flag of the newly-independent nation. 'Back then, none of us would have believed it if we'd been told that the Soviet Union only had two more years to live,' he recalls. 'We were preparing ourselves for around ten years of struggle – even for armed struggle, although we didn't want that – and for long prison sentences.'

After the students won their battle in Kiev in 1990, Dykiy and his comrades travelled to the Lithuanian capital, Vilnius, to support independence protests there; the Kremlin had sent in the tanks after the Baltic republic had declared its intention to leave the Soviet Union; 14 people were killed and hundreds more injured during a siege at the television station. 'We were all basically risking very serious criminal charges, verging on treason,' he says. 'At that point it was very easy to be sentenced to death, but as I was still only 17, the worst I could get was ten years in jail. All the other guys wore masks and used false names.'

When he returned to Kiev, he was summoned to KGB headquarters for questioning. 'The KGB officer looked at me like an entomologist studying an insect. He said: "So, student, do you think you'll be imprisoned as an enemy of the Soviet state? *No!* Read this…" He gave me a report written by some 15-year-old girl who I'd never met and whose name I didn't know, saying that during the student strike I'd got her drunk and raped her. Then he said: "Now you understand what you'll be charged with, and what treatment you'll get in prison." It was even scarier than seeing the Soviet tanks in Vilnius.'

Dykiy had long ago left politics and was teaching science at Kiev-Mohyla Academy. It was his students who begged him to get involved again. He had initially suspected that Pora was yet another glossily-branded NGO founded with the intention of soaking up funds from Western donors, regurgitating all the politically-expedient clichés about open societies and fair elections while doing little more than providing lucrative jobs for its directors. 'I just thought it was another PR project that wouldn't achieve anything; [the yellow Pora leader] Vlad Kaskiv might get offended about this, but I still think that in the beginning it was,' Dykiy says. But when his own students began to be arrested and interrogated by the secret services, as he had been years before, he realised that the situation had turned critical, and that his help was needed.

Nevertheless, he didn't have high hopes for the election campaign. 'I didn't believe even in the remote possibility of a victory,' he says. 'I was sure we would lose, but not doing anything meant I wouldn't be able to look my students in the face any more. I realised that staying outside all of this would be immoral, so I found some of the lawyers I knew from my student times and organised a series of lectures on what to do when you're arrested or when you're in court.'

For many Pora activists, the fight wasn't just about the presidential elections; it was about the very nature of Ukraine itself. They saw the polls as a way to finally, after more than a decade of independence, break free from the influence of Russia and assert a truly Ukrainian identity. The fact that Kuchma's candidate, Viktor Yanukovych, was backed by Moscow was yet another mark against him. For them, the battle for democracy was cultural as well as political; all Pora's propaganda material was in the Ukrainian language, not Russian. 'That was a conscious decision,' says Anastasia Bezverkha, a 22-year-old who became the press secretary for the 'yellow' wing of Pora. 'When you do something for Ukraine, you have to do it in Ukrainian. That's why doing something in Russian was out of the question. Yanukovych said if he won the elections he would make Russian a second state language, which we all protested against 100 per cent.

'It's not just that we're dependent on Russia for gas and oil. You also have this culture and socialisation which is all Russian. This is a way that Russia penetrates our inner politics – through language, through culture, through pop music like *chanson* [Russian songs about the outlandish exploits of criminals]. It's not that I don't respect people who speak Russian, but if you live in Ukraine, you have to know the language and respect the people who speak it.'

Pora's answer to Yanukovych's promises of closer ties to Moscow was a sticker showing President Putin in camouflage fatigues, pointing at the camera and asking: 'Do you want to go to Chechnya?' It was crude, yet it illustrated their view of what kind of government Yanukovych wanted to get more intimate with: one which would wage dirty wars against anyone seeking independence. Yet although Ukrainian patriotism was a driving force for many Pora members, the movement was never overtly nationalist. One of yellow Pora's leaders, Yevgen Zolotariov, recalls that some of their early posters used traditional Ukrainian images depicting Cossacks or the national poet-hero, Taras Shevchenko, but these were quickly discarded in favour of pop-culture graphics influenced by Hollywood films like *The Matrix*. 'Those national themes were a dead end,' Zolotariov says. 'They didn't correspond to the moment, they didn't look modern.'

Nevertheless, there were extreme nationalists and anti-Semites who tried to attach themselves to Viktor Yushchenko's campaign; small groups which considered themselves the equivalent of

European far-right parties like Jean-Marie Le Pen's Front National, and wanted a 'Ukraine for the Ukrainians'. Yushchenko spoke out against racism, but many of them remained, on the fringes, right to the end.

Yanukovych continued to be the unwitting provider of much of Pora's best propaganda material. On the campaign trail in the city of Ivano-Frankivsk, he was hit by an egg thrown by a protester. First he hesitated, then fell to the ground dramatically, groaning and holding his chest as if he had been shot. He was rushed into intensive care where he was pictured on television, wearing hospital pyjamas and congratulating the policemen who had 'saved' him. Pora activists gathered outside the cabinet building in Kiev, clucking like chickens and complaining that the huge egg which they had brought with them had been unjustly accused. The egg became a running joke; there was even a video game in which the player could defend Ukraine from tyranny by firing eggs at a cackling nebbish called 'Ya'.

This was not exactly adult politics, but it wasn't meant to be; it was fun and it attracted increasing numbers of young people. By the elections, Pora would claim to have recruited more than 30,000 members, although as in Serbia and Georgia, such figures were impossible to verify. 'Everyone wanted to be part of Pora, even the people you wouldn't expect to, like the girls who wear high-heeled shoes,' says Yulia Yastremska, an 18-year-old from Lviv. 'It was the most amazing time in my life, and I don't know whether I'll ever experience anything like it again.'

Yastremska was one of 300 activists who attended a joint yellow-and-black Pora seaside training camp near the town of Yevpatoria on the country's Crimean peninsula in early August. Amongst the advisers was Pavol Demeš of the German Marshall Fund of the United States, who had been involved in both Slovakia and Serbia, alongside veterans of the 1990 student movement and the Gongadze protests, while a representative of the pro-opposition television channel 5-Kanal, owned by Yushchenko ally Petro Poroshenko, advised them on how to deal with the media. In the morning they lounged on the warm sand and learned about the intricacies of election law and tactics for mobilising the masses. Some passed around a Ukrainian translation of Gene Sharp's book, *From Dictatorship to Democracy*, which was being distributed through the Maidan website. In the afternoons, when it became almost too hot to think, they frolicked in the sea or toured the historical sights of Yevpatoria. In the evenings there were bonfire parties and poetry readings. It was almost idyllic.

Andriy Valchyshyn, who helped to set up the camp, was also a member of the Ukrainian scouting organisation, Plast – as were other leaders of the student resistance, he says. Being a scout, he suggests, was an ideal revolutionary apprenticeship. But he laughs at media reports that the Yevpatoria camp was some kind of junior spy school: 'There was no weapons training and we didn't learn how to climb up ropes or anything – although there were agents of the security services all around the camp. We just learned about the mission and how to achieve it. It was inspiring, particularly because there were people from all the regions of Ukraine, we got to know each other and a certain kind of camp spirit emerged, people started to feel they were strong and they were all part of one team.'

Black Pora had its own training camp too, amidst bucolic surroundings in the Carpathian mountains. The schedule was strict; television and alcohol were banned. In the morning there were physical exercises; in the evening they sang Ukrainian songs together around the campfire. By the end, they had planned their strategy for the elections. Now it was time to put it into practice.

By the summer, students were already on the move in Sumy, Yushchenko's hometown in the north-east, near the Russian border, where a decision to amalgamate three universities and appoint a new, pro-Kuchma dean had sparked a strike. Professors were sacked and students expelled. Demonstrations erupted on campuses all around the country.

At this point, a variety of different youth groups were mobilising, as well as the two Poras, including Clean Ukraine, an independent direct-action initiative, and Student Wave, the youth wing of Yushchenko's party, Our Ukraine. 'Yushchenko's Komsomol', one Pora activist mockingly called it, comparing it to the Soviet-era state Communist youth organisation. But Student Wave had the power to summon the numbers when it was time to take to the streets. 'We did a huge amount of the work,' says one of its members, Sergiy Odarych. 'The yellow Pora did less work but it had a great PR campaign and it became a brand name. They did not have many people, they just put up stickers and spray-painted on the walls.'

Like many in the student resistance, Odarych wasn't just a member of one organisation; he also joined Pora and Clean Ukraine. As his friend Andriy Valchyshyn says, 'One day they were Pora, the next day they were Clean Ukraine or Student Wave. For different actions they just changed their T-shirts. It wasn't a problem, they just wanted to do something.' Pora's Olexander Solontai points out that, in a country with a fractured political landscape and scores of rival parties, it's hardly surprising that a range of youth movements emerged. To outsiders, they simply looked like a bunch of radical youths shouting slogans and waving flags. But as Odarych suggests, it was Pora's intriguing name and rebel mystique which would capture the public imagination – exactly as it had intended.

Another youth organisation, Znayu ('I Know'), preferred a far more sober approach. It was a voter-education campaign funded by European and American foundations which ran public information adverts on TV and a toll-free hotline with a professional call centre to process queries about the election, and staged quirky public-awareness events. Student stunts might be fun, but the real businesss was convincing people to go and vote, says its co-ordinator, Dmytro Potekhin.

Potekhin had been involved with the unsuccessful Gongadze protests as part of Za Pravdu, alongside many of the Pora leaders. 'We planned our activities with that failure in mind,' he says. 'I usually cite Ivan Marović of Otpor, who said that "every success must be preceded by failure". So the protests of 2000 and 2001 were a necessary failure.

'In Ukraine, the situation wasn't as clear as in Serbia and Georgia. In Serbia, there was a dictator, they'd had wars and bombing. In Georgia, there was a very serious economic crisis, there were electricity cuts several times a day. In Ukraine, there was at least the beginning of the development of a middle class, and the regime was much more efficient at fooling people through the media they controlled.

'Also, Ukrainians are peaceful, they don't like riots and things like that. They get used to things, they don't go on the streets and protest. That's reflected in the leadership – Yushchenko was popular because he was not an activist like Mikheil Saakashvili in Georgia, for example; he was a more peaceful guy, trying to resolve conflict. Our experience from Ukraine without Kuchma was that you can't mobilise people sufficiently with a purely negative campaign. Our campaign had to be built not on radical demands, but on positive stuff.'

One of Znayu's trainers was Aleksandar Marić of Otpor. In Belgrade, he was among a group of Otpor activists who had set up an organisation called Centar za Nenasilni Otpor – the Centre for Non-Violent Resistance. Some media reports portrayed it as a strategic hub of the international revolutionary network; a suggestion which annoyed its staff, as the Centre mainly worked on educational projects for young people growing up amidst the ethnic tensions of Kosovo and southern Serbia. 'It has never taken part in training activists in Georgia, Belarus, Ukraine or anywhere as an organisation,' says Marić – although some of its staff did undertake freelance 'assignments' in other countries.

The Ukrainian authorities eventually realised, many months too late, that foreign activists like Marić posed a potential threat. On his final visit to Ukraine, he was arrested at Kiev airport and then deported, it was said, in the interests of national security. 'We knew it was just a matter of time before the authorities made a nervous move,' Marić says. 'We were tailed by the secret police, but that was nothing new, we had lived with that in Serbia. They knew everything about me, my whereabouts and my movements. Frankly speaking, I expected to be expelled even earlier.'

Kmara, too, had been conducting training sessions for youth activists. Keto Kobiashvili hadn't been particularly impressed when she had first made the 900-mile journey from Tbilisi earlier in the year. 'I'm not an expert on Ukraine, but I *am* an expert in revolution, and I know how to motivate people,' she says. 'In the spring when I was there, they were very disorganised, they didn't know what they wanted, they were afraid, they were not motivated enough. There was training in PR and fundraising, which was funny for me because activists don't want academic seminars, they want to know how to fight. If you want to do something, you can do it, you can *find* money. But when I was there the second time, I was excited because now they were organised – *very* organised. It was really impressive.'

The opposition campaign was gathering pace, but questions were being asked about how close Pora was – yellow Pora in particular – to Yushchenko's Our Ukraine bloc. Black Pora would claim that Our Ukraine was the controlling influence on yellow Pora. 'It was very partisan – it was 100 per cent partisan,' sneers one black Pora member. However, yellow Pora's press secretary, Anastasia Bezverkha, hotly denies that they were controlled by Our Ukraine: 'This was an accusation against us, that we were just a part of Yushchenko's campaign, but we were not,' she says. 'At certain points we were criticising what Yushchenko was doing. We had common goals, but we were separate.' Some in the opposition still remembered how Yushchenko had signed a letter condemning the Ukraine without Kuchma protests during his time as prime minister, and some suspected the motives of some of the former Kuchma confidants who had become influential figures within Yushchenko's entourage. The majority of Pora activists, however, did support Yushchenko, although some preferred Yulia Tymoshenko or the Socialist leader, Olexander Moroz, and others simply wanted anybody but Yanukovych in power.

Suspicions centred around the rumoured existence of a shadowy 'Pora Council' overseeing the movement's strategy. This body included politicians who were involved with Yushchenko's Our Ukraine party, alongside the former Ukraine without Kuchma organiser, Taras Stetskiv, and various other prominent activists – as well as others of even more surprising and potentially compromising origins.

'It was not public, but it was a real centre of decision-making,' admits yellow Pora leader Vladyslav Kaskiv. 'We had to work in these half-clandestine ways. The people who took part in that council, some of them held important positions in Kuchma's administration, some of them were in business and their businesses would have been under threat, there were people from all sorts of political forces, not only Our Ukraine; there were people who were working in international organisations and they simply had no right to do political work in public. They are still incognito. This was a serious business that required organisation, financial resources, political management, communications systems, it wasn't something that could have been done in an amateur way.'

Yellow Pora undoubtedly had good connections, and questions were inevitably asked – as they had been in Serbia and Georgia – about where the money was coming from to pay for the wages of the co-ordinators and produce all the glossy leaflets, stickers, badges and T-shirts. At the time, Pora's spokespeople would only say that their funding came from 'Ukrainian businessmen'. The obfuscation was understandable; complete openness would have left them open to attacks in the government-dominated media. What they most wanted to avoid was the charge that they were taking cash from the old Cold War enemy in the West. However, months later, in a post-conflict report, Vladyslav Kaskiv would state that the training of activists was supported by around $130,000 provided by Freedom House, the Canadian International Development Agency and the German Marshall Fund of the United States. He said that most support – $1.5 million in financial donations and an estimated $6.5 million in donations in kind, such as free printing and transport – was provided by Ukrainians.

Towards the end of August, the two Poras held a joint congress, and decided to join forces – the rising sun of the blacks combined with the ticking clock of the yellows. The unity would prove to be temporary, but in the field, if not at the leadership level, it seemed to work. Meanwhile, the public was still unaware that two Poras existed. As *Ukrainska Pravda* later observed: 'Pora activists themselves talk reluctantly and with reservations about the division into "yellows" and "blacks". The arguments vary – from "this division is imaginary", to recognition that the activists of both – especially in the regions – are often the very same people. On the other hand Pora activists have their fears that focusing attention on certain differences can be perceived by many as proof of a "rupture" in Pora and this consequently would lead to disappointment and thus would only harm the common cause.'[10]

A BOMB IN THE OVEN

A few days after the Pora congress, something happened that would completely transform the election campaign. On 5 September, Viktor Yushchenko met the head of the Ukrainian security services and his deputy for dinner. He wanted to find out what course of action they would follow during and after the polls; whether they would intervene to preserve the status quo. The next morning, he was taken ill with what he thought was a gastric illness. As the days passed, his condition deteriorated and, as ugly blisters and pustules erupted all over his skin, he flew to Vienna for specialist treatment. The doctors suspected poisoning but couldn't say for certain. Yushchenko, however, was certain: this was an assassination attempt. 'Look at my face,' he urged MPs in parliament. It was hideously disfigured; bloated, pockmarked and scarred like a lunar landscape. Further medical investigation suggested that he had been poisoned with a potentially lethal dioxin.

The suspects were people close to the government, or business clans who feared for their future and had resorted to the tactics of the Soviet-era KGB. But it wasn't clear whether the intention was to kill Yushchenko, to get him off the campaign trail for a while, or simply to make the formerly smooth-faced, square-jawed politician appear so repulsive as to be unelectable. If there was a plot, however, it backfired: Yushchenko's drug-wasted, deformed features were both an accusation and a living reminder of how far some of those in the shadows were prepared to go to keep the opposition from power.

At the same time as the alleged assassination attempt, police surveillance of the Ukrainian youth movements intensified. Security officers photographed and videotaped Pora actions; activists were followed; student halls of residence searched and phones tapped. 'It was no secret that they were listening to our conversations. That's a normal thing in this country, that's just the basics,' says Vladyslav Kaskiv. 'It started after the camp at Yevpatoria. Then in October they decided to destroy us. They wanted to to discredit us first, demoralise the leaders and then physically lock us up.'

On 15 October, not long after Otpor's Aleksandar Marić was expelled from the country, police raided Pora's headquarters in Kiev. At first they found nothing incriminating. Plainclothes officers then carried out a second search behind closed doors with no one else present, and said they had discovered a stash of explosives. They detained two activists on charges of terrorism and 'illegally forming an armed group', and suggested that Pora was suspected of causing an explosion earlier that year in a Kiev market, in which one person had died. The activists said they had been framed.

It was the beginning of a two-week wave of repression which coincided with the last fortnight of the presidential election campaign. Police raided the Pora offices in Lviv and trawled its computers for information. The college buildings of the prestigious Kiev-Mohyla Academy were also raided by special forces searching for Pora members and 'suspected terrorists'.

Pora staged a parodic stunt outside the ministry of internal affairs, showing off fake explosives with a string of sausages as their fuse; a large dog dressed in a Pora T-shirt then gobbled up the sausages. But many found it difficult to laugh. Before Yanukovych arrived to hold a public meeting in the northern city of Chernihiv, a serene, dreamy place which is home to some of Ukraine's most ancient churches, 15 Pora activists were seized by police and held until his speech had ended. 'I was going to my class at university when a car stopped and a young man asked me to get in,' recalls one of them, Tanya Pekur. 'There was a policeman standing nearby and I started to shout that I didn't want to get into the car but the policeman turned away and didn't react. I was forced into the car and he took me to the police station. They didn't tell me why I had to stay there. I asked them to let me go because they had no grounds to keep me there. They said we were just having a "simple conversation" and I should stay. But when I tried to go, a young policeman threatened me. It was all just a pretext to keep us away so we wouldn't disrupt Yanukovych's meeting.'

The next day, police burst into the flat which Pekur was sharing with her boyfriend, another Pora activist called Olexander Lomako. They slapped Pekur in the face, dragged Lomako away, then searched the premises. 'I knew they would "find" something while they were searching,' Lomako says. 'In one of my jacket pockets they found some counterfeit money, and inside the oven they found explosives.' To Lomako, the charges were ridiculous: 'For one thing, we had just cooked dinner – we wouldn't have done that if I had been keeping a bomb in the oven.' Nevertheless, he was facing three to five years in jail if convicted. It was, he believes, part of a campaign to neutralise Pora's key activists. 'I wasn't surprised that the authorities went to such extreme measures,' he says. 'Actually, I was waiting for it.'

Over the next few days, as part of the ongoing operation to root out the 'terrorists', police searched the offices of the Freedom of Choice Coalition and Znayu, where they seized lists of volunteers and campaign material. A number of Pora leaders were also raided, including Vladyslav Kaskiv and Mykhailo Svystovych.

Svystovych was at home, he says, snoozing through a pleasant daydream about blocking the runway at Kiev airport to prevent Kuchma and his allies fleeing the country, when the security services arrived and woke him. While they searched his apartment, he telephoned the Maidan website and the news of the raid was online before it had even finished. When the interrogating officer asked how Pora operated, Svystovych presented him with one of Gene Sharp's books and told him about Otpor, Kmara, and the Polish Solidarity movement. 'At the beginning he was listening carefully but it's hard. It's not about his IQ. It's just for the person from a hierarchical structure, it's hard to grasp non-hierarchical organisations that are almost impossible to destroy no matter how many people you arrest,' Svystovych wrote shortly afterwards in a report for the Maidan site. He ended his account with some tips 'from Soviet times' for younger, less experienced revolutionaries: go to the toilet before you leave your apartment, even if you're just going out for cigarettes; take a shower when you can, and wear warm clothes – you never know whether you'll be spending the next few days in a cold, dirty cell. 'Smile, friends!' he concluded optimistically. 'We will win anyway! Carthages get ruined. Dinosaurs die out…'[11]

From the beginning of the election campaign to polling day at the end of October 2004, more than 350 Pora activists were reported to have been arrested. Some were assaulted in custody; one was half-suffocated with a plastic bag over his head; drugs and bullets were planted on two young women. This was not on the scale of the Milošević government's offensive against Otpor in Serbia, but nevertheless, like the poisoning of Yushchenko, it recalled the old KGB methods of dealing with dissidents. A sharp jolt of panic coursed through the movement. 'We were hiding some people from the authorities because we thought they could even be killed,' says Yaryna Yasynevych. 'We arranged for them to stay with people from small towns or villages who had no connection with us, or we rented flats, we changed their mobile phone numbers and we only let a few people know where they were.

'That's when we realised that Otpor's example was so important, because having no leaders meant they couldn't be targeted. We were only living through this for a few weeks, but Otpor lived through the same thing for a year, and we understood how hard it must have been for them.

'This was when the government and Yanukovych showed what was inside of them. But they couldn't stop us, because when one activist was arrested, another came and took his place.'

Ukrainian television gave extensive coverage to the anti-terrorist operations, but as in Serbia, where Otpor had been labelled a paramilitary threat, the rhetoric was undermined by reality. 'People heard what they were saying, that we would shoot people or kill them, and then they saw us on the streets, and we looked entirely the opposite of what was being said, and they understood it wasn't true, that we weren't criminals,' says Yasynevych. 'Their propaganda wasn't working; it wasn't even convincing the ordinary policemen who had to put pressure on us.'

All the national television channels were strongly behind the Yanukovych campaign. They either ignored Yushchenko, portrayed him as some kind of divisive nationalist, or as a puppet of Washington who would devastate the industrial east with neo-liberal economic policies. By contrast, Yanukovych was depicted as a competent and successful prime minister who had ensured that wages were paid on time, incomes and public spending were rising, and the price of bread was falling. Yushchenko could count on one friendly TV station, 5-Kanal, to back his campaign, although its signal only reached half the country. Outside the internet, truly independent mass media was almost non-existent.

In this environment, new technology was a vital organisational tool. Both yellow and black Poras coordinated actions through their websites and used mobile-phone text-messaging to rally activists outside police stations after people were arrested, or assemble instant 'flash mobs' to make brief protests before slipping away as quickly as they appeared. The Maidan site was publishing reports of actions and detentions around the country, and mainstream journalists and opposition politicians would use it to pick up grassroots information which had been phoned in by scores of regional stringers. But partly because of its relatively low profile, Maidan escaped the police dragnet which was closing around the youth resistance. 'In the minds of many people, Maidan is a website – and it *is* a website, but it's also an organisation,' explains Andriy Ignatov. 'This helped us because it didn't attract fire like other organisations did. We didn't look for conflict although we were writing very harsh stories and doing very deep intelligence work.'

The students were ready now. On 16 October, Student Wave held a show of strength near Kiev-Mohyla Academy. As Yushchenko spoke, thousands of students chanted his slogan in unison – *Freedom can't be stopped!* – while Ukraine's leading rock bands, VV and Okean Elzy, played hard and loud. Thousands of electoral observers were ready to monitor the polls on 31 October, while Pora was busily setting up strike committees in universities and higher education institutes right across Ukraine to organise protests in case of fraud.

The government was ready, too, and it warned that it was prepared to use force if there was civil unrest. The chief of the Kiev police, Olexander Milenyn, gave a sinister interview in which he suggested that his officers had new methods to stamp out subversive activities. 'There won't be any revolution here,' he promised. 'We are ready for the unexpected. We even have our "ninjas" – a recently formed subdivision, trained in special measures. We also have new means, which for now I won't speak about. I'll only say their use has been approved by the health ministry.'[12]

It had been a dirty, aggressive, sometimes surreal campaign. But now, after months of preparation, it was time for the showdown at the ballot box. The Ukrainian writer Oksana Zabuzhko summed up the mood: 'On the night of the elections, I'll be in the streets, too. I don't know what is going to happen there. That is, I don't know what forces will be turned against us, and what will be the final result. But even if the worst happens, and Putin's guards help turn my country, for God knows how long, into a criminally governed reservation for degenerate Stalinist types, we'll be in the streets to say this was not our choice.'[13]

THE ORANGE WAVE

The official results from the first round of the election gave Yushchenko a lead of less than one per cent. Neither he nor Yanukovych had reached the 50 per cent threshold necessary for outright victory. There would have to be a second round of voting – a run-off between the two leading candidates three weeks later, on 21 November 2004: Viktor against Viktor for the future of Ukraine. Despite pressure from the European Union and the United States, which had said it would reconsider its relations with Ukraine if the presidential election wasn't fair, there were reports of widespread violations at the polling stations. This was enough for yellow Pora; they realised that the second round would be even more corrupt, and that there was no chance of an honest result: it was time to take the resistance to the next level. They set up a tent camp near Kiev-Mohyla Academy and began a two-week rock 'n' roll extravaganza – *It's Time for Freedom* – with bands playing and speakers every night. However, black Pora took a rather different view of the camp. 'It looked great on TV but it wasn't necessary, what was necessary was to go to the regions and work there to campaign against Yanukovych and try to stop the elections being rigged in your own town,' says Mykhailo Svystovych. 'Then if they *are* rigged, everyone immediately go to Kiev.'

The fearful delirium of the election campaign still lingered; a new wave of raids and random arrests seemed imminent. 'We started hiding at other people's apartments, we were only speaking for a short time on mobile phones, we were moving to different locations so they couldn't track us down,' says Yevgen Dykiy. 'We didn't believe in the possibility of victory and we were already working on the scenario of what we were going to do when the authorities started to crack down on us. With our close friends and family, we were saying that immediately after our defeat, some of us would have to run away abroad or maybe go to jail. I was sure we would go to jail for quite some time and I prepared myself to continue my scientific work in prison.

'We were discussing whether to keep our resistance non-violent to the very end, or if the authorities actually resorted to using force, whether we should have the right to retaliate in some way. Officially, Pora's position was non-violent, but privately, different people thought different things. Two of my students brought me to a place where they had several crates of Molotov cocktails and asked me to hide them somewhere. Through all the next few weeks, these crates full of bottles were sitting under a bed at one of my friend's places, a rock musician. He was scared to death.'

A few days before the second round, yellow Pora made the decision to co-ordinate its activities directly with Yushchenko's headquarters. Its activists believed that Yushchenko had won outright, and that their role now was to defend the people's choice. Alongside the Maidan website, they helped to organise what became known as the 'Orange Ribbon' initiative to spread the chosen colour of the Yushchenko campaign: to turn Ukraine orange. Tens of thousands of orange ribbons and scarves were distributed throughout the country, in what proved to be a triumph of viral marketing.

Yushchenko's campaign managers had spent many months

preparing to beat fraud at the polls, training thousands of people in election law and distributing hundreds of video cameras to document violations. But according to one senior yellow Pora figure, Yevgen Zolotariov, most still wanted to proceed cautiously until the second round of voting was over. 'There weren't too many people at Yushchenko's headquarters who realised the necessity of mass actions; I can count them on the fingers of one hand,' Zolotariov says. 'Yushchenko and the majority of the people at his headquarters thought those actions weren't necessary at all. After the first round of elections, there was a meeting between representatives of Yushchenko's headquarters, black Pora, Clean Ukraine, Student Wave and us. At the meeting, the representatives of Yushchenko's headquarters were trying to convince us not to prepare for any sort of mass actions. They were telling us that if we wanted to contribute anything to the success of this campaign, we should go to eastern Ukraine, promote Yushchenko's ideas and serve as election observers. We didn't agree.'

Nevertheless, what was called a 'scenario for mass action' was ultimately agreed and signed off by the head of Yushchenko's campaign headquarters, Oleksander Zinchenko. Nobody knew how successful it would be, and some of them doubted it could work at all. But it was a meticulous document which detailed the activities which would unfold in the days after the second round of voting, assigning specific responsibility for everything from organising transport to printing leaflets and providing people to carry banners. Under the heading of 'Setting up a tent camp on Kreshchatyk', it named Pora leader Vladyslav Kaskiv as the person responsible for setting events in motion.

Pora might have described it as 'defending the people's choice', but what the plan appeared to envisage was nothing less than a mass outbreak of civil disobedience. There would be a marathon rock concert and protest rally, broadcast live on television from Kiev's Independence Square: the Maidan. This would be a non-stop, full-colour, high-tech, multimedia, rock 'n' roll uprising – a perfect twenty-first century revolution. The world's media would be watching, and the television pictures would look spectacular. They gave the city authorities a few days' notice that they would be staging some kind of event at the Maidan, although few had any idea about the real nature of their agenda.

The second round of the election, the run-off between Yushchenko and Yanukovych, was all they had expected. Ukrainian and Western observers reported that the process was even more flawed than the first round; they detailed widespread intimidation, the violent seizure of ballot boxes by black-clad toughs, the use of fake pre-printed ballot papers, and the reappearance of those old Ukrainian favourites, the 'unknown persons' who had made such a spectacular impact in Mukachevo in the spring, travelling by bus and by specially chartered trains from one polling station to another, casting multiple votes. Even more audaciously, a pro-Yanukovych team had surreptitiously gained access into the electoral commission's computer and electronically manipulated the results in favour of its candidate, according to taped evidence which emerged later.

Most exit polls showed Yushchenko leading, but the official results would give Yanukovych just over 49 per cent, with Yushchenko three percentage points behind. Viktor Yanukovych was set to succeed Leonid Kuchma as the president of Ukraine.

That evening, the first tents appeared at the Maidan, as the 'scenario for mass action' had envisaged. Pora had dismantled its protest camp near Kiev-Mohyla Academy the night before and moved into the city centre, where several thousand people gathered in support of Yushchenko. But it wasn't until the following day that the true scale of public discontent began to emerge. Early that morning, the crisp winter air on the Maidan was pierced by cries of 'Freedom can't be stopped!' Students rushed around, erecting more tents, assembling cooking units and hanging banners along Kreshchatyk. Young men dragged benches from the street, one by one, to form barricades around the encampment. Within hours, a tent city had been established, complete with field kitchens and unarmed sentries, and nearby, a huge video screen, mounted on a stage between colossal loudspeakers. Vladyslav Kaskiv had been counting on around 15,000 Pora activists to join the protest. Yushchenko's team believed they could summon tens of thousands

more. None of them was prepared for the sheer mass of .
which began to flow into the Maidan. People just kept coming and
coming, until there were around a quarter of a million gathered
there, singing, dancing and chanting. Those who remembered the
disappointment of the Gongadze protests could hardly comprehend
it. Here was the uprising they had dreamed of for so long: an Orange
Revolution.

Around the country, people who had spent the past few months
campaigning against Yanukovych switched on their television sets
and saw the huge crowd gathering at the Maidan. Some remember
breaking down in tears; they knew this meant the election had been
stolen. But they also realised it meant that Ukrainians had started
to rise up. They began to make their way to Kiev, despite the police
roadblocks set up to turn them back. Many of them would not
return home for weeks.

'This was the first time I believed we even had a chance,' says
Yevgen Dykiy. 'Even the day before, I was still convinced that people
were apathetic, that there wouldn't be enough of us and that we'd
be destroyed. But – just for myself – I determined that I wouldn't
be able to live normally if I didn't come out and do it now. I said to
myself, whatever happens, I will be part of it and my conscience will
be clear. And somehow, many people thought that way. The fact that
there were suddenly so many of us was very unexpected, and for the
leaders of the revolution it was just as unexpected.

'The tent camp was a genius idea, it transformed what would have
been a rally into an ongoing event. Because no matter how many
people you get together for a rally, at some point they will disperse.
But the tents completely changed things. They showed this would be
a long-term thing.' Within a fortnight, thousands of people would
be living in more than 1,500 tents; it was a magnet for like minds
and a statement of total conviction.

Protesters marched into nearby buildings, announced they were
taking over and began working in shifts, serving up thousands of
hot meals. With the backing of Kiev city council, toilets and waste-
disposal systems were put in place. A map was issued showing
the 'free territory' of the Maidan; telling people where they could

charge their mobile phone batteries. An
...cy was established with the addresses of
...e who were offering beds for protesters from out
...usinesses donated sleeping bags and woollen socks.
...ding and *valenky* – felt boots – were trucked in. First-
aid ...vere erected and medics distributed vitamins and cold
cures.

The people of Kiev responded with a remarkable outpouring of generosity; headscarved babushkas brought pots of borscht, black bread, sausages and pickled cucumbers for the tent campers. There were huge piles of clothes, mounds of loaves, thousands of tea bags, stacks of medicines. Soon the protesters had so much, they were giving it away to children's homes, homeless people, even tourists. The Socialist MP Yuri Lutsenko, one of the key lieutenants of the revolution, recalled a conversation between one tent-city resident and a passing well-wisher: '"What can I bring you to eat, man?" He said, "We've got enough food." "What can I bring you to drink then?" "We've got enough to drink." "But what do you need?" "A fire extinguisher and a carpet."'[14]

The tent city was like an independent republic – part Glastonbury, part Paris Commune. It was a temporary autonomous zone where higher values prevailed, says Pora activist Tetyana Boyko: 'There was so much positive energy. People were kind and loving, they would share everything down to the last piece of bread. It was like thousands of friends together.'

The temperature fell to −10° and snow began to fall, settling softly on tents and pavements. But the wintry city felt more vital than it had for years; the crisp air crackled with political energy. It was as if Kiev, by some strange alchemy, had turned orange; every other person was wearing some kind of orange ribbon, scarf or hat: glamorous women tottered past on vertiginous heels wearing orange headbands; young toughs with buzz-cut hairstyles sported orange jackets; elegant ladies in their finery festooned their pet dogs with orange ribbons; some teenage girls even dyed their hair orange. There was a real sense of possibility, a feeling that momentous upheaval was imminent. The beat of the ubiquitous chant – '*Yush-chen-ko! Yush-chen-ko!*' – was echoed in the rhythmic honking of car horns, over and over again.

Inside the tent camp, people danced around braziers to Ukrainian rock music and good-time Europop blasting out of speakers hitched up to lamp posts. A radio station, Gala FM, had set itself up in the heart of the camp and was broadcasting live to Kreshchatyk. Groups of demonstrators chanted the name of their leader to the rhythm of songs by Kylie Minogue and The Prodigy – '*Yush-chen-ko!*' – while a huge screen relayed 5-Kanal's continuous coverage of political developments. Bus shelters were turned into impromptu social clubs, with people strumming guitars as others huddled around them, tapping their feet under blankets, or jigging frantically to the wild squalls of an accordion. Children and pensioners lined up to have their photos taken with the protesters, while street traders drifted around selling orange hats and balloons, and fashion stores clothed their shop-window dummies in orange jumpers and skirts: the revolution instantly marketed to its participants by canny entrepreneurs.

Advertising hoardings were turned into samizdat bulletin boards, covered in poems, letters, drawings and hundreds of messages from supporters. There were scores of digitally-altered pictures poking fun at Yanukovych and his Russian backers: Yanukovych and his aides depicted as a posse of gun-toting mobsters, Kuchma and Yanukovych as Leonardo DiCaprio and Kate Winslet on the prow of the *Titanic*, Yanukovych and Putin locked in a pornographic embrace; images depicting the government as a bunch of drunks, gluttons and thieves.

A bizarre, rambling speech made by Yanukovych's wife, Lyudmila, accusing the tent city protesters of being American-financed drug fiends, offered yet further creative inspiration. 'It's simply an orange orgy there,' she said of the Maidan. 'There's rows and rows of felt boots – all of it American-made! See! And mountains of oranges! Oranges! Gosh! It's just... a nightmare. And look here, guys; those oranges aren't just any oranges – they're loaded. People take an orange, eat it, and take another one. See! And the hand keeps reaching, keeps reaching for it... and they keep standing, keep standing! Eyes simply glazed over!'[15] Soon afterwards, the tent camp was adorned with oranges pierced by syringes and felt boots with 'made in USA' scribbled on them.

As the days progressed, the revolutionary campers began to look increasingly bedraggled, their clothes encrusted with dirt, their hair unkempt, stinking of woodsmoke from the cookfires and braziers. Some were dressed like soldiers gone AWOL in their military fatigues, some like anarchists at a peace rally, others like tourists on a wet day at Wimbledon. Their tents were decorated with the names of the cities they had come from: Kiev, Lviv, Odessa, Poltava, Kharkiv...'People's security' officers patrolled the camp's perimeter, watching out for intruders; alcohol was banned and drunks were summarily ejected: this was revolutionary discipline. Visitors were treated to sweet tea and sausage sandwiches. When questioned, all the campers seemed to repeat the same phrase: '*We will be here until the end.*'

'Something strange has happened here – people's minds have been transformed,' said Iryna, a 19-year-old physics student who was living in the tent camp. 'More than anything, this is a revolution of the mind. Of course there will be years of changes, because for so many years so many bad things happened in our country. Yushchenko cannot change this overnight, but this could be the point when changes start. I know it will take a long time, but I just don't want things to get worse than they are now. We will win, it's only a question of time.'

The optimism was infectious. 'The change has already been made, the whole nation is definitely transformed,' said Sergiy, a twenty-four-year-old information technology student. 'The revolution is mental and sociological, it's about the way people feel as Ukrainians, they're no longer allowing themselves to be manipulated. There's a new generation which is setting the mood for the older ones. We've been more exposed to Western culture and beliefs. Our politicians couldn't indoctrinate us like the Communists did to the older generation because we live in a more globalised society, we have access to outside media sources like the internet. If you're isolated, you can be moulded by the government, but that's not possible here now.'

Next to the camp was the huge stage on the Maidan, with its constant stream of speech-making politicians, rowdy rock bands, choirs and folk singers. The music revived the spirits and thawed the chill as people swayed in time to the rhythms, arm in arm, while the snow drifted around them; hard-faced men shed tears to emotive patriotic ballads, elderly women nodded their heads to hip-hop beats, small children frolicked and leaped in time to thrash metal riffs. The anthem of the revolution came from the crowd itself: 'Razom nas bahato, nas ne podolaty' – *'Together we are many, we will not be defeated'*. A group of young musicians called Grinjolly had heard the slogan chanted at a protest rally in their home town of Ivano-Frankivsk; they rushed back to their studio, and within four hours had set the slogan to a thunderous hip-hop rhythm. 'The words were written by the people, so we just had to come up with the melody,' one of them said.[16] *Razom Nas Bahato* was basic but effective: *'Falsifications – no! Manipulations – no! Yushchenko – yes! Yushchenko – yes! Our president – yes, yes!'* The song was posted on the internet and thousands began to download it. The unknown band who previously had spent their time composing advertising jingles had become revolutionary icons.

Yushchenko's celebrity supporters joined him on the Maidan stage, among them champion boxers the Klitschko brothers and the Eurovision song contest winner Ruslana. Ruslana sang live, wearing a bright orange jumper and waving a clenched fist high in the air. She would later use the Maidan as the backdrop for a promotional video. Georgian musicians who played during the Rose Revolution in Tbilisi also flew in to join the party.

'It was a very special experience for a musician to play on that stage at that time,' says Oleg Skrypka, the charismatic, tousle-haired singer with the rock band VV. 'A lot of people were ready to die for the cause. It was like a war, but at the same time it was like the carnival in Rio de Janeiro.' VV – Vopli Vidopliassova, a name taken from a character in a Dostoyevsky novel – had been playing gigs for Yushchenko throughout the election campaign. 'At the beginning, musicians who supported Yushchenko were the exception; most musicians supported Yanukovych and a few were neutral,' says

Skrypka. 'They couldn't imagine that Yushchenko would win. They thought it was dangerous to be with Yushchenko, they thought it would damage their careers. Only rock bands and traditional singers joined Yushchenko, not pop singers. There is a traditional expression here, "I will not go to the barricades with this person" – that's how I felt about pop singers. Pop is prostitution, so it was normal for them. It was like at a market when you discuss the price; they discussed the price being offered by each candidate. But when they saw Yushchenko winning, they became the number one revolutionaries.'

Away from the Maidan party, earthy folk players and bearded troubadours – inheritors of the tradition of the *kozbars*, travelling balladeers who passed their lyrics down through the generations – set up wherever they could, entertaining both protesters and police. Here, believes Skrypka, was the true soul of the revolution revealing itself. 'You had the showbusiness on the big stage and then the really patriotic musicians playing on small stages for our "soldiers",' he says. 'They were singing patriotic songs, songs with passion, songs about the history of Ukraine which was repressed during the Soviet Union.'

Despite the traditional soundtrack, this was a digital-age revolution. The protesters used text-messaging services to distribute bulletins and orders to hundreds of mobile phones; telecommunications companies even had to set up temporary phone masts in central Kiev because of the overwhelming demand. Bloggers posted instant reports on the internet. But national television was still under the control of the authorities – until, a few days in, a remarkable thing happened: journalists began a revolt against censorship and biased reporting, with strikes at the main three channels forcing an agreement to institute more objective coverage. In the most celebrated case, the sign-language interpreter for the UT-1 channel staged a unilateral act of rebellion during a newscast, ignoring the script and announcing instead that the election had been rigged. 'I am not sure you will ever see me again,' she said as she signed off.

Every evening, a high wave of pure energy rolled over the city. Some nights the crowds were estimated at more than a million people. It felt like Berlin or Prague in 1989: it felt like nothing so beautiful and honest could ever be denied, that it would simply keep gathering strength until it inevitably prevailed, and the corrupt and perfidious would simply have to move aside, acknowledging the righteous force which was surging onwards to the promised land. 'Our orange movement is not so much a political campaign as our Woodstock and our May 1968, our Dadaism and our revolutionary velvet,' gushed the Ukrainian newspaper *Den*.

The power of the crowd was inspiring, nurturing, soothing. It drew people in and made them feel safe, made them believe. The Ukrainian blogger Veronika Khokhlova recalls how one night she met a friend, a student called Tanya, who had been out on the streets for ten hours dressed only in a thin coat and an orange scarf, and was planning to be back there at six the next morning, yet didn't look cold or tired. 'Tanya and her friend started singing the Ukrainian national anthem. They didn't sound phoney; they were singing for themselves, not loudly, and in beautiful voices, and it moved me to tears. An hour later, we were at Independence Square again, at another huge rally, listening to Mr Yushchenko on the loudspeakers again. Tanya, along with everyone else, was shouting "Yushchenko! Yushchenko!" and I, standing next to her, found myself shouting too, with confidence and inspiration I hadn't felt before.'[17] Deep in the crowd, all doubts dissolved.

Amongst the orange banners of Yushchenko, the Ukrainian flags and the Pora emblems were the flags of Poland, Georgia and Belarus. Leaders of Kmara and Otpor came to marvel at their legacy. Democracy activists flooded in from other former Soviet countries, eager to pick up any new tricks which they could use back home. Vladyslav Kaskiv of Pora held meetings with groups from Azerbaijan, Kazakhstan, Russia, Belarus and Moldova, lit up by the brilliance of the orange wave. 'In my opinion,' he said, 'it is not so much our techniques as the hope that Ukraine is giving them that is more important for those movements.'[18]

But it was not all celebration; there was trepidation too. From the very first days – especially in the first days – there were persistent rumours of Russian special forces crossing the border, or riot police tooling up to crack skulls, or thugs handing out wooden staves, or armoured personnel carriers gunning their engines for battle, or an imminent curfew. A week after the second-round vote, reports suggested that more than 10,000 interior ministry troops had been mobilised to smash the protests, as in Hungary in 1956 or Czechoslovakia in 1968. The opposition made ready to defend itself, but by morning the troops pulled back, in circumstances which still remain unclear. Nevertheless, behind the scenes, the government's power over its security apparatus seemed to be seeping away. The opposition had been reaching out to key figures in the army and the security services for many months. It had started to pay off.

'I spoke to many of them, we had negotiations and that's why I'm convinced there would have been no bloodshed even if the situation had become more acute,' says the yellow Pora leader, Vladyslav Kaskiv. 'I knew that not a single general would give an order to attack. We knew that certain military detachments would have joined our side, some would have stayed neutral, but I don't know anyone who would have attacked us.'

Yevgen Dykiy set up the medical centre in the tent camp. Initially he forecast that the main problems would be broken bones and gunshot wounds from clashes with police; he and his colleagues struck a secret agreement with a hospital in Kiev, allowing them to bring in wounded people for treatment without any paperwork, so they couldn't be traced. 'But instead of the secret field service we had planned, we ended up mainly treating colds and flu symptoms,' he smiles. 'I'm so proud that our revolution was very civilised – not a single storefront smashed, not a single car turned upside down. Everything worked, shops stayed open. There were four weddings on the Maidan, and not a single funeral.'

Within a few days, the blue-and-white colours of the Yanukovych campaign began to appear in central Kiev, as thousands of his supporters arrived from the mines and factories of the east. A group of them set up a small parallel tent camp on a nearby hill, and for a short while, conflict seemed likely. But there were never enough Yanukovych followers to challenge the orange supremacy, and neither side seemed ready for a physical fight. Orange envoys started visiting the Yanukovych camp, chatting, arguing and joking with their opponents, giving them food and warm clothes, chanting 'East and West together!' and 'Glory to the coal miners!' – defusing the tension with kindness…'One day, two marches met, one of Yushchenko and one of Yanukovych,' says Pora activist Alina Shpak. 'When we started to give them flowers and sandwiches, they were astonished. They were shocked. And maybe that's why, the next day, many of them didn't turn out on the streets again, they just went home.'

Many of the tent city dwellers insisted that Yanukovych's supporters in the east were simply wretched pawns, indoctrinated by the mendacious transmissions of state television. Stories circulated that the Yanukovych protesters had been promised money and accommodation if they came to Kiev, but were then abandoned, unpaid, without food or shelter. Certainly, a few of them joined the orange campers after experiencing their generosity. Viktor, a burly fellow in heavy boots, said he had come from Donetsk, where he laboured in a huge metalworks. He had voted for Yanukovych in the first round of the election and had journeyed to the capital to do something about what he thought were the extreme nationalist, anti-eastern prejudices of the orange mass – but he ended up becoming a resident of the tent city. 'The boss came and told us, "Guys, the opposition is trying to put us on our knees, they're trying to portray us as inferior." So I came here to fight for our interests,' he explained. 'But when I got here and I saw how people were behaving towards us, it changed my mind completely.'

But the east had been wholeheartedly, genuinely behind Yanukovych, and many weren't ready to accept that their man had lost. There were real fears that Ukraine might simply crack apart under the political strain, the faultline between east and west splitting the country. Some eastern regions threatened to secede to escape what one provincial mayor called the 'orange plague'. They believed that Yushchenko would sell out the country to the West. If Ukraine was to be run by a wealthy clique, they preferred it to be theirs.

'I come from the east, from Donetsk region, and there most people thought this whole thing was totally funded by George Bush and other foreign powers,' says Pora activist Nelly Verner. 'During the first days of the revolution, I called my parents because I was so excited by what I was seeing here on the Maidan and I wanted to tell them about it. I said, "We have a real revolution here, it's totally incredible what's happening!" They told me to stay away from it all. Several days later I called again and my mum said, "Don't call me any more, you're earning big money there from other people's blood." She thought there was some kind of civil war going on here and we were being paid to physically fight people from Donetsk in the streets.'

Many Russian newspapers projected the same picture, speaking of the Maidan crowd as an ugly weapon of blackmail, of the opposition as ciphers for the Western imperialists of the new world order who wanted to ride the engine of successive revolutions, extending their domination, state by state, right up to Russia's borders – and, then, into the very walls of the Kremlin itself...

And while Western governments condemned the election result as unfair, President Putin came forward to congratulate Yanukovych on his win and warned of outsiders trying to push Ukraine into 'mass mayhem'.[19] It would prove to be a strategic blunder which did little for Moscow's already tarnished reputation in parts of Ukraine, and it provoked both resentment and dark humour: 'A Ukrainian man shows up at work, with all his clothes rumpled,' one joke began. 'When his colleagues ask what happened, he replies: "I turn on the TV this morning, and there's Putin praising Yanukovych. I switch to another channel, and there's Putin again, praising Yanukovych. So I turn on the radio, and Putin is there too, praising Yanukovych. So I figured there was no use turning on the iron."'[20] Nevertheless, many tent campers went out of their way to stress they were not anti-Russian; they disapproved of Putin, not his people. 'This so-called anti-Russian sentiment is just another fiction, they're trying to infiltrate this into our minds, that there's a split between Russian and Ukrainian-speaking people,' said 24-year-old Sergiy. 'I have friends in the east and the west. There's no conflict between the people, it's a conflict between different political interests.'

But taking this message to the industrial Donbas region in the east proved all but impossible. Pora – which had never really been able to operate effectively in the east – tried to erect one small tent in Donetsk's main square, where a huge statue of Lenin still gazed down paternally over the city. It didn't even last an hour before it was demolished. 'We had this slogan, "It's time to love", says Anastasia Bezverkha. 'We set up this tent in Donetsk with the message, "We bring you love from the Maidan". There were five people from Pora, three girls and two boys, and one tent with a flag. The tent stood there for 20 minutes and then 40 people came and tore it into little pieces and beat all our people up. And the slogan was nothing more than love. We couldn't do anything about it.'

A CITY UNDER BLOCKADE

All the main government buildings in Kiev had been blockaded by 24-hour pickets; the apparatus of power was frozen. On 23 November, Yushchenko swore an oath in parliament, boldly if symbolically declaring himself president. The same day, thousands of protesters marched on the presidential administration building, making ready to storm the doors and take control. The mood was fraught and edgy; the building was ringed by armed police and there were rumours that troops were billeted inside, ready to shoot dead any insurgents who breached the cordon. Yevgen Dykiy was alongside Vladyslav Kaskiv, marshalling a column of Pora youths, none of whom knew what might happen next. 'We were standing there with loudhailers, waiting for an order from the Maidan to start marching,' Dykiy says. 'When you're doing something, you're not thinking, it's an adrenalin rush, you're just getting things done, but when you're waiting, you start thinking. When we were distributing gas masks and metal chains so these kids could link themselves together, I had these mixed feelings about whether I had the moral right to take them there. On the other hand, I knew that even without us they would be going there and we had the knowledge how to do it with fewer losses. But we were really very nervous.'

'We'd been preparing for that for a month and a half,' says

Kaskiv. 'We were absolutely ready, there were thousands of people marching towards the building and I know there were people in our ranks who were absolutely convinced they were going to die. But the critical moment never came.'

The order to take the building was never issued; this was the first of many times that the protesters came close to seizing state institutions, but pulled back at the last minute. The opposition leaders decided it could set off a chain reaction of violence and retribution which might consume the entire country. Instead, they decided to wait for the Supreme Court to decide whether the elections were legitimate. 'We could have followed the Georgian scenario,' opposition MP and Pora Council member Taras Stetskiv said later. 'But we were restrained by the fear of the split of Ukraine.'[21] Some of the young Pora activists were dismayed; they thought the hour had come to make the decisive strike: 'We thought the revolution would be finished that day, like in Serbia when they took the bulldozer to the parliament, and there would have been no compromise with Kuchma later on,' says Oleksiy Tolkachov. 'Non-violent resistance is very good, but there are some moments when you have to work quickly and strongly.'

But Yushchenko continued to stress the need for calm, restraint and discipline, and within days, an international delegation including the Polish president, Alexander Kwasniewski, the European Union's foreign policy chief, Javier Solana, and the speaker of the Russian parliament, Boris Gryzlov, had arrived in Kiev in an attempt to negotiate a solution. The world's television cameras were focused on the crowds on the Maidan, and a violent crackdown seemed increasingly unlikely.

Every day, students would mass at breakfast time and begin a series of marches around the city: from the Maidan to the presidential administration building and to parliament, maintaining their grip on the government's pressure points. The revolution was in perpetual motion. 'We were on our feet all day and we were tired, but we were in such a high emotional state because we knew we were doing the right thing,' says Tanya Botanova, a student at Kiev-Mohyla Academy. 'We were singing the Ukrainian national anthem and chanting so much, we lost our voices. It didn't feel like a crowd, it felt like a nation marching.

'You know, there are some stereotypes about Ukrainians – they are passive, they are too tolerant, they are too easy-going, they are apathetic. But when it came to it, we were not passive when the authorities stepped over the line.'

Outside the presidential compound, young women like Botanova sang folk songs and danced all night in front of the riot police. They weaved orange ribbons into security barriers and pushed flowers into the grilles of riot shields, invoking memories of the Vietnam war protests of the 1960s. 'Militsiya z narodom!' they chanted – *The police are with the people!* Hundreds of brightly-coloured blooms were strewn across the blockades: red, pink, purple, yellow and, of course, orange. The main players would meet at campaign headquarters each evening, with discussions sometimes stretching deep into the night. A few hours later, as dawn broke, the whole cycle would begin again. And every day, new protesters would arrive in Kiev from the provinces as the momentum continued to build.

It seemed to be working: Kuchma called for fresh elections, stepping back from his previous unqualified support for Yanukovych, who was now looking increasingly isolated. Negotiations continued between the authorities and the opposition to find a solution to the political crisis. While the talks were going on, Pora picketed Kuchma's dacha outside Kiev, putting ladders up against the fence so they could get a good look at the building. 'I think Kuchma finally realised there and then that we could get him physically, that a few thousand hot-tempered guys could climb over his fence,' said Taras Stetskiv a few weeks afterwards. 'Then he would have to order his guards to shoot. And then there would be a total mess. But frankly speaking, we never meant to climb over the fence. The blockade of the dacha was only psychological pressure on Kuchma. We knew that it would drive him mad in three seconds.'[22]

A compromise was ultimately agreed, reforming the country's electoral legislation to ensure a fairer vote and reducing the powers of the president. Stetskiv believes it demonstrated that Yushchenko was never a genuine revolutionary; the orange leader was, Stetskiv said, 'programmed for compromise'.[23] Inside the tent camp, many were deeply disappointed with the outcome – it felt like a betrayal. 'It demoralised the activists, they couldn't understand it,' says Vladyslav Kaskiv. 'These people were criminals and wanted to take over power, so why go to negotiate with them? It made it possible for the old elite to come back after the revolution.' But others believed it was the only way to a peaceful victory. 'Friends of mine thought we would have to storm the presidential administration,' says Andriy Ignatov, the Maidan website activist. 'But the controversy would have hurt the legitimacy of the presidency. The risks were high. To me, it was like, if you were confident there were good chances of victory in the Supreme Court, you should do the right thing.'

On 3 December, the Supreme Court annulled the results of the second round, blaming mass violations of the law: there would be a re-run of the poll on 26 December. Here, finally, was the victory over the cheats and con men that the protesters had been fighting for. The Orange Revolutionaries had prevailed; at the Maidan, people cried with joy as the decision came through. Yevgen Zolotariov was directing a contingent of Pora activists outside the cabinet building when he heard the news: 'We were standing there, preparing to break inside, so when the decision came, we had to change our plan quickly. I remember quite a few people were very disappointed because they were ready for action. Some of them were even trying to beat me up,' he laughs. The blockades were dismantled and many of the protesters began to pack up their belongings and head back out into the provinces to prepare for the final ballot.

Meanwhile, a small group of Pora activists and Yushchenko supporters decided to take their message into the heart of Yanukovych territory in the south and the east of the country. On 10 December, around 50 cars – Mercedes and Jeeps, a cranky old Russian Zhiguli and a limousine supplied by the taxi drivers' trade union – set off from Kiev on a journey which would last ten days and cover more than 2,000 miles: the 'Convoy of Friendship'. They took with them an exhibition of photographs from the Maidan, two rock bands and a crew of graffiti artists. They flew the yellow and orange flags of Pora and Yushchenko, but as the journey unfolded, they picked up the blue and white symbols of Yanukovych's supporters, mixing them together in a gesture of national unity. 'The idea came from when lots of cars were driving around Kiev with orange flags, honking their horns to the beat of the '*Yush-chen-ko!*' chant,' says Nelly Verner, who wore an orange coat with a blue scarf on the journey. 'We wanted to tell them about what was happening, because in Kiev we felt this strong sense of freedom, we were almost flying with hope, and we thought it would be easy to bring that feeling to others.' It didn't quite work out that way.

They stayed anywhere they could find a place to sleep for the night; in hotels, in people's houses and on freezing campsites, huddled together under blankets to stay warm. As the convoy rolled onwards, they sang revolutionary songs to keep their spirits up. Some cities welcomed them; they would set up their exhibition, make speeches about the great orange dream, and then the bands would set the pulse racing. 'The main thing was the dialogue,' says Dirk Lustig, a Swiss businessman who lived in Kiev and took his own car on the tour. 'There were hundreds of hours of discussion, talking to people about what happened in Kiev, what we'd seen there, reassuring them, telling them that we weren't against them, telling them their voices were important, saying that they should vote for whoever they wanted to vote for rather than who they were told to vote for, even if it was Yanukovych. Whenever we got to any village or town I would wind the car windows down, turn the volume way up and put on *Razom Nas Bahato*. That was the key message of the trip – *together we are many*.'

But it was not a message that some people wanted to hear. On the way to Odessa, in the deep south where ties to Russia remain strong, they were held up by an improvised roadblock for several hours. Hundreds of angry pensioners and drunken youths screamed abuse at them, calling them fascists and shouting, 'Americans go home!' And when they reached the eastern Donbas region, there were disagreements within the convoy over whether they should proceed to Donetsk, where Yanukovych had once been the governor and where his support was at its keenest. Some said it was too dangerous; a few thousand blue-clad protesters had gathered there and burned effigies of Yushchenko and his ally Yulia Tymoshenko. In the end, the decision was made for them; as they progressed towards the city, they were ambushed by local thugs just as night fell. 'It was like a cowboy film,' says Lustig. 'We were trying to drive our cars all together in a block, but they were circling all around us on the highway, throwing nails and bottles and stones. They were real bandits, guys with old Mercedes and gold teeth, and they were stirring up other ordinary people who started throwing eggs at us. Lots of our tyres were destroyed. The police tried to help us and they got their tyres destroyed as well.'

They decided it was time to move on, and they didn't even attempt to reach Luhansk, the other industrial powerhouse of the region. 'Maybe we were getting a bit paranoid by this time, but we were really afraid,' says Verner. 'Compared to the euphoria we felt when leaving Kiev, I was thinking, "Why are we doing this? People cannot be convinced, they have their own ideas and that's all they want."'

But the dark mood lifted as they reached Yushchenko's home town, Sumy, where people ran to hug and kiss them in the streets, and as they made a triumphant return to the Maidan, they found Kreshchatyk lined with Pora flags and drummers beating out a welcoming tattoo. Fireworks went off as the entire convoy parked right in front of the stage. It was 24 December; two days before the polls opened for the final vote.

In those last moments, there were still fears that some pro-Yanukovych diehards might mount some desperate last-ditch intervention. Yanukovych's campaign manager had announced that Pora's 'real members' – armed gangsters, snipers and explosives experts – were waiting to reveal themselves when the time was right, and pro-Yanukovych television advertisements contrasted an idyllic future Ukraine, where 'children will be smiling in their sleep', with the alternative promise of a pernicious orange future of civil war and fascist resurgence. But the election passed without major incident. With the new election law in place, fraud diminished significantly, and the con men's hearts, it seemed, were no longer in it. 'We knew there would still be falsifications but we knew they would be on a much smaller scale, and that we could stop them, especially with the new law,' says Mykhailo Svystovych. 'We could feel victory was very close. We knew we couldn't let it slip out of our hands.'

The result gave Yushchenko victory by 52 per cent to Yanukovych's 44 per cent. The opposition leader who had almost died for his cause would be the next president; Ukraine appeared to have made a decisive shift away from the power cliques and business clans who had run the country since independence in 1991; away from the 'managed democracy' which had allowed votes but not choice. This was, some said, the final step in the independence process; the severing of ties with the Soviet past. 'We have drawn a new place for Ukraine on the map of the world,' stated Yushchenko. The political map of Europe, at least, had changed. Yet despite the weeks of mass protest, this was still a relatively close result, indicating that considerable numbers of Ukrainians had not been infected with orange fever. The split between the west, where Yushchenko again won heavily, and the east, where Yanukovych commanded a huge majority, still remained.

It was around this time that the questions about who was really behind the revolution returned with renewed force. Where, asked the international media, had all the tents and the television screens and the banners and the stickers come from? Who had paid the bill? Was it the West, seeking to ensure that its favoured candidate won, and that its influence dominated the New Ukraine? Was it all just a seedy plot?

The British newspaper, the *Guardian*, set the tone which others around the world were to follow. One of its journalists, Ian Traynor, reported that the US government and the pro-democracy foundations it funded were repeating tricks developed since the campaign to destabilise Slobodan Milošević in 2000: training the opposition, backing student movements, funding exit polls. 'The operation – engineering democracy through the ballot box and civil disobedience – is now so slick that the methods have matured into a template for winning other people's elections,' he wrote. After Serbia and Georgia, now Ukraine. 'If the events in Kiev vindicate the US in its strategies for helping other people win elections and take power from anti-democratic regimes, it is certain to try to repeat the exercise elsewhere in the post-Soviet world,' he concluded.[24]

Another writer for the *Guardian*, Jonathan Steele, pointed out that many other elections in former Soviet countries had been rigged, but the 'furious noise' of complaint from the West had been absent: 'The decision to protest appears to depend mainly on realpolitik and whether the challengers or the incumbent are considered more "pro-Western" or "pro-market".' Intervening in foreign elections under the guise of promoting democracy, said Steele, was part of a phenomenon which he called the 'postmodern coup d'etat', the old CIA-sponsored putsch adapted for the post-Soviet era. 'Instruments of democracy are used selectively to topple unpopular dictators, once a successor candidate or regime has been groomed,' he argued.[25] He pointed out that much of the global media coverage was so besotted with the revolutionary glamour of the Maidan that it overlooked the significant proportion of the Ukrainian population which had voted for Yanukovych.

A third *Guardian* columnist, John Laughland of the British Helsinki Human Rights Group, was even more damning. He ridiculed what he called the 'fairy tale about how youthful demonstrators bring down an authoritarian regime, simply by attending a rock concert in a central square'. Pora, he wrote, like Otpor and Kmara, had been 'created and financed in Washington'.[26] Much was made of the fact that James Woolsey, who at the time was the chairman of one of the leading democracy foundations, Freedom House, had previously been the head of the CIA.

The reaction from Pora activists was a mixture of incredulity and rage. This was, they said, a movement made in Ukraine, with very specific roots in Ukrainian political history, and the people who had made it happen were ordinary Ukrainians who had endured the long nights in Kiev's snow-covered streets to change their own country's history. 'It wasn't a Western-inspired revolution at all,' says Mykhailo Svystovych. 'Nobody was laying any hopes on Western support. We are grateful that we got that support during the revolution, but if it hadn't happened, we would still have won... and it maybe would have been even better. We would have stormed the buildings in the end and there would have been no compromise deal. And the politicians would have had to pay more attention to the people if the people had physically put them into those chairs and not simply elected them.'

But it couldn't be denied that Western countries had invested huge amounts in 'democracy-building' programmes in Ukraine; the *New York Times* estimated that the United States spent around $28 million in 2004; other newspapers suggested that even greater sums had been paid out.[27] The money had provided training for politicians and journalists, and funded election observers and exit polls, preparing the ground for the revolution. Some saw this as a sly method of ousting governments which didn't conform to Western strategic and economic desires, but the US said that all it wanted to do was promote sound democratic practices. Lorne Craner, the president of the state-funded International Republican Institute, insisted that no outside forces, however powerful, could have sparked the upsurge of popular emotion which was seen on the Maidan. 'There's this myth that the Americans go into a country and, presto, you get a revolution,' he said. 'It's not the case that Americans can get two million people to turn out on the streets. The people themselves decide to do that.'[28]

Juhani Grossman, the director of Freedom House's election participation project in Kiev, which helped Znayu and, to a lesser extent, Pora, says the accusation of interference in another country's political affairs was simply invalid because his organisation's work was carried out on the basis of an agreement with the Ukrainian authorities to promote democratic commitments. 'It was never the national strategy of Ukraine to have unfair elections,' he says. 'There are many things foreign NGOs shouldn't do. These should be limited by the laws of the land. If Ukraine had a policy of unfree elections or hadn't signed up to these international agreements, it would perhaps have been inappropriate for us to be here.' However, as others pointed out, supporting free elections would hardly help a government which hoped to retain power through fraud; as in Serbia and Georgia, supporting democracy inevitably helped the 'democrats': the opposition. In such situations, opposing electoral fraud effectively meant – throwing off the linguistic cloak of abstraction, and looking at what was really happening, on the ground – assisting regime change.

Of course, it was even harder to estimate how many millions of Russian roubles had been poured into the Yanukovych campaign, and how many Russian 'political technologists' – Moscow fixers and their bagmen – had helped to develop its strategy. None of this, however, would alter the views of those who saw the Machiavellian hand of Washington manipulating the entire globe for its own nefarious purposes.

There was also much debate about how significant a part Pora had really played in the events of the past year. Was it a kind of radical vanguard, awakening the dormant desires of a downtrodden population, as the yellow Pora leader Vladyslav Kaskiv suggested, or just a colourful sideshow, a telegenic circus act which was irresistible to the media? The black Pora leader, Mykhailo Svystovych, cautioned against claiming too much influence: 'It wasn't Pora who made the revolution – the people made the revolution, the mass of unorganised people,' he says. 'Yes, our principles spread around society, but it wasn't us who imposed these on everyone – no, people grasped these ideas independently of us. The participation of huge masses of ordinary people was what really mattered.

'Yushchenko was the symbol of the revolution, but he wasn't the organiser of the revolution. He was the alternative to the regime, and some of the people who took to the Maidan supported him, but some were simply against the regime. So it was thanks to people's desire not to live any longer in this criminal state, and their willingness to stay on the Maidan, and thanks to the military who were willing to either stand aside or take the side of the people.'

Oles Doniy, one of the key figures in the independence protests of 1990, believes that Pora and the Maidan tent city had become new Ukrainian myths, like the student hunger strike more than a decade earlier. 'Myths are very important, they are stronger than reality, they inspire you, make you act,' he says. The authorities' crackdown on Pora just before the election had created a romantic image of good versus evil, a glowing parable of a cruel state crushing the innocent aspirations of its beautiful sons and daughters. 'Thanks to this myth, people don't just see this as a struggle between the authorities and politicians,' Doniy suggests. 'To legitimise the victory, it was important to show that it was not just former ministers who were fighting against the present ministers, but that there was a young, romantic generation involved. Unfortunately, not all of the romantic dreams of the people who participated will become true, but that doesn't decrease the importance of these events.'

Nevertheless, even among some of the most committed participants, there was a sense of realism about what lay ahead. 'This revolution is not the end, it's the start, there's a lot of work to be done. That's a fact,' says Pora activist Alina Shpak. 'The country has not changed absolutely, in many places it's exactly the same as it was. But it's very important now to avoid disappointment. When people were out in the streets, they wanted immediate results, but there are no such things. The previous system was built up over ten years, it can't be changed in a few months. It will take time.'

A CLASH OF COLOURS

The revolution was almost complete, but the most hardcore of the revolutionaries refused to accept that the party was over. The orange-clad crowds had dispersed, but a final few remained in the tent camp on Kreshchatyk. Pora urged them to leave, saying the camp had become an unsanitary eyesore. 'It is no longer needed, now it has become a nuisance to the residents of this city,' said Vladyslav Kaskiv. 'I frankly can't understand the people still there.'[29] Piles of damp, rotting clothing lay on the street amid the discarded remnants of the past few turbulent weeks, now no more than so much dirty litter. But the campers were no longer under anyone's control; they vowed that they would stay until Yushchenko was inaugurated as president. 'There was a decision to shut the camp but we couldn't put it into practice,' says Yevgen Dykiy. 'At the point when the decision was taken, Pora activists were a minority in the camp. On one hand there were all these positive tendencies for self-organisation, it governed itself, but then on the other hand you could feel some anarchy there. A great number of people in the tent camp thought they were the main revolutionaries, they didn't care about any decisions from any kind of headquarters. People who worked had gone back to work; those who stayed there were somewhat marginal elements, and they followed no orders.'

On 20 January 2005, Yanukovych finally conceded defeat, albeit reluctantly. 'The right of force has won against the force of the law,' he told his supporters.[30] Six days later, Yushchenko was inaugurated, and a hundred thousand people gathered at the Maidan for one last time to watch as he ascended to the presidency. 'This is a victory of freedom over tyranny, of law over lawlessness,' he declared.[31]

Afterwards, the tent camp was finally dismantled. The protesters held a small farewell ceremony, took photographs and exchanged telephone numbers, and left the Maidan. Three days later, the yellow wing of Pora held what it called its 'grand closing ceremony' at a Kiev hotel. It was attended by foreign dignitaries and prominent politicians from the Yushchenko bloc, and serenaded by the Eurovision star Ruslana, dressed in a bright yellow Pora T-shirt. Yushchenko didn't attend, but sent a message: 'I am proud of your courage, honour and faith in your own strength to struggle and to be victorious.'[32]

It was here that the decision was announced that Pora would become a political party to compete in the parliamentary election the following year – an echo of Otpor's ultimate decision to enter politics in Serbia. This was the vision of Vladyslav Kaskiv and those close to him: 'Pora will not allow the old corrupt political guard that ruled over Ukraine these past 14 years to change its colours again, we will not allow the villains and corrupt officials that are now again changing their stripes by putting on the orange colours to seize power again in Ukraine,' Kaskiv would explain. 'Pora will stand and protect the democratic victory of the Ukrainian people.'[33]

Black Pora activists were furious. They believed that forming a political party contravened the spirit of the movement. At their own conference in January, they vowed to continue the struggle as a watchdog organisation, as Otpor had done initially, cajoling and criticising the new authorities whenever necessary, pushing them to live up to the promises made in the heat of the revolution, to exorcise the demons of the Kuchma years and 'cleanse' the country. 'When we created Pora, we wrote down a principle – no one should take any dividends from participation in the movement,' says Mykhailo Svystovych. 'A political party is a trip to power. It means certain people will become part of power under the name Pora: that is taking dividends. A party has a certain ideology, but Pora was above ideology, we had both the right and the left.'

The differences which had been submerged beneath the passions of the past months had resurfaced, more bitterly than before. Black Pora even staged a demonstration outside parliament, demanding that authorities should not grant official registration to the yellow Pora party. Rank-and-file yellow Pora activists found it all hard to understand. 'During the revolution, the difference between the yellow and black Pora wasn't really felt, it was just different coloured T-shirts. We were very much alike, we were all after the same goal,' says Nelly Verner. 'Now black Pora was saying we stole something from them, we took over the brand name. They kept saying that on television and in the media. It looked like the only thing they were doing was accusing us. It was a little sad because I wanted us to be all together.'

Vladyslav Kaskiv – who was the main focus of black Pora's rage and contempt – says that all the arguments were simply products of a healthy new democratic process. He denies being irritated by his former allies' persistent criticism. 'Democracy *is* irritating sometimes,' he smiles. 'There's always criticism and every political leader in a democracy should have to constantly explain what he's doing. That's what we were struggling for. I never had the goal in life to build a political career, I'm doing this because of the moment and the responsibility I have now under these circumstances. But despite that' – he smiles again – 'I should acknowledge that I enjoy it.'

The Pora party was registered, although not immediately, as a significant number of the signatures in support of its application were found initially not to be authentic. But as in Serbia, some still argued that the movement should simply have disbanded after the revolution and bequeathed its name, untainted, to history. 'It would have been more honest if the name wasn't used any more,' says Yevgen Dykiy. 'If any of the activists wanted to pursue political careers, they were free to create other organisations but without using the brand name.

'But I can also understand Vlad Kaskiv, he was risking more than any of the ordinary members, he really invested a lot: a lot of time, a lot of money,' Dykiy continues. 'It's very logical that this political brand should now help him in the future. If I were in his shoes, I wouldn't be able to resist the lure to build on what Pora was, so I don't share the criticism that he's receiving. I think the decision he took was not immoral. Maybe I'll even vote for them…'

ONE POINT FIVE PER CENT

The orange coalition collapsed even more rapidly than it came together. Within months, Yushchenko had dismissed the government led by the new prime minister, Yulia Tymoshenko, amidst allegations of corruption, economic mismanagement and vicious infighting between senior politicians. Then a second administration crashed amidst a crisis caused by an increase in the price of Russian gas imports, which many thought was Moscow's revenge on Ukraine for turning to the West during the Orange Revolution. Although freedom of speech was now flourishing, there was disillusionment that the 'bandits' so vehemently denounced by Yushchenko during his election campaign had not gone to jail. Even those who maintained that the revolution had been a definitive step forward for Ukraine were disconcerted: it wasn't meant to be this way… 'I didn't expect such an open confrontation,' says Mykhailo Svystovych. 'I knew these politicians weren't ideal, but I didn't know it would be that bad…'

At parliamentary elections in March 2006, it was the party of Viktor Yanukovych which won the most seats, and Yushchenko's party which suffered the greatest losses – although the total number of seats won by the former orange revolutionaries still far outweighed those of their opponents. However, the result enabled Yanukovych to return to power as prime minister, throwing Ukraine back into political turmoil as the two Viktors clashed once again, and both orange and blue protesters returned to the streets of Kiev – leading many to question what, if anything, the revolution had really achieved.

The new Civic Party Pora also fared badly in its first electoral test. It had formed an alliance with another small party, Reforms and Order, and ran with a list of candidates headed by the celebrity boxer Vitaly Klitschko and a manifesto of civil rights and free-market economics. But as in Serbia, the youth movement's popularity didn't translate into electoral support. It attracted only 1.5 per cent of the vote; not enough to win seats in parliament. 'We repeated the result of Otpor,' said one disconsolate Pora activist.

But whatever the results, election observers said that these had been the country's fairest polls yet, and that the ultimate victors were not the politicians, but the people who had struggled for genuine democracy in Ukraine – even if the result caused political instability. Vladyslav Kaskiv agreed: this, he said, had been the real point of the Orange Revolution; it hadn't been about Yushchenko or Yanukovych, but about something much more important – justice: 'Because of the revolution, Ukrainians will never again allow someone to steal power,' he said. 'Of course the authorities will change, dozens of times, but the principles will remain unchanged.' At the Maidan, Kaskiv suggested optimistically, Ukrainians had made a historic step forward: they had fought for and won the freedom to decide for themselves.

CHAPTER FOUR

ORANGE DREAMS AND BLUE JEANS

KYRGYZSTAN, AZERBAIJAN, BELARUS... AND BEYOND

George W. Bush thrust out his hips and jerked his body to the beat. As Georgian dancers in traditional costumes swirled lithely to the music's sensual pulse, the American president couldn't restrain his enthusiasm, and burst on to the stage, clapping his hands in jubilant approval. It was May 2005, and Bush was making a surprise visit to the Georgian capital, Tbilisi, where he was welcomed by enraptured crowds who hoped that he was bringing not only endorsement for their struggle from the most powerful nation on earth, but the promise of protection, and of economic benefits to come.

The following day, tens of thousands of people gathered in Freedom Square to hear Bush address the nation alongside President Mikheil Saakashvili. 'Bushi! Bushi!' they yelled as he acknowledged their applause, a shimmering throng of red-and-white Georgian flags catching the sunlight. In few other places that year would he be greeted with such enthusiasm, such fond admiration.

In a meticulously-crafted speech, Bush sought to link the 'Rose Revolution' to his own agenda: spreading democracy around the world. He argued that democracy movements in Ukraine, in other former Soviet states and in the Middle East had been inspired by what had happened in Tbilisi in 2003. Georgia, he said, was a 'beacon of democracy' for the world. 'We are living in historic times,' he said, speaking of a 'global democratic revolution', a world where freedom was advancing, overturning tyranny in its wake. 'Now, across the Caucasus, in Central Asia and the broader Middle East, we see the same desire for liberty burning in the hearts of young people,' he declared. 'They are demanding their freedom – and they will have it.'[1]

Giga Bokeria, one of the founders of Kmara and now a prominent member of parliament in President Saakashvili's party, said he believed that Bush's visit sent out a message – to Russia in particular – that the United States would support democratic movements wherever they emerged. It was a theory which would be tested in the months to come.

Bush's trip to Tbilisi, coming soon after Ukraine's Orange Revolution, appeared to be part of a wider campaign to identify him with successful twenty-first century 'people power' movements. In February 2005, before a summit with Vladimir Putin in Slovakia, the American president had held a meeting with a group of people who were billed as 'champions of freedom' from former Communist countries. It included some of those who had played a crucial role in the region's youth resistance groups over the past few years – Ivan Marović from Serbia, Giga Bokeria and Tinatin Khidasheli from Georgia, Vladyslav Kaskiv from Ukraine – alongside veteran dissidents from Poland, Hungary, the former Czechoslovakia and the Baltic countries.

'It took place when we were riding this wave of emotion, we were celebrating victory, and we thought the entire world was sharing the taste of that victory with us,' recalls Kaskiv. 'I asked George Bush to understand that it was now clear that democracy and freedom wouldn't stop at Ukraine's borders, and that changes, however fantastic they might seem in some countries, were possible. To which George Bush, to my surprise, said, "Yes, the next should be Moldova", where they had elections a few weeks later. So it showed me that he understood my point and I didn't need to convince him any further.'

The invitation to meet Bush was somewhat ironic for Ivan Marović because, during the previous year's US presidential election, he had been contacted by members of the grassroots anti-Bush campaign, moveon.org, who saw Otpor as an inspiration. Like others involved in non-violent resistance around the world, Marović also believed that the US government's attempts to bring democracy to Iraq by force were deeply misguided. He says that he attempted to explain this to the American president.

While Bush was congratulating the instigators of the revolutions in Serbia, Georgia and Ukraine, a wave of paranoia was sweeping through the rest of the former Soviet Union. The international media repeatedly posed the question: where next? Leaders of countries with grubby human rights records became increasingly nervous, fearing the onward march of what they believed was a concerted, Western-funded regime-change programme. Islam Karimov, the hard-line president of Uzbekistan, where opposition parties were banned and dissidents jailed and allegedly tortured, said he would not tolerate such a scenario in his country. 'It is unacceptable to use democracy to take over power or organise a coup,' he said, warning that he had the 'necessary force' to prevent it.[2] It was a promise he would fulfil within the year, when his security forces put down an uprising in the Uzbek town of Andijan, killing 187 people, according to official figures – although eyewitness reports suggested that hundreds more had died. In Russia, new laws were brought in to limit the role of foreign civil rights groups; while the Belarussian president, Alexander Lukashenko, simply stated: 'There will not be any rose, orange or banana revolutions in our country.'[3] A Belarussian opposition leader was immediately jailed for stealing computers from the US embassy – which denied that anything had been stolen. The message could not have been clearer.

The president of the Central Asian state of Kyrgyzstan, Askar Akayev, also voiced concerns that any revolution in his country could lead to a civil war. 'We need to reject political forces who want to repeat the revolutionary scenarios that were used in Georgia and Ukraine and funded by Western financial groups,' he said.[4] He spoke darkly of extremists and provocateurs who had been trained by unnamed foreigners to stir up unrest. And yet Kyrgyzstan, a remote, impoverished and relatively obscure former

Soviet republic on the border of China, didn't immediately appear to be primed for a democratic uprising. During the 1990s, Akayev had gained a reputation as one of the most promising democrats in Central Asia, but as the decade came to a close – as in so many former Soviet republics – corruption and nepotism were flourishing as the economy stagnated and opposition activity was increasingly discouraged. Although there had been sporadic demonstrations against Akayev's rule, the political opposition was weak and quarrelsome. Nevertheless, as parliamentary elections approached in February 2005, the Kyrgyz authorities felt the need to bring in new rules to thwart street protests, and to prevent a former foreign minister turned opposition leader, Roza Otunbayeva, from standing in the polls.

Otunbayeva had been working for the United Nations in Georgia and had watched the Rose Revolution unfold in the streets of Tbilisi. Her disqualification sparked a series of small demonstrations and the emergence of a new Kyrgyz youth movement called KelKel, which was modelled on Otpor, Kmara and Pora. KelKel, which said its name meant 'Renaissance' or the more unwieldy 'Coming Together for the Common Good', was founded in January 2005 and drew attention to itself at the Otunbayeva protests by handing out lemons, a reference to the oranges of the Maidan. One of KelKel's founders had worked as an election observer in Ukraine and had returned full of hope and fervour; the fears incarnate of Central Asia's more authoritarian leaders. KelKel said it had been inspired by left-wing writers like Karl Marx and Noam Chomsky as well as the civil rights campaigns of Martin Luther King and Gandhi. 'We wanted a country where the state was accountable to its citizens, instead of being an organised mafia for controlling resources and power, instead of mimicking a democracy while supporting some of the most corrupt practices and mentality,' says one of its activists. KelKel believed that Akayev was manipulating the constitution to allow him to hold on to power until his death, when the presidency would be bequeathed to one of his children, who were standing as candidates in the elections.

KelKel members were trained in the now-familiar techniques of non-violent resistance, translations of Gene Sharp's *From Dictatorship to Democracy* were passed around, and they were aided by American-funded democracy foundations – but this was not a movement with the nationwide reach of Otpor or Pora. Nevertheless, the authorities came up with a novel method of dealing with the potential threat: they set up a rival youth organisation, also called KelKel, also using the lemon as its symbol, which distributed leaflets praising the Akayev government and cautioning against 'velvet revolutions'. The original KelKel's website was hacked, and web pages advertising the pro-government group appeared in its place. 'They threaten us with lemons,' ran its slogan. 'We simply squeeze them.'[5]

But none of this could prevent the unrest that followed. After the elections, scattered protests broke out around Kyrgyzstan as demonstrators claimed the polls had been rigged in President Akayev's favour. Government buildings were occupied in the southern towns of Osh and Jalalabad, and as the demonstrations spread to the capital, Bishkek, people complaining about alleged election fraud were joined by others who simply wanted to express their discontent about the ugly contrast between the wealth of the ruling elite and the poverty suffered by most of Kyrgyzstan's citizens.

On 24 March 2005, several thousand people gathered outside a clinic run by a wealthy Kyrgyz doctor who had gained international celebrity for his unconventional methods of treating drug addicts, and who had become a vital presence in the opposition. They began to march on Bishkek's Alatoo Square, the site of the presidential palace, the White House. Few expected the outcome to be revolution. 'On that morning, we were not sure what was going to happen, yet we felt quite determined to get something done,' says a KelKel activist. Women handed out tulips to the security forces, while, in another intentional echo of Kiev, KelKel attempted to pitch a few tents.

The demonstration proceeded relatively calmly until a group of unidentified men wearing white caps started throwing stones at the protesters, who responded with missiles of their own. This would prove to be the flashpoint which would make its mark on Kyrgyz history. Youths started fighting the riot police, attempting to force their way through the cordon around the White House, and despite calls for restraint from the protest leaders, what had begun as a peaceful rally was rapidly transformed into a seething, angry mass.

Emboldened by the raw power of their emotions, the crowd rushed through the White House gates as the soldiers guarding it retreated. Demonstrators rampaged through the corridors, smashing computers, throwing sheaves of official documents out of the windows and beating up two senior officials. Correctly gauging the prevailing mood, President Akayev had already fled, taking only the suit that he was wearing at the time. He would eventually resurface in Moscow; an apparently untouchable figure who had ruled for 14 years, spontaneously deposed within an hour, not so much by a revolution as a riot which had got out of hand. He said he was the victim of an American-backed coup.

The sheer speed of the Kyrgyz government's collapse surprised even those who were involved. Policemen deserted their posts and slipped away into the twilight, and as darkness fell, Bishkek became a lawless zone, with looters roaming the streets, burning shops, sacking shopping malls and loading cars with stolen goods. 'People threw off their shoes and tried on the latest Italian designer fashions,' reported one observer. 'Young girls struggled to drag away computer equipment, while old ladies made off with packs of macaroni.'6 Some said the looting and vandalism were retribution against businesses linked to the president's clan; others blamed unemployed youths or Akayev loyalists who they said were trying to discredit the protests; there were also reports of people being paid to cause mayhem. The opposition, unprepared for seizing power, set up a 'people's council' in the presidential palace and tried to restore calm, with KelKel activists manning the doors, searching anyone who left in case they were smuggling out 'souvenirs', and organising teams of night watchmen who patrolled the city centre and held vigils at key sites to prevent further damage.

It would become known as the 'Tulip Revolution', but in the chaos of the moment, it wasn't clear exactly what had happened during this improvised rebellion which owed little to the calculated strategies which had brought the opposition to power in Belgrade, Tbilisi and Kiev. Nevertheless, ordinary people had exerted real influence for perhaps the first time in a state where the rule of the elite had gone unchallenged. The next day, the Kyrgyz opposition press was jubilant: 'Akayev and his clique thought they were ruling a nation of slaves and plebeians who would never rise from their knees. They were mistaken,' declared one newspaper.[7] Whatever its outcome, the Kyrgyzstan uprising demonstrated how the events in Ukraine and Georgia had unleashed desires which had begun to resonate way beyond their origins, and that it would take more than a few inept and unenthusiastic policemen to stop them.

MARLEY AND MUGABE

Over the course of 2005, new youth resistance movements began to emerge all over the world, in Africa and the Middle East as well as the former Soviet Union, sometimes in places where direct action had previously only involved gunfire. *'It's spreading,'* Otpor had declared in 2000, but the television pictures from the Orange Revolution and the instant global access provided by the internet had enthused young democracy activists everywhere. All they needed, it seemed, were the principles of non-violent resistance, a smart logo, some inspiring slogans and enough money to print a few colourful T-shirts. Some of them, however, would quickly discover that it wasn't that easy. Newspaper articles reduced it to a formula: how to bring down a dictator in a few easy lessons. But in many places, the formula just didn't work, at least not immediately; real life proved more complex than a set of simple rules and catchy slogans. Repressive governments were also reading those same articles, and learning. But although the element of surprise was quickly disappearing, there was no shortage of idealistic young people who were willing to try it.

In Zimbabwe, where President Robert Mugabe, once the national liberator from colonial rule, had become increasingly autocratic, they could only operate deep underground. The country was in crisis, with widespread food shortages, massive inflation and soaring unemployment. Protest was harshly suppressed, although a shadowy group emerged calling itself Zvakwana in the Shona language and Sokwanele in the Ndebele language – both words meaning *Enough*. It had no offices, no leaders and no spokespeople, and its only public communications came in the form of emails. But its black 'Z' logo began to appear on walls and billboards all over the capital, Harare – once, most audaciously, all along the route taken by Mugabe's motorcade, causing it to be diverted in case the president took offence. Zvakwana/Sokwanele took its ideas from Solidarity in Poland and the American civil rights movement of the 1960s, and some of its members had been trained by Robert Helvey and Srdja Popović of Otpor.

However, an open, public movement was impossible in Zimbabwe; it could mean not only imprisonment but, its activists feared, torture and death. So they left matchboxes containing messages of dissent in public places, stapled subversive notes to telephone cards, or scattered condoms emblazoned with a suitably suggestive message taken from the lyrics of Bob Marley: *Get Up! Stand Up!* They also distributed CDs of rebel anthems – songs by Marley, Hugh Masekela and Thomas Mapfumo – and videotapes showing government forces preparing themselves to put down demonstrations. It wasn't much, but it was all they could do. After the motorcade incident, the Zimbabwean police assigned a team of investigators to track them down, interrogating politicians, journalists and musicians for leads, but each time they seemed to evaporate into the ether, like restless spectres, before they could be caught. 'In Zimbabwe, it is easy to give up hope,' one of them told an American newspaper. 'What a movement of this nature is doing, in my estimation, is keeping the hope alive.'[8]

The Egyptian Movement for Change, which was known as *Kefaya*, or 'Enough', also adopted some of the tactics used by the peaceful revolutionaries in the former Soviet Union. Kefaya was one of the groups which defied a long-standing ban on street demonstrations to insist that President Hosni Mubarak should not stand for a fifth term in elections in 2005, and be replaced by a freely-elected leader. Some of its supporters wore the orange headbands of Ukraine, others flew the yellow flags of the Kyrgyzstan uprising; some of them were secular activists, some Islamists, some socialists. While pro-government media accused them of being agents of foreign influence, this was hardly a movement which would have been welcome in Washington. 'If things really change here, America's illusions that its interests in the region would be advanced by democracy will be laid bare,' suggested one Kefaya activist. 'A real democratic government in Egypt would be strongly against the US occupation of Iraq and regional US policies, particularly over Palestine.'[9] While its numbers were small, the very existence of Kefaya was a sign of a new kind of outspokenness in Egypt. Where it would lead, however, remained uncertain.

However, the most remarkable reinterpretation of Ukraine's Orange Revolution would take place in Lebanon. After the prime minister, Rafik Hariri, was killed in a car bomb attack in February 2005, hundreds of thousands of people flooded into Martyrs Square in Beirut, to demand that Syria, which they blamed for Hariri's murder, withdraw the 15,000 troops it had stationed in Lebanon since the civil war began there almost thirty years previously. There were deep sectarian divisions within Lebanese society, but the protests brought together people from estranged religious faiths in an unprecedented display of unity. Young demonstrators set up a tent camp in the square; this was, they said, in a reference to Lebanon's national symbol, a 'Cedar Revolution'.

'For the first time we felt that as a people, we had a voice and that we were powerful. It was a liberating experience,' says Joumanna Nasr, a 20-year-old student who worked for a youth group called Pulse of Freedom, which published its website direct from the tent city. 'We waved our Lebanese flags with pride and with dignity. It didn't matter whether the person standing next to me was a Muslim, Christian, or a Druze; whether he was from the north, the south, the Beqaa Valley, Beirut, whether he had been to the best university or had barely finished high school. This was the beauty of these demonstrations – everyone was there. For the first time, our love for our country was more important than any other identity. We wanted to regain our national dignity and sovereignty. It was beautiful.'

Within weeks, despite massive counter-demonstrations by supporters of the pro-Syrian Islamic party Hezbollah, the Lebanese government resigned and the Syrian troops began to pack up their equipment and move out of the country. Watching from Belgrade, Otpor's Srdja Popović was ecstatic: 'This was an amazing achievement, without one single bullet fired, in a very violent environment. Beirut was a synonym for civil war for years. That was the way they dealt with things. If they had a problem, they took up the guns. What they did will change the face of the Middle East in the years to come.' Not everyone agreed with Popović's optimistic analysis; the 'Cedar Revolution' ended quickly, most politicians returned to their familiar sectarian divides and, within months, Lebanon was at war again. And yet, for a few short weeks, Beirut had witnessed something special, however temporary and fragile it proved to be.

ORANGE NIGHTS IN BLACK GOLD CITY

Heydar Aliyev remains the dominant figure in his country, despite the inconvenience of having been dead for several years. Aliyev was a KGB boss and a senior Communist Party figure during the Soviet era. When he became the president of Azerbaijan after it gained independence from the Soviet Union in the early 1990s, the country was at war with neighbouring Armenia over the disputed territory of Nagorno-Karabakh – a war it effectively lost. Aliyev signed a ceasefire and helped to restore some national pride.

In 2003, the man who had led Azerbaijan for so many years suffered a heart attack while making a speech on live television. The presidency was passed on to his son, Ilham Aliyev, a wealthy businessman. But even after his death, the face of 'Heydar Baba' – 'Grandfather Heydar' – continues to gaze down, wisely and benevolently, from huge billboards by the roadside. Sometimes he is pictured smiling indulgently, at others he appears to be passing on a word of fatherly advice to young Ilham. Lenin is long gone, but in Azerbaijan the cult of personality remains, a testament to dynastic continuity.

The country's recent history is summed up by the architecture of the capital, Baku, on the shores of the Caspian Sea. The ornate mansions built around the turn of the twentieth century, when Caspian derricks pumped around half the world's oil, are the former residences of magnates like the Nobels and the Rothschilds, who made fortunes here. Not far away are clusters of brutalist concrete housing blocks from the Soviet era. Then there are the new buildings, the mirrorglass-fronted towers and luxury apartment complexes of the new oil boom, which began in the era of 'Heydar Baba', who signed lucrative deals with petroleum multinationals to start a new rush for the Caspian's black gold in the 1990s. But while the economy grew and the new oil wealth enriched the business elites, it failed to reach many ordinary Azeris. A short walk from the designer fashion stores and flashy restaurants of downtown Baku are the raddled, grimy backstreets where people scratch out a living in grim conditions. Outside the capital, the situation is even more desperate, particularly for the hundreds of thousands of refugees from the Nargorno–Karabakh war.

These were the stakes in play when parliamentary elections were called in 2005; not only power, but control of huge natural resources. Azerbaijan was a country with growing geopolitical significance. It had just opened a pipeline pumping oil from the Caspian to the Mediterranean to supply Western markets at a time of increasing concern about global energy insecurity, and it was also a Muslim country which was proud of its Western friendships. Situated between Russia and Iran in a strategic location for the Americans' 'war on terror', Azerbaijan was one of the few Islamic nations to have sent troops to serve with the US-led coalition in Iraq.

When Ilham Aliyev succeeded his father in the presidential election in 2003, the opposition had accused the West of overlooking fraud at the ballot box in favour of an orderly transfer of power which would ensure stability for its business interests. They took their grievances to the streets, and in the ensuing riots, bones were broken and hundreds of people were arrested. In 2005, the opposition said, the West must not put profits and global security priorities above democracy. Indeed, some of its more cunning spokesmen argued that by ignoring the people's will, Western countries were risking the rise of radical Islam in Azerbaijan. The stability offered by President Aliyev, they said, was a false investment. The president's New Azerbaijan Party saw things differently, of course. It argued that it had turned the country into one of the world's fastest-developing economies and created hundreds of thousands of jobs. It said that it was following a peaceful, evolutionary path to reform, and that economic growth would be threatened by political instability.

Azeri opposition activists had been listening intently when George Bush made his speech about the onward march of liberty in neighbouring Georgia, and were eager to warm themselves around his 'beacon of democracy'. The revolutions in Tbilisi and Kiev had given them hope that something similar might be possible in Baku. In his inauguration address at the start of his second term in office, President Bush seemed to be speaking to them directly: 'It is the policy of the United States to seek and support the growth of democratic movements in every nation and culture, with the ultimate goal of ending tyranny in our world,' Bush declared. How strongly and under what conditions that support might be expressed remained to be seen, but the Azeris took his words literally. Three of the leading opposition parties had decided to work together in an alliance they called Azadlig, or 'Freedom'; they had also adopted orange as their campaign colour.

Around the same time, three separate Azeri youth movements had begun agitating for change. One of them, Yokh! ('No!'), was led by Razi Nurullayev, a 31-year-old, multilingual law graduate who had translated works on non-violent resistance by Gene Sharp and Robert Helvey into Azeri and had made two trips to Kiev to meet the Pora leader Vladyslav Kaskiv and other Ukrainian youth activists and study their methods. Nurullayev was a realist: 'I was very encouraged by what I saw in Ukraine, but I realised they had many things we did not have here,' he says. 'They had the plan, they had the people, they had a lot of money, they had very good international support – and their police were friendly. They also told me it would be much harder for us here, because the regime would learn from what happened in Ukraine, Georgia and Kyrgyzstan. It would learn how to stop us.'

Yokh! made some initial impact with its bright green T-shirts and graffiti – Nurullayev believed that it was senseless to copy the Ukrainians' orange, as it had no significance within Azeri culture – but despite its limited membership, it quickly attracted unwelcome attention from the police. On his return from a conference in Amsterdam, Nurullayev was arrested and detained for five days. 'They were asking me why did I travel so frequently, which foreigners had taught me and where, and who was behind this,' he recalls. Yokh! also came under pressure from opposition politicians who wanted it to commit itself to the Azadlig bloc. Nurullayev refused, believing that the movement would never be credible if it wasn't independent of political parties. He was no admirer of the opposition leaders, believing them old-fashioned and incompetent.

Nurullayev appealed to foreign embassies and democracy foundations for financial aid, but found there was little interest in an Azeri version of Pora or Kmara. 'We made so many proposals but we only raised €1,000. How can you make a revolution with €1,000? It's impossible,' he says, rather forlornly. 'So we had to do everything ourselves, with our own resources.'

Another Azeri youth movement, Magam – *It's Time* in Azeri – also had to rely on its own membership for money and improvise its actions around whatever resources were available. Its activists clubbed together to publish an orange-covered edition of Gene Sharp's *From Dictatorship to Democracy*, buy cans of orange spray-paint and photocopy small, cheap leaflets on orange paper. When they ran out of propaganda material, they simply customised other opposition groups' leaflets, ripping off the logos and adding their own messages with marker pens. They took their name and their logo, the ticking clock, from Pora, although they only had a tiny fraction of the Ukrainians' membership: a couple of hundred at most. Like Yokh!, they worked when darkness fell, operating like a peaceful guerrilla group, spraying slogans – 'Free Elections or Revolution!' – and then slipping away into the night.

One advantage that Magam did have, however, was charisma. Its leader, 26-year-old Emin Huseynov, in his khaki cap, combat jacket and black polo neck, resembled an iconic rebel hero – an impression

complemented by the Che Guevara watch on his wrist. Huseynov
was one of those who had been severely beaten during the election
demonstrations of 2003. He had worked as a reporter for an Azeri
news agency and was assigned to cover the inauguration of Viktor
Yushchenko in Kiev, then travelled on to Georgia to see how the
Rose Revolution was organised. When George Bush made his speech
in Tbilisi's Freedom Square, Huseynov was there, standing at the
front of the crowd just a few metres away from the American leader,
holding up a placard bearing the words, 'President Bush, please help
democracy in Azerbaijan'. He recounted the story in an open letter
to Bush many months later: 'When your translator spoke, I held the
placard even higher, because at this time you looked at the people in
front of you and waved to us. It was exactly at this time that you read
my placard. This was clear, you even greeted me. I looked in your
eyes, listened attentively and engraved your words on my brain.'

For Huseynov, the driving force was anger; a cool, clear fury
at what he believed was the moral degeneration of his country.
'Corruption here is like a drug, nobody can live without it,' he says.
'It starts when a child is born in hospital, and you have to give the
doctor money. Then when the child grows up and goes to school,
you have to pay bribes to the teachers there too, because you won't
get an education. So corruption is our first experience of life, and by
the time we are in our twenties, we already have a clear knowledge
of this corrupt way of life. We all went down this road, we saw all
this with our own eyes. That's what made us do what we are doing.

'Azerbaijan has a lot of oil, but the money is just going into a few
people's pockets. All these buildings, all these restaurants, all these
bars, they are part of those people's wealth. If you have oil you can
do things two ways. One is like Norway, where they are establishing
infrastructure for the people. The second way is like Nigeria; they
have a lot of oil but the people are poor. We don't want Azerbaijan
to be like Nigeria, we want the money from oil to be shared out, to
be invested in education and welfare and social systems so everyone
in this country gets a chance, instead of it being kept in Western
bank accounts.' Naturally, this was not a view shared by the Azeri
government, which saw itself as honest, benevolent and fair, and

insisted that it was making steady progress in an orderly transition to European-style democracy.

What followed would be one of the most bizarre and bitterly-contested election campaigns of recent times. For the opposition, it began positively, with American and European officials firmly telling President Aliyev to ensure a free and fair vote. Azadlig was doing relatively well in the opinion polls and, under pressure from the West to prove their commitment to democracy, the Azeri authorities allowed the opposition bloc to stage a number of demonstrations. The opposition continued to believe that the polls would be rigged, but when orange flags flew in Baku for the first time, they allowed themselves some cautious hope.

That hope would not survive the next three months. At the end of July 2005, Ruslan Bashirli, the leader of the third Azeri youth movement, Yeni Fikir ('New Ideas'), travelled to Georgia to attend a democracy conference, accompanied by a recent recruit to the organisation. A few days later, on his return, he was arrested. The Azeri prosecutor announced that he had a covertly-filmed videotape showing Bashirli drinking brandy with two secret agents from Armenia – Azerbaijan's bitter enemy in the war over Nagorno-Karabakh – and discussing how to organise a revolution in Baku with the help of an American democracy foundation, the National Democratic Institute. He was alleged to have accepted $2,000 for his cause from the Armenian spies. The video was replayed again and again on the main Azeri television channels; one of them interspered the footage with images of Azeris killed or mutilated during the war with Armenia. This, they said, was treason. Bashirli was charged with plotting a coup. 'Now the Azeri public has seen the true face of the opposition and is fully convinced that in order to take power, it is prepared to collaborate with anyone, including the secret services of Armenia, which has occupied 20 per cent of the lands of our republic [in the territory of Nagorno-Karabakh],' said the state prosecutor.[10]

The prosecutor denied that the case was politically-motivated, but Bashirli's comrades were convinced that he had been framed by the Azeri secret services in order to discredit the movement and the opposition in general. 'This was a carefully planned KGB-style sting operation,' insisted Yeni Fikir's deputy leader Said Nuri shortly afterwards. Yeni Fikir alleged that the new recruit who organised the trip and accompanied Bashirli to Tbilisi, and then testified against him, was an undercover agent.

In the days after Bashirli's arrest, the headquarters of the Popular Front Party of Azerbaijan, where Yeni Fikir had its offices, was besieged by stone-throwing demonstrators, some of them refugees from the Nagorno-Karabakh war. Senior politicians called for the Popular Front itself to be banned. 'It's clear that the authorities are trying to destroy us and undermine trust in the democratic movement,' said Said Nuri. 'We believe this is the start of a wave of repression.'

Nuri was more right than he could have known. A few days after he made these comments, he was also detained on charges of preparing to overthrow the government. Nuri was immediately hospitalised; he suffered from the blood disorder thalassaemia and his condition rapidly deteriorated after his arrest. When a few of his friends gathered outside the hospital in silent protest – members of Yokh! and Magam as well as Yeni Fikir – they were hustled away by police. Nobody was allowed to visit him, and police officers were stationed near his hospital bed.

The following day, a third senior Yeni Fikir member, Ramin Tagiyev, was arrested for his role in the alleged plot. The three young men would ultimately receive harsh sentences: seven years in jail for Bashirli, four years for Tagiyev, and a five-year suspended sentence for Nuri.

Soon after Nuri's arrest, his friends discovered a cache of grenades in a plastic shopping bag, concealed amongst the flags in the Yeni Fikir office; they believed it had been planted as a pretext for yet more arrests. 'The day after that, the president's convoy was due to come down this street,' said activist Ahmad Shahidov. 'We think they wanted to come and say our members wanted to murder the president, then arrest us all as terrorists and put an end to us.'

But despite all that happened, Yeni Fikir still clung to the innocent belief that the higher powers of the West would come riding to their aid; that George Bush would see them as the next 'champions of freedom'; 'demanding their God-given rights', as he had told their Georgian neighbours. 'In 2003 [during the Azeri presidential election] it was different because the foreign countries didn't know what to do – they chose stability over democracy because of the oil,' said Shahidov. 'But now Western countries, especially the United States, think the main factor is democracy. We're waiting for support from the United States, because the United States is one of the most democratic countries in the world and we believe it will support the democratic process here. We are not alone.'

However, while the US continued to press for a fair vote and expressed concern about the crackdown on the opposition, the American ambassador to Baku made it clear that American economic, military and democratic interests in the region were indivisible, while George Bush wrote to the Azeri president, Ilham Aliyev, assuring him: 'I look forward to working with you after these elections.' An Azeri government spokesman said it meant that Bush understood there was no alternative to Aliyev in Azerbaijan, while a former US diplomat in the region suggested that because both government and opposition declared themselves pro-Western and anti-corruption, the US had little to lose, as long as stability was maintained.[11]

Georgia, which wanted to maintain friendly relations with its energy-rich neighbour, also decided to remain neutral. President Mikheil Saakashvili said that Ilham Aliyev was a leader who 'represents great hope for his people and whose achievements are obvious', while the influential MP Giga Bokeria insisted that it would be wrong to try to 'teach democracy' to Azerbaijan. No Kmara cadres arrived in Baku to assist their Azeri brothers and sisters; some of the Rose Revolution veterans questioned not only the Azadlig opposition bloc's popularity, but also its ability to govern the country any more fairly and democratically than President Aliyev. Two delegations of Ukrainian Pora activists did attempt to visit Azerbaijan, but they were denied entry and deported. It looked like the young Azeri radicals might end up alone after all. In a televised interview, Aliyev derided their efforts:

'People here, when they see those orange T-shirts, they can only laugh at that,' he said.[12]

There would be yet more twists in the plot before the elections on 6 November. Rasul Guliyev, the leader of the Azerbaijan Democratic Party, one of the other parties making up the Azadlig bloc, had been living in exile since the mid-1990s. He was a former speaker of parliament and a sometime ally of the former president, Heydar Aliyev, but had left the government and was subsequently accused of embezzling millions of dollars. Less than a month before the 2005 elections – in which he had been registered to stand, despite being a wanted man – Guliyev made a dramatic announcement that he would return to Azerbaijan, whatever the consequences. His statement generated widespread anticipation; Guliyev was seen by both sides as someone who could ignite public fervour. On the morning of his arrival, hundreds of troops were deployed across the capital, the road to the airport was blocked by checkpoints with barbed wire and water cannon, and anyone who tried to reach the airport to greet him was turned back. Scores of opposition supporters were arrested.

But Guliyev's plane did not land, in circumstances which remain murky. He said his flight was not given permission to touch down; the Azeri authorities say it simply chose not to. The plane was diverted to Ukraine, where Guliyev was briefly questioned by the authorities before being released.

The days that followed brought yet more surprises, as a number of senior Azeri officials, including the ministers for health and economic development, were arrested and accused of conspiring with Guliyev to seize power. Television news bulletins showed footage of the bundles of dollars and expensive jewellery which were allegedly found at their homes.

For the Yokh! movement's leader, Razi Nurullayev, this was the latest in a series of bad signs. Unlike the other Azeri youth groups, Yeni Fikir and Magam, he didn't believe in the inevitability of a great orange future. He had decided to stand for parliament as an independent candidate so he could, at least, put up his posters without interference. 'What can we hope for?' he asked. 'That the international community will know that this government is not democratic and never will be democratic. The opposition has no money and no clear programme, so there will be no revolution now. This is part of a process of longer-term change.'

Murad Gassanly, a 26-year-old adviser to the Popular Front party, who lived in London and had worked for the British Labour Party but had returned to Azerbaijan for the 2005 elections, also had lower expectations than the radical youth. 'This is not Georgia, this is not Ukraine,' he cautioned. 'This regime makes Eduard Shevardnadze look like a European liberal. What we can do at this election is damage the regime; we can seriously undermine it. We have an unprecedented level of international interest here now, and if the regime falsifies the election, it will be impossible to keep it a secret. What we want to do is dismantle the system whereby the parliament is a rubber stamp for the president, make the parliament independent and create a pluralist system.'

After the coup allegations, the Azadlig bloc was no longer permitted to hold rallies in central Baku. When they tried to stage a demonstration without official permission, they were dispersed quickly and firmly by the flailing batons of the riot police. Afterwards, at Azadlig's headquarters, which had been turned into a makeshift treatment centre, the floors and tables were spattered with blood. The authorities said they were simply upholding the law and combating the illicit activities of reckless provocateurs.

After all the conspiracies and the subterfuge and the arrests and the street-fights, there was little surprise when international election observers reported widespread violations at the polls – although the authorities insisted that democratic progress had again been made President Aliyev ordered the elections to be re-run in a handful of constituencies where he acknowledged that there had been irregularities, but that wasn't enough for the opposition Azadlig bloc, which had won fewer than ten out of 125 seats in parliament. They hoped that the Azeri people would respond to their call to take to the streets and overturn the results.

Azadlig's initial strategy was to wait until the authorities granted them a permit to demonstrate, to avoid another violent clash with the police, so they didn't start their protests immediately, as the Serbs, Georgians and Ukrainians had done. But, as Razi Nurullayev of Yokh! had realised months earlier, the Azeri government had learned some lessons from Ukraine: the permit, when it was finally issued, only allowed the opposition to hold a rally three days after the election in the remote Victory Square, a few metro stations north of the city centre, out of sight of the everyday crowds. This was no Maidan, yet it was a place that seemed to symbolise the opposition's view of Azeri political life: a scruffy concrete arena ringed by apartment blocks, a decrepit Soviet factory and a petrol station, watched by ranks of armed police with metal shields and riot helmets and two giant posters of Heydar Baba.

Nevertheless, optimism was running high as the demonstrators unfurled their gaudy banners and made their way down the dusty, windswept road leading to the square, led by a young man perched atop a tall wheeled gantry, the image of a heroic pioneer leading the believers into battle, his flag flashing orange against the crisp blue autumn sky. A tight knot of Yeni Fikir and Magam activists in orange headbands quick-marched past, turning their placards towards the massed lenses of the international media: *Stop trading our democracy for oil*, they urged… *Don't lose a friendly Muslim country… President Bush, don't fail us now…*

The politicians' speeches summoned up the utopian visions of Kiev and Tbilisi as they vowed to stand firm against injustice and challenge the election results in the courts and the squares of Baku. The crowd's rhythmic chants mimicked the slogans of the Orange Revolution, hyped up by the wild antics of the young activists who leaped and crouched, bounced and capered in unison. 'The orange revolution is beginning here, right in front of us!' yelled a Yeni Fikir activist, Ahmad Shahidov, over the noise. 'Now, today, we will insist on staying here all night. We will do it! Everyone wants it, the opposition leaders will demand it, the citizens will do it. We will continue our fight until we win!'

But it was clear that the Azeri opposition could not match the resources of its Ukrainian counterparts; there were no high-tech television monitors or rock bands or even portable toilets, the sound system crackled weakly, and as the sun set, the rally fell into darkness; they hadn't been able to rig up any lights. Even more importantly, they simply could not rally enough people to their cause; most estimates suggested that no more than 20,000 people had joined the demonstration. And despite the young activists' belief that this would be the beginning of the Azeri uprising, that the tents would go up and the revolution would start here and now, the opposition leaders ordered the crowd to leave as soon as their two-hour protest permit expired, fearing confrontation and casualties. Minutes afterwards, the square was almost deserted, and street sweepers set to work with brooms, clearing away the orange detritus.

This would set the pattern for the weeks that followed; brief rallies on the outskirts of Baku which dispersed as soon as they reached their time limit. With little access to national television channels or the city's central squares, they found it hard to spread their message. When opposition activists finally defied the law and attempted to stage a sit-in, they were beaten bloody and dispersed with cold efficiency. The momentum began to wind down. The Azeri 'revolution' was over before it had even begun.

THE ALCHEMY OF RESISTANCE

There was little agreement about why Baku had not risen up as Kiev, Tbilisi and Belgrade had done before it. Some said that the Azeri government was too strong, while others said that the opposition was too weak, incompetent or unpopular. Apathy, they argued, had been the real victor: the Azeri people were not seriously discontented with President Aliyev's rule, and they had voted for stability in a country with a recent history of bitter conflict, situated in a particularly volatile region. Ivan Marović of Otpor argued that the opposition had simply failed to seize the moment: 'Nothing happened in Baku because nothing happened on the night of the elections,' he said. 'You know the day by the dawn, and they seemed to have no plan before the elections. Money and international support are not the most important things.'

But for Emin Huseynov of Magam, the international response was crucial. Yes, the opposition didn't have enough money, he agreed, nor did it have a strong voice in the media, and it was damaged by the scandal surrounding the aborted return of Rasul Guliyev and the subsequent purge of alleged coup conspirators. But a crucial factor was that, unlike in Serbia, Georgia and Ukraine, the West decided not to get involved. 'They closed their eyes to the falsifications,' Huseynov said. 'It's possible that their economic, energy and geo-strategical interests were behind this, but it is a fact that the West again closed its eyes to the falsifications of elections in Azerbaijan.' The sour taste of betrayal would linger for months to come.

The failure of the Azeri uprising also raised the question of whether there really was a 'formula' for a successful twenty-first century revolution. Although the political situations in Serbia, Georgia and Ukraine were very different, there were some consistent factors: an unpopular government with authoritarian tendencies; poor social conditions; a united political opposition with the ability to put large numbers on the streets; a thriving network of civil rights groups; support from Western governments and democracy foundations; some access to the media for the opposition to get its message out; a rigged election; the clever use of independent election monitors and exit polls; and a state security apparatus with wavering loyalties to the government and an unwillingness to open fire on the people. All the successful revolutionaries adopted non-violent tactics and worked hard on their action plans. And they all had vibrant youth movements which showed no fear of repression and could reach out to people who distrusted politicians.

'Young people have more courage, more passion and more desire to change situations; they take part in risk-taking operations more willingly than older people,' says Pavol Demeš of the German Marshall Fund of the United States, who had been involved with many of the youth resistance movements. 'They have a different vision of their future; they are more pro-European and pro-democratic than the older generation. Plus they have much better communication skills, they know how to make use of modern technologies like the internet and cellphones.'

But Demeš cautions against giving youth too much credit. 'Youth movements play a powerful and often decisive role, but if it was only them, things would not change,' he says. 'Sometimes journalists exaggerate this and turn it into some kind of Western movie – the good guys, the youngsters in their T-shirts, come in and defeat the dictator. Things don't happen like that at all. It's a collaborative exercise.'

What still remained unclear was whether the tactics of non-violent resistance would work in countries where the authorities were both willing and able to use extreme force to wipe out any opposition – even to murder their own citizens, like the Chinese government at Tiananmen Square in 1989. Even in such desperate circumstances, Srdja Popović believes that the Gene Sharp doctrines remain valid, but that they will take far, far longer to make an impact: 'Of course it's easier when you have an electrified situation with a history of election frauds like in Georgia or Ukraine,' he says. 'But even in the narrowest possible space, like Lebanon, if the people are organised well and use the right tactics, they will succeed.' In Belgrade, he pointed out, success had not come instantly; there had been long years of trial and error before Milošević eventually fell.

There also seemed to be no blueprint for what, if anything, these youth movements could achieve after their revolutions. In Serbia, Otpor tried to be a watchdog organisation and then a political party. In Georgia, Kmara shut itself down and many of its leading members either went into government or returned to work with civil rights groups. In Ukraine, 'black' Pora became a watchdog organisation while 'yellow' Pora became a political party. In all cases, most of the rank-and-file activists simply drifted away. They could help to change their countries, but they found it harder to ensure that the politicians who came to power afterwards remained true to the principles they had espoused at the moment of revolution.

Some of them, however, found themselves in growing demand as travelling advisers, bringing their expertise to other countries in similar situations. An informal network had emerged, held together by personal connections and online communication, providing tactical advice and fraternal sustenance across borders:

the resistance was being globalised. Various Otpor, Kmara and Pora veterans were employed by international democracy foundations to train activists abroad, as they had once been trained, working with people from Belarus, Zimbabwe, Iran, with the opposition to the left-wing president of Venezuela, Hugo Chavez, and with exiles from the hermit state of North Korea.

They were accused of being itinerant revolutionaries-for-hire – mercenaries, even – an idea all of them found ludicrous because it not only exaggerated their ability to mobilise a foreign population but also overlooked the issues of poverty, corruption and authoritarianism in some of the countries where they worked. 'Whatever the critics say, we don't teach them how to overthrow governments, mostly because if they're really committed, they'll do it anyway,' says Ivan Marović. 'We pass on our knowledge and offer them a kind of solidarity and an idea that there's somebody outside who cares about them, and it's not the Americans who have their interests there, but people from some remote country like Serbia which doesn't have any interests there. It's very important to help the growth of indigenous power in these countries so their problems aren't solved by international interference but through internal pressure. And nobody gets killed in these revolutions; it's not like Iraq, it's genuinely liberating.'

And yes, it could be exhilarating, too... 'I criticised Aleksandar Marić when he came back from Ukraine and journalists asked him, "Why do you do this?" And he said, "It's because of adrenalin." I asked him why he said it, it sounded so unprofessional, like it's some kind of extreme sport or something,' says Marović. 'But actually, I can tell you I'm also doing it because of adrenalin. I admit it. I enjoy helping people who're in deep shit.'

For Marić, his involvement in Serbia, Georgia and Ukraine was a matter of pride. 'Three dictatorships were ousted, three nations were given an opportunity to get the authorities that would be slightly better than the previous ones,' he says. 'It's a long road towards a civilised democratic state, but I am glad to have helped here in Serbia and in these two countries – and, in future, possibly some other country – to make that first leap.'

Marović and Popović developed projects designed to pass on their knowledge to the next generation: do-it-yourself guides for twenty-first century revolutionaries. Popović established his own organisation, the Centre for Applied Non-Violent Action and Strategies, and published a book called *CANVAS Strategic Nonviolent Agenda*, mixing smart digital-age graphics with advice and anecdotes from the insider who had been there and done it, aimed at young activists who found Gene Sharp's prose a little too tepid. Marović helped produce a computer game called *A Force More Powerful*, in which players could plan an uprising against the ruthless military junta in 'Bedorven', subvert the hardline religious government of 'Ulmar', or campaign to bring the soldiers of democratic 'Soporia' home from an unjust war.

Meanwhile, new resistance movements could often count on assistance from wealthy allies; US government-financed groups like the International Republican Institute and the National Democratic Institute continued to provide what was referred to as 'technical assistance' to democracy activists around the world, while the American government agency USAID even celebrated its support for the 'multi-coloured revolutions' by publishing a full-colour magazine entitled *Democracy Rising*. Others went further still: organisations like Freedom House and the International Centre for Non-Violent Conflict overtly promoted 'people power' and peaceful subversion. 'A focal point of training and assistance should be how to organise and sequence non-violent protests and mass demonstrations; strikes and other forms of industrial action; boycotts that exert domestic pressure on regimes and their financial backers; and non-violent civil disobedience,' a Freedom House document stated.[13]

Many of the key players in the global resistance network gathered in the Albanian capital in June 2005 for the Tirana Activism Festival, a weekend of intense discussions and intensive partying hosted by the Albanian youth group Mjaft, and attended by representatives of Otpor, Kmara, Pora, Yokh! from Azerbaijan, Zubr from Belarus, Pulse of Freedom from Lebanon and a plethora of other groups from the Balkans. As one journalist noted at the time, some of them would probably go on to hold high office, while others would be jailed as political prisoners.

The weekend ended with the signing of a common declaration: 'Every indigenous struggle for freedom and democracy is our fight, and we hereby commit ourselves to stand by one another.' Echoing article five of the NATO treaty, it continued: 'Any attack against one or more of us will be considered an attack against us all and consequently, if such an attack occurs, each of us will assist and defend the so attacked and react accordingly. All for one and one for all!'

At this point, many of them felt they were still in the ascendance, charged with youthful energy and leading a new wave of global democratisation. As Ukraine's orange revolutionaries had insisted, *freedom can't be stopped*. But their methods would soon face their biggest test yet. It would come the following year, in Belarus.

BRAVEHEARTS AND GLADIATORS

There's an old joke about Belarus which advises visitors to turn back their watches by 20 years when arriving in the country: back to Soviet times. The Belarussian capital, Minsk, was razed to the ground during World War Two and rebuilt as a model Stalinist city, its landscape dominated by dour, imperious buildings. The iconography of those years remains ubiquitous: many of its Communist-era statues, monuments and street names are unchanged, jangling against the signs and symbols of global capitalism: a McDonald's burger bar stands on the corner of Lenin Street, next to posters bearing the hammer and sickle; a chic boutique calling itself La Dolce Vita plies its trade on Communist Street; songs by Eminem and Beyoncé play in the cafés where boys show off their Hugo Boss and Moschino fashions and girls sport T-shirts emblazoned with provocative English words like 'Flirt' and 'Enjoy' – but the secret police still go by their old name: the KGB.

It was in Belarus, back in 2001, where the first attempt was made to imitate the Serbian revolution in an attempt to prevent President

Alexander Lukashenko from winning another term in office. For his Western critics, Lukashenko, with his comb-over hairstyle, luxuriant moustache and unrestrained enthusiasm for strident soundbites, was one of most preposterous and repellent European leaders of recent times. For his Belarussian supporters, he was *Batka* – 'Daddy'. Lukashenko was a country boy who got his first taste of power as the manager of a Soviet collective farm in the 1990s, before ascending to the presidency in 1994. Within two years he had begun the process of dismantling any opposition to his rule. He disbanded parliament, installed another which was more favourable to him, won a referendum which greatly extended the powers of the presidency, and replaced the red-and-white Belarussian flag with the one it had used in the Soviet era.

Around this time, his Western critics began to refer to him as 'the last dictator in Europe'. Lukashenko denied it – almost: 'They tell me, "You are a dictator." My position and the state will never allow me to become a dictator but an authoritarian ruling style is characteristic of me, and I have always admitted it,' he said.[14] In 1999 and 2000, several opposition activists disappeared. Their bodies were never found. The European human rights organisation, the Council of Europe, concluded that high-ranking apparatchiks were involved in their disappearance.

But Lukashenko was undoubtedly popular, just as Slobodan Milošević had once been. What he offered was the reassurance of stability, an alternative to the turmoil of neighbouring Russia, where the free market had thrown the country into economic and moral chaos after the Soviet social system collapsed. Lukashenko appealed to those who feared they might lose their secure state jobs in Western-style privatisation programmes. Unlike Russia, he only allowed the free market limited access to Belarus, preferring to maintain a system of central control. He called it 'market socialism' and claimed he had conjured up an economic miracle, although it was underpinned by benevolent trade deals and discount energy supplies from Moscow, which saw Belarus as the closest of its former Soviet brothers and was determined not to let it look west to Europe like its other neighbours, Lithuania and Poland, had done, and as

Ukraine would in 2004. Whatever the differences between the stern Putin and the bellicose Lukashenko, Belarus was an ally which Moscow was keen not to lose.

It was in Belarus, in the run-up to the 2001 presidential election, where the first youth group modelled on Otpor emerged. According to its self-made myth, Zubr – meaning 'Bison', one of the country's national symbols – was founded in early 2001 by 40 young people who gathered in Belovezhskaya Forest, a nature reserve near the Polish border where the last of the bison roam, and where the document which announced that the Soviet Union had ceased to exist was signed a decade earlier. Zubr's first public pronouncement had an ecological theme. A group of mystified journalists was led to a public park in Minsk where an unidentified spokesman read out a statement: 'The forest is the natural environment of the bison, and freedom is our natural environment,' it said. 'Lukashenko is destroying forests and strangling freedom.'[15]

Like Otpor, Zubr built its reputation with situationist pranks. Its activists staged a happening in which men in white coats chased a raving 'madman' wearing an ice hockey mask – coincidentally, President Lukashenko was an ice hockey fanatic. A few even repeated the action at Lukashenko's old farm, with the presidential impersonator stopping passers-by and asking them, 'Do you know me? I'm your old boss. I'm back!' The fake doctors then appeared, looking for their 'patient', who, they said, had escaped from a mental hospital.[16] Zubr went on to distribute portraits of the 'disappeared' dissidents, and put up posters depicting alternative heroes like Che Guevara, the Dalai Lama, Mel Gibson's Scottish insurgent leader from the film *Braveheart* and Russell Crowe as the rebellious slave in *Gladiator*. At the time, such stunts felt fresh and innovative. 'Zubr was using completely new methods and tactics, it was very creative and colourful and very different from the old opposition,' says one of the movement's early recruits.

With the 2001 election in Belarus coming so soon after the Serbian revolution, many in the West hoped that the trick could be repeated. Foreign funding flowed in for democracy projects and the independent media; Gene Sharp advised the opposition and Otpor veterans provided training for young activists. However, Lukashenko warned that the 'Belgrade scenario' wouldn't work in his country: 'I won't sit in a bunker like Milošević,' he declared. 'I'm not afraid of anybody. I will defend myself.'[17] And he did, closing independent newspapers, barring election observers and persecuting protesters; tactics which would serve him well in years to come. All opposition was driven to the margins, where it could be portrayed as the perilous yet simultaneously impotent fantasy of cranks and desperados.

The 'Belgrade scenario' proved to be a grand failure. The official election results gave Lukashenko around three-quarters of the vote, with the opposition candidate, Vladimir Goncharik, on around 15 per cent. The opposition alleged fraud, but their demonstrations lasted only a few days before they resigned themselves to their defeat and dispersed. 'If the majority of citizens votes for a dictator despite dictatorship, then that's it, until the next elections,' says Aleksandar Marić, who advised Zubr. Ultimately, the West took little notice, the minds of its leaders elsewhere: two days after the election, the date was 11 September 2001.

Lukashenko would use the next few years to consolidate his control of Belarussian society. This was a time of narrowing horizons for anyone involved in the opposition, the independent media, or any kind of culture which could be interpreted as subversive. Yet more newspapers were closed down, foreign democracy groups were expelled from the country and a law was introduced giving the authorities the right to ban political parties if there was any kind of disorder at their demonstrations. In 2004, Lukashenko staged a referendum on whether to allow him to stand for the presidency as many times as he chose, giving him the option of becoming president for life. In the run-up to the vote, he announced that the West was trying to destroy the country by force, to turn Belarussian women into prostitutes, to pump its citizens full of drugs and to spread homosexuality. Of his 'disappeared' opponents, he sneered: 'Don't you understand that the issue of the missing people is a broken record?'[18] His inevitable victory in the referendum was again followed by street protests, but they were broken up by riot police, and some of their leaders were sentenced to two years of 'corrective labour' – sent to remote villages and put to work, a kind of internal exile.

In this environment, large-scale demonstrations became increasingly risky. Zubr actions dwindled into fast-moving hit-and-run raids and the movement was only able to operate covertly, concealing its premises and personnel. It proved hard to sustain the momentum and vitality of its first, frenetic months. By 2004, according to one of Zubr's former co-ordinators, Tatyana Elovaya, several long-serving members had resigned. 'Some of them just grew up, had a family,' she says. 'Some of them got disillusioned by many years of unsuccessful fighting for freedom, some of them just wanted to make money in other opposition organisations.'

Elovaya, who had joined Zubr as a teenager and had been arrested for protesting around 100 times, was expelled from the movement; she says she was suspected of working for the KGB. She accuses Zubr of being too dependent on foreign funding, and some of the movement's leaders of spending too much time at meetings and conferences in the West while not being radical enough where it mattered, on the streets and squares of Belarus: 'There was a confrontation between those people, the "street fighters" who really wanted to work and were ready to give their lives for the motherland, and those who were getting money for Zubr projects and were touring Europe.'

Zubr's leaders saw it differently; they say that they were attempting to keep the spirit of resistance alive. Meanwhile, the arrests continued. Iryna Toustsik, one of the few Zubr members who dared to speak publicly, was held for five days after a group of Zubrs dressed as Santa Claus handed out oranges in solidarity with the Ukrainian revolution. The police told her she was being detained for being in possession of subversive fruit. 'They laughed when they were taking us away,' she says, 'but they said we shouldn't have been doing it.'

Like many young activists, Toustsik had been kicked out of university for her political views and now spent her time taking food packages to jailed student activists and working to set them free. She says that the authorities regularly attempted to recruit the imprisoned youths as informers: 'At first the police start threatening them, saying they'll be expelled from university and their parents will be thrown out of their jobs,' she explains. 'Then a person from the KGB comes and says, "Listen, you will end your university studies with the best diploma, you will get perfect marks, you will have a good job, just answer us: where is Zubr's headquarters and who are its leaders?"'

The KGB didn't just offer incentives to students. Although it wasn't clear how successfully state security had infiltrated the Belarussian opposition, there were persistent rumours that undercover officers had comprehensively penetrated the youth resistance and bullied or bribed some leading opposition activists into becoming informers. 'It's the KGB's job and they do it well,' says one observer. 'They have their eyes and ears on every level of decision-making, they find out about plans for actions even when only five or six people know about them.'

Tatyana Elovaya tells a similar story: 'It's common knowledge that in our opposition, one in seven people is a member of the KGB. I think that's not far from the truth,' she says. 'Many people got frightened, they were threatened that their relatives or people close to them would be killed or they would have problems at university. Others are attracted by money, or by guarantees that there won't be criminal cases against them. That's why the question of secrecy is so important, you never know where the real threat is coming from.'

The secret services in Ukraine and Georgia had never been this tough, but Lukashenko had no interest in posing as a Western-style democrat. The Belarussian authorities had noted the impact that youth movements had made in Serbia and Georgia, and brought in the compulsory subject of 'state ideology' in universities in an attempt to inoculate against dissent. 'We have lessons about the period of Lukashenko's rule, and there are ideology books talking about the great achievements of Lukashenko,' says Iryna Toustsik. 'There is a test, and one question asks how you rate the ideology of Lukashenko. There are three answers to choose from: "good", "very good" and "perfect".'

The state also had its own youth organisation, the Belarussian

Republican Union of Youth, to provide teenagers with an 'ideological and patriotic upbringing' – in the tradition, it said, of the USSR's Communist Youth League, the Komsomol. 'If you don't like Lukashenko, leave Belarus,' one of its spokesmen declared.[19] Subversive jokers labelled it the 'Lukamol'. Unlike the Russian youth group Nashi ('Our Guys'), which was set up in Moscow after Ukraine's Orange Revolution to counter the potential influence of student resistance movements and demonstrate public support for the rule of President Putin, the Belarussian Republican Union of Youth was believed to have considerable influence. Meanwhile, dozens of opposition activists were expelled from university, as Toustsik had been, for 'failing' at their studies.

Even dissent which wasn't overtly political was dealt with severely. In 2004, several Belarussian rock bands played a concert in Minsk which was intended as a satirical 'celebration' of Lukashenko's first decade in power. It was met with a disproportionate show of force. Roadblocks were set up to prevent people reaching the capital, at least 20 people were arrested and others were driven out of the city in police buses and dumped by the roadside. Afterwards, the musicians – among them NRM, the most popular rock band in Belarus – found themselves on a secret blacklist; they were banned from radio and television and any major concert they tried to arrange was mysteriously cancelled. The ban was enforced informally, in private conversations between officials: 'telephone justice'. 'Like in Soviet times, they deny it all, they say they know nothing,' says Pete Paulau, NRM's guitarist.

The band, whose full name translates as Independent Republic of Dreams, had played at the Maidan in Kiev during the Orange Revolution, and they understood the reasoning behind the blacklist. 'Rock music has the power to motivate people; any concert we played would turn into a protest meeting,' says Paulau. 'We don't sing about politics, but we do sing about the situation here. In one of my songs, I sing, *I'm illegal in my own country, I'm illegal in my own city, I'm out of the game.* It's not about Lukashenko, it's about my life.' As in Serbia during the Milošević years, it felt as though the country was attempting to drive out any pernicious subversive influences, and heading ever deeper into isolation.

Belarussian state television portrayed the world according to Lukashenko. A typical news bulletin would open with admiring footage of the president, followed by good news from the collective farms or the state factories, with a personal interlude from the presenter, either praising Lukashenko or attacking the United States and other Western countries. Most of the foreign news coverage depicted the outside world as a profoundly disturbing place, plagued by disease, war and terrorism, unlike safe, serene Belarus. When it was mentioned at all, the opposition was condemned or derided; one feature about Zubr cut images from its protests into riot footage from the Serbian revolution, to the musical accompaniment of a song about the IRA by an Irish rock band, the Cranberries: 'Zombie'. Nevertheless, the Zubrs were happy with the publicity, as it was all they could get.

Independent newspapers – those which remained – found themselves increasingly marginalised. The Belarussian information minister accused them of acting as agents of the US government, although he denied they were being persecuted: 'We have no problem with free speech in Belarus.'[20] Perhaps, joked one journalist in Minsk, because there wasn't much free speech to have a problem with. By 2005, there were only two national independent papers left, and they were subject to increasing restrictions and a series of punitive court cases. One of them, *Belaruskaya Delovaya Gazeta*, was printed across the border in Russia because no Belarussian printworks would handle the job. 'Some foreigners who come to Belarus say it's not an absolute dictatorship. They say, "People go to nightclubs in Minsk, you have independent newspapers,"' says its deputy editor-in-chief, Iryna Khalip. 'But there is no contradiction between nightclubs and a dictatorship, and you cannot buy an independent newspaper in a shop or a kiosk in this country, because we are not allowed to distribute them there.

'It would be very easy to give in, to say, "OK, we are losers, we have to look after our own lives and earn money." Some journalists from our newspaper made that choice and are now working with the government newspapers. I cannot condemn them, because they have lives and children and it's very difficult. But when you are in such a situation for some years, it becomes a habit to resist, to fight, to be an idealist.' Nevertheless, Khalip believed that it was only a matter of time before her own newspaper was shut down and its staff had to resort to guerrilla publishing. She was right: within a few months, its printing contract was mysteriously cancelled and publication was suspended.

The Orange Revolution in Ukraine coincided with increased pressure on Lukashenko from outside Belarus. The US Congress passed a Belarus Democracy Act, assigning large sums to democracy programmes, and the American Secretary of State, Condoleezza Rice, included the country in a list of what she called the world's last 'outposts of tyranny', alongside Burma, Cuba, Iran, North Korea and Zimbabwe. Nevertheless, even some people within the opposition had to admit that, economically at least, Belarus didn't have the same problems as some of its regional neighbours. Under Lukashenko, it was one of the few former Soviet countries that was richer than it had been under Communism. 'The situation here is difficult but it's not tragic,' says the Zubr movement's press secretary, Alexander Atroshchankau. 'If you said to people that we have to live in poverty and we're starving, it wouldn't be true.' The opposition, he said, had to focus instead on the moral failings of the government.

Atroshchankau took heart from the Ukrainian revolution, but he knew that such huge protests would be much harder to instigate in his own country. 'The situation in Ukraine was absolutely different – they had opposition politicians in parliament and in local governments, they had a television station, and the repression wasn't so cruel,' he says. 'It couldn't be compared to the situation in Belarus – it could only give us spiritual encouragement. Also, Lukashenko knew now what we were planning.'

Indeed, the authorities did seem to have been studying the Ukrainians' methodology. Zubr activists like Atroshchankau who visited the tent camp in Kiev were hauled off the train on the way home and questioned; Otpor veterans trying to visit Belarus to hold training sessions were turned back; Pora members who did get in were detained. Two Georgian activists, Giorgi Kandelaki and a fellow Kmara member, who came to investigate the Belarussian opposition, were sentenced to 15 days in jail, accused of instructing people 'how to hold civil disobedience campaigns and riots patterned on the coloured revolution in Georgia', according to a KGB spokesman.[21] After Kandelaki's first night in the cells, the investigating officer dropped in to offer some of his own brand of dark humour: 'Well, Mr Kandelaki,' he quipped, 'how do you enjoy Belarus?'[22]

A series of laws was introduced to prevent any repetition of the events in Ukraine. Universities were given the legal authority to expel students for political activity. It became a criminal offence to train people to take part in demonstrations and to 'discredit' Belarus or its government. Foreign assistance for political activity was banned. 'No money will ever overthrow the existing government in Belarus. Remember that!' said Lukashenko. 'That's what I tell those who bring money into this country in bags and suitcases. We know practically everything. And if we are silent, that does not mean we do not know!'[23] Lukashenko also said he intended to strengthen the KGB; he said he needed officers with the qualities of Felix Dzerzhinsky, the founder of the Soviet secret police force which was responsible for hundreds of thousands of deaths during Stalin's rule. 'We shall create a powerful secret service in order to defend the interests of the state and our people. It's the most important thing,' he explained.[24]

The reason for the systematic build-up of state powers soon became clear. Lukashenko announced that the next presidential election would be held early, in March 2006, giving his opponents as little time as possible to prepare their campaign and build up their resources. It was a deft pre-emptive strike. However, the opposition – a ramshackle coalition of liberals, nationalists, conservatives and Communists – had managed to decide on a unity candidate to run against Lukashenko, a genial academic called Alexander Milinkevich. But even this show of unity was not absolute, and Milinkevich would not be the opposition's sole contender: Alexander Kozulin, the forceful leader of the Belarussian Social Democratic Party, Hramada, also announced that he would stand.

Milinkevich said that the opposition had to approach the election as if it was a war. 'I will not promise you victory, but I can promise that I will go forward with you to the very end. I will go into the streets. I will go into the public squares,' he told his supporters.[25] In return, they gave him a pair of running shoes – a symbolic gift suggesting he would have to walk every street in Belarus to reach the voters as there was little chance of any objective media coverage.

As 2005 came to an end, Iryna Khalip published an impassioned open letter to her opposition comrades. She talked of her country, which she said she now found hard to recognise. 'It starts speaking in an incomprehensible language, full of threats and orders; it takes you at gunpoint, spies, eavesdrops, writes denunciations and murders your friends,' she wrote. 'Maybe it has gone crazy, and everything is hopeless. Maybe it's better to disappear, to leave, to melt into other countries and cities. Many people have done that.' And yet she pledged not to give in to despair and defeatism, to overcome the 'bitterness of losses'; to return Belarus to sanity. 'The most important thing is that this year is to become ours,' she urged. 'It must become the year of freedom.'[26]

AN ELEGANT VICTORY

Despite all its problems, the Belarussian opposition at least had a symbolic emblem: blue denim, with its echoes of Soviet-era counterculture, when jeans were objects of desire and totems of imagined liberation. On 16 September 2005, during a small demonstration in remembrance of the 'disappeared', the police had confiscated the red-and-white Belarussian flags the protesters were waving, the symbols of Belarus before Lukashenko. One of them, a Zubr activist called Nikita Sasim, stripped off his denim shirt, tied it to a pole and waved it high in the air. He was beaten unconscious and hospitalised.

A few weeks afterwards, Sasim, alongside the journalist Iryna Khalip and Iryna Krasovskaya, the wife of one of the 'disappeared', announced that the sixteenth of the month would now be marked by regular protests, with denim – Sasim's improvised flag – as their symbol. They called it 'Jeans Solidarity'. 'We decided that if our [red-

and-white] national flag was to be forbidden, we would choose another symbol,' said Iryna Toustsik of Zubr. 'Jeans were always what free people wore. And of course, you could never imagine Lukashenko wearing jeans.' Small groups gathered in city squares with strips torn from old pairs of jeans tied around their arms, and people lit candles in darkened windows – although some believed that this was no more than foolhardy self-incrimination.

Jeans Solidarity intensified its activity as the election approached, distributing underground newspapers, leaflets, stickers and posters depicting ranks of strutting policewomen in miniskirts or a gang of leather-clad, moustachioed bikers, with a wave of blue denim scrolling towards them. It was also involved in a guerrilla graffiti programme: 'Fed up!' and 'We want a new one!' screamed its slogans; rare signals of discontent on the clean and orderly streets of Minsk.

The other leading Belarussian youth movement was the Young Front, which had started as the youth wing of the conservative nationalist Belarussian Popular Front party. Like the Zubrs, the Young Front's activists had become more familiar with the Belarussian prison system than they might have liked. The movement's leader, Pavel Severinets, had been banished to a distant rural area to serve a term of 'corrective labour' after being convicted of organising street protests. Two of its other senior members were also serving sentences. Its offices had been raided, its computers seized and its website hacked.

The vice-chairman of the Young Front, Siarhei Lisichonak, admitted that Lukashenko's decision to call early elections was a major setback. 'I was part of the team which prepared the opposition campaign; we wanted to repeat the Ukrainian Maidan, and the time needed to realise this plan was no less than half a year,' he said. 'We co-operated with different international friends and partners to realise this plan, to be prepared, but Lukashenko moved and our plan was not possible to implement. Other groups which had other tactics, their plans became much more relevant than our strategic one. We needed to take instant action.'

The Young Front decided to join Zubr and a new underground propaganda group called Khopits ('Enough') in the Jeans Solidarity and 'Fed Up!' actions, as well as working on Milinkevich's presidential campaign. But Lisichonak found that the political landscape had changed dramatically since the previous presidential election in 2001. 'That election campaign now seems very liberal compared to this one,' he said. 'I remember those days, I wrote dozens of articles saying it was not democratic then, but right now when I look back on that, I have to laugh – "Oh my God, in those days we were punished only with *fines*?" Now we get ten or 15 days in jail for anything minor.'

Nevertheless, the opposition could count on the moral and financial backing of the United States and the European Union. The *New York Times* reported that the US government and the EU were spending millions of dollars to 'promote democracy', as they had done in Serbia, Georgia and Ukraine. Foreign governments, democracy foundations and opposition activists met in safety outside Belarus to share out the aid and plan campaign strategies – or, as Lukashenko believed, to plot regime change. Two new radio stations, one funded by the EU and another backed by the government in neighbouring Poland, began transmitting across the borders into Belarus, in an attempt to disseminate alternative views.

But some expressed concern about how effectively the Western money was being spent, and about its impact on those who were receiving it. Tatyana Elovaya, who was involved with Alexander Kozulin's campaign, suggests that some youth activists and people involved in the wider anti-Lukashenko campaign were more excited by the prospect of financial rewards than the fight for liberation. 'My firm conviction is that when you are paid for an idea, you will never succeed,' she says. 'It spoils people, especially the young, because they don't worry about the result and they think only about their salary. I'm very sorry that it turned out like this.'

Despite support from the West, Milinkevich was convinced that the opposition had little hope of victory. 'It is impossible to win the elections, because there are no elections,' he said.[27] He saw the polls as the beginning, not the end, of the struggle; it was, he said, like Poland in 1980 when the Solidarity movement began its campaign against the country's Communist government – not like in 1989 when, after years of martial law and repression, Solidarity eventually triumphed. President Lukashenko said he had information suggesting he would win at least 75 per cent of the vote. Milinkevich agreed, although he had no doubts that the figure would be achieved by fraud.

Lukashenko appeared to want an unassailable mandate: what a Belarussian official had once referred to as 'an elegant victory' – a phrase which formed the basis for many caustic jokes during those days. He conducted an unusual but supremely confident campaign, appearing constantly on state television but doing no overt electioneering. Instead, a massive propaganda drive outlined the virtues of the state that he had created. Posters and billboards with the slogan 'For Belarus' were placed at prominent roadside sites all over the country, in metro stations, shops and cafés, even in the Minsk franchise of McDonald's. Some depicted the honest, weather-beaten face of a factory worker, others a young child in the classroom, a war veteran, or a babushka bringing in the harvest. Their messages spoke of 'stability' and 'independence', the blessings of peaceful quiescence.

The posters were complemented by a nationwide 'For Belarus' concert tour, featuring the country's leading unprohibited pop stars. Belarussian television even showed a group of singers performing an adoring tribute to their beloved president, a song called 'Listen to Your Daddy'. 'He is a hard nut to crack, he wouldn't teach you anything wrong,' it counselled the viewers. 'He can call everybody to order, he is really cool, he can easily redress all grievances, he is reliable and calm. When you look at him, you can easily see, who is the master in the house...'

Nevertheless, all the presidential candidates were given the chance to make half-hour broadcasts on national television. For many Belarussians, it was the first chance to hear forthright, open criticism of Lukashenko. 'For the majority, this was a shock, some of them still do not believe it,' says Siarhei Lisichonak. 'It was like hearing that Father Christmas does not exist.'

The opposition had no doubts that the final showdown would

not take place at the polls, but after they closed, on the streets of Minsk. The authorities took a similar view, insisting that they would not tolerate the kind of protests which had been seen in Ukraine and Georgia. Lukashenko said that the West was attempting to destabilise Belarus with the help of an 'extremist' opposition, and called on the security services to 'act ahead of the situation'.[28] They did. In the run-up to the election, hundreds of opposition activists were arrested; many were given short jail terms which ensured that they would miss the vote.

The head of the KGB, Stepan Sukhorenko, turned up the pressure, saying that he had received intelligence suggesting that the post-election protests would serve as the cover for a violent coup: 'According to the scenario, it is planned to set off several explosive devices in the crowd,' he announced. 'The bleeding victims will untie the hands of the organisers of the protest to organise the second stage of the scenario – to seize the buildings of administrative bodies and train stations and to block railroads, which should completely halt the functioning of the state, and on this wave, to seize power by force.'[29]

All potential outside influences were targeted. Organisations representing the Polish minority in Belarus – believed to be a fount of subversion – were harassed. A group of Ukrainian politicians, including Vladyslav Kaskiv from Pora, was detained by the KGB at Minsk airport and sent back; Kaskiv was told that he was on a list of known terrorists. Giga Bokeria from Georgia was denied accreditation as an election observer. 'Our exclusion can be explained by a general fear of the Georgian experience,' Bokeria told the Georgian media. 'This time they have formally identified us as threats and denied us entry to the country.'[30]

Lukashenko outlined the nature of these threats during a three-hour speech at a Soviet-style congress in the capital. He said that the West was determined to wipe out Belarus, as it had Yugoslavia, or plunge it into bloody turmoil, as it had Iraq. He again laid out his achievements – 'a stable, prosperous, civilised country' – saying he had avoided the 'destructive privatisation and shock therapy' which had devastated other former Soviet states.[31] He promised that the opposition would be 'dismantled in a tough way' after the election.[32] When the opposition presidential candidate Alexander Kozulin attempted to get into the congress, he was roughed up and arrested.

The KGB chief, Stepan Sukhorenko, announced more revelations about the planned 'coup' and warned that opposition protesters could be charged with terrorism offences and face life sentences, or even capital punishment. At a press conference in Minsk, Sukhorenko screened a video which he said showed a man who had been trained in terrorism tactics by former Soviet army officers and Arabs at what he called a 'Kmara camp' in Georgia, with the involvement of American instructors and the Georgian security services. He said that the instructors had proposed a plan to bomb four polling stations at schools in the capital during the elections. On the eve of the polls, Lukashenko echoed the KGB boss's message, vowing to crush anyone involved in fomenting unrest: 'We will break their necks immediately, like a duckling's.'[33]

As election day dawned on 19 March, the atmosphere was fraught with nervous uncertainty. But despite the official denunciations and the anonymous text messages warning that 'provocateurs are preparing bloodshed', which were sent to all the subscribers of one of the main Belarussian mobile-phone companies, thousands began to gather in the centre of Minsk after the polling stations closed. In October Square, a wide, bleak expanse just across the road from the president's official residence, ice and snow lay deep on the pavement and a brisk wind seared the skin as Milinkevich addressed the crowd: 'Belarus has become a completely different country now', he declared. 'Now it's a free Belarus, which will not be brought to its knees.'[34]

Nevertheless, the official results delivered all that had been expected, and more: Lukashenko was re-elected with 83 per cent of the vote, even more than in 2001; Milinkevich won around six per cent, with Alexander Kozulin just over two per cent. It was, indeed, another 'elegant victory'. Milinkevich demanded a re-run; it seemed unlikely that he would get it. Western observers condemned the conduct of the elections, but their Russian counterparts said they had been exemplary. None of these reactions was unusual; this was a script which could have been written months in advance. 'I was not surprised that Lukashenko got 83 per cent – I wouldn't have been surprised if he got 120 per cent,' said Alexander Atroshchankau of Zubr. 'He wanted to show he is supported by so many people, but the result is that nobody believes this. If he said he got 55 per cent, people might think, "Well, maybe it's true." But only crazy people will believe these figures.'

Some independent opinion polls conducted before the 2006 election suggested that Lukashenko's support was higher than 50 per cent, others estimated that it was around 40 per cent, although all the figures were disputed. Some of the opposition protesters admitted that Milinkevich probably could not have won outright even if the polls were fair, but said that what they wanted was the chance to decide freely and to know the truth. 'We don't know how popular Lukashenko is, but we *can't* know because he falsifies the elections,' said one. 'If he did it fairly, maybe he could win and then no one could complain. But this faking! It's just ludicrous, it's a farce.' Others insisted that the opposition must take some of the blame: 'Their campaign was a failure,' one complained.

The following night, thousands gathered again in October Square. The old red-and-white Belarussian flags flew gaily above the crowd, alongside those of Ukraine, Poland and the European Union, the bison silhouette of Zubr and the black banner of the local anarchists. People tied denim strips and blue ribbons around their arms; others wore blue scarves bearing the message 'Belarus to Europe' or the home-made red-and-white headbands of the Young Front. Girls swaddled in layers of scarves waved blue balloons; boys wrapped their shivering shoulders in the flag. A little sound system pumped out Belarussian, Russian and Ukrainian rock anthems between the politicians' speeches, while the crowd – the overwhelming majority of them young and middle-class – stamped their feet and swayed to the beat. 'This is not Lukashenko's city, it's our city!' declared one of the speakers. Others talked of Belarus reaching towards Europe, and of their inevitable triumph. The chant went up, again and again: *Long Live Belarus!* This, they said, was their Maidan, although it was clear even then that no revolution was imminent; that Minsk would not be like Kiev in 2004.

Just as the demonstration seemed to be turning into a street party, the mood changed. People suddenly stepped back, opening up an empty space in the middle of the crowd, and a small group of youths rushed forward to nail down tent-pegs. Other protesters linked arms in a tight, protective circle around them. Within 15 minutes there were around a dozen tents on the square, decked with red-and-white flags. Nothing like this had been attempted in the city before; there was an instant sense of urgency in the air, in anticipation of impending violence. The youths laid down blankets on the cold, damp brickwork, and started making sandwiches and opening thermos flasks of tea.

Dasha Kostenko was among them. 'We put up the tents, put down the rugs and sat down on them. It was then that I started to tremble. The realisation of just *what* we had done dawned on me. And the realisation that all my previous life, very possibly, was now going away, like the sand through my fingers,' she wrote in a diary which was subsequently published on the internet. 'I was trying to hide my tears under my hood, so that the journalists would not see them. It is an unattractive sight when a person is trembling and twisting from sobbing. Then I calmed down: what was done, was done. There was no way back.'

She had realised that her future could be one of prison or exile. 'There remained only one thing to do, and I did it. I called a person whom I loved for the past two years, and told him about it. I had wanted to do it for a while, but did not dare. And now there was nothing to fear.'[35]

Inside the circle, they began to sing, to ease their nerves and take their minds off the cold as much as anything else. Kostenko recalls the lyric that affected her the most deeply, from a song called 'Faraway the Beautiful'. 'My voice broke off at the words: *I can hear the voice, the voice asks me strictly: and today, what have I done for tomorrow?* I will try to remember this song, in the surrounding of people who protected us with their bodies, for all of my life. This evening was probably the best and the most important thing in my life.'[36]

The final decision to set up the tent camp had only been reached during late-night discussions after the first day's demonstration had ended. Some of the instigators had been members of Zubr or the Young Front in the past and some were involved with Khopits, but significantly, none of the youth movements' leaders was involved in making the critical choice: this was a new autonomous coalition. They had become disillusioned with the opposition leaders who had ordered the crowd to go home the night before instead of occupying the square, and who didn't seem to have a plan for victory. They realised that they couldn't leave everything to the politicians and decided to take the initiative. Telling only those who needed to know, they bought tents and food supplies, arrived in the square by car and dashed into the crowd, pursued by a group of plainclothes agents. The police tried to grab the tents from their hands, but they managed to put most of them up and organise some kind of rudimentary security system to protect themselves.

One of them was Tatyana Elovaya: 'It was clear that neither Milinkevich nor the people from other opposition headquarters knew about our decision,' she says. 'I am absolutely sure that if this information had been leaked to them, nothing would have happened. It wasn't only the authorities who didn't want this camp, but the old opposition people too.' Elovaya says that Milinkevich even suggested that they should pack up and leave, but she raised a megaphone and shouted defiantly: 'We're staying!'

Some of the campers, those who had been expelled from their universities and had little chance of getting a state job, simply felt they had nothing left to lose. 'I'm not afraid of the police,' said a young Belarussian woman called Nira. 'I've fought this regime for five years and now I've lost my fear. If the police come, most people will run away, but we will stay and face them.'

Another of the campers, an Estonian called Silver, was more pessimistic: 'To be honest, when most people leave for the night because it's too cold and there is no entertainment like there was in Kiev, the *militsiya* will come and kick hell out of us. I'm Estonian so the worst that can happen to me is that I will be deported – it doesn't matter. But everyone else is Belarussian; this is their life, and they will lose everything.'

Police began to search people going into the square and arrested some of those trying to smuggle in tents, sleeping bags or food; some were given ten-day jail sentences for carrying flasks of tea. Many of the flags were hoisted on extendable fishing rods because poles were too difficult to hide from the police. The only toilet was a manhole cover over a sewer, above which, to maintain some kind of privacy, they erected a small tent. 'At first the smell was awful there,' wrote Dasha Kostenko. 'I cried out, encouraging, "Did you think that revolution smells like roses?", and dived into the tent.'[37]

The tiny encampment resembled the meagre colony of tents set up during the Ukraine without Kuchma campaign in Kiev in 2001, years before the Orange Revolution. But inside the magic circle of entwined arms, everything felt transformed; a kind of pioneer community was emerging during the bone-chilling, sleepless nights. The campers even looked different, decorating themselves with the stickers and symbols which were rarely seen on the streets; hugging each other close and sharing every morsel of food. The tents were spray-painted with the words 'Khopits', 'Young Front' and 'Indymedia Belarus', the Minsk branch of the global direct-action website, as other youth activists joined the camp.

During the daytime, folk singers and rappers entertained the campers. The rock band NRM performed an a cappella set, with the refrain of a new song capturing the mood: *Our enemies can do what they like with their witchcraft in their snakepit, but still we will win...*

'I am not a romantic person, but I believe we have created an isle of freedom in this sea of dictatorship,' said Alexander Atroshchankau. 'I am so proud to be among these people. In Kiev, you could see thousands of orange ribbons, but in Minsk you can be arrested for wearing a denim ribbon, they can just stop you and say you were swearing at the police. This camp encourages people, it shows people are not afraid to stay in the centre, 200 metres from the residence of Lukashenko, among all these police.'

State television reports depicted them as an insanitary nuisance, a tiny bunch of drunken fools, gibbering and swaying to the music in a narcotic trance, deranged by visions of their 'so-called revolution'.

The camp was isolated and vulnerable; several people were dragged away by snatch squads as they left the square at night, and some who appeared to be protesters were undercover agents disguising themselves with the badges of freedom while identifying their targets. And yet, somehow, there was a strange optimism, as if some kind of psychological breakthrough had been made.

'The people living in the camp have defeated the fear in their souls,' suggested Atroshchankau. 'They are not the same people they were a few weeks ago. For me, a few months ago I went to demonstrations but I didn't feel positive, it was some kind of depression, but I knew my friends were behind bars and I had to go there to tell people about it – it was my duty. Now we are going there because we want to be there, in the only part of Belarus where there is freedom and democracy.'

For some of them, this was not just about free elections or looking west to Europe, but about establishing a genuine Belarussian identity; about the country's language and traditions. By no means all of those on the square sympathised with this kind of cultural nationalism, but some felt it with growing passion. 'Almost every night I have dreams about how things could be,' said Iryna Toustsik. 'I dream of watching concerts with Belarussian rock groups like NRM who are forbidden to play now, of reading Belarussian magazines and newspapers, of reading the truth about our people. I dream of a free Belarus...'

Each evening, thousands would join them in the square, but for most of the day and night they were on their own, no more than a few hundred strong – 'a flock of lambs surrounded by black wolves', one said – and their only protection was the watchful presence of the international media.[38] 'All I can do is come here every evening,' said one of the evening protesters. 'I cannot be a hero like these people in the camp.' Some opposition politicians also chose not to commit themselves too deeply. 'There were a lot of politicians in the central office of the campaign, and all of them were so keen to explain to foreign journalists how democracy is so important for Belarus,' says Siarhei Lisichonak. 'They were so brave, but then they left us in the square at the most critical moment, when we needed them most.

They all said they would defend democracy, but in the night they were all gone and the youth were alone.'

Tatyana Elovaya believes that the campers had seized the moral leadership from the politicians: 'The events showed who was who,' she says. 'At the end, nobody would even pay attention to the politicians and their declarations. Everybody knew they were not the people who were deciding the future of Belarus.'

Despite their optimism, most of the campers knew that the end would inevitably come, probably sooner than later; that they were offering up their young bodies as sacrifices in a gesture of tragic defiance. Nevertheless, they did what they could to ensure that they would know in advance about any police raid: 'We had an internal system of counter-intelligence which was listening to the police frequencies and getting information from our people in the interior ministry and KGB in order to avoid provocations,' says Elovaya. 'Every hour we were receiving information that they were preparing to storm us.'

After four nights, the moment came. At 3 a.m., armoured trucks entered the square and police in masks and riot helmets surrounded the camp. 'Deeply respected citizens,' announced the officer running the operation, 'by staying here you are breaking the law, so we demand that you move away.'[39] But the campers didn't run. They sat down in their circle and grasped each other's hands tightly. Some tried to call their families, or started to pray; others began to chant, as they had in Kiev: *The police are with the people!* But the police moved in quickly and started dragging them out, and eventually, the last of them were marched away, hands above their heads, towards the waiting vans, and driven off to prison. A few gave the clenched-fist salute or flashed peace signs as they went. Street cleaners arrived to sweep away the miserable heap of scattered possessions and limp canvas which remained, and by the time the city awoke, there was no sign that the camp had ever existed. On state television, a scandalised report showed syringes, packets of drugs, pornographic magazines and scores of crisp $100 bills which police had 'found' in the tents after they were demolished.

March 25 2006 – the anniversary of the short-lived independent

Belarussian republic of 1918 – would be the seventh and final day of sustained protest in Minsk. Squadrons of muscle-bound, black-clad policemen blocked off October Square and forced the demonstrators down the pavement and away from the centre, but they managed to reassemble in a snow-covered park nearby. When the rally ended, Milinkevich told people that they should disperse and reconvene the following month, but Alexander Kozulin boldly announced that he would lead a march to the detention centre where the tent campers were being held. 'It was very significant because it was the first time that people didn't just go home after a rally,' says Iryna Khalip. 'Even when Mr Milinkevich said, "Now we're going home and we'll meet again in a month's time", many in the crowd thought, "We cannot go home because our brothers and sisters are in prison, we have to go there and demand they are released." Many of us crossed this mental barrier.'

But before the marchers reached the jail, they were halted by a battalion of riot police. Kozulin, with red and white flowers in his hands, walked up to the commanding officer and tried to negotiate. He was quickly dragged away. The police advanced on the demonstrators, hammering on their metal shields with their batons, then attacked. They closed in on a middle-aged woman, thrashing at her limbs with truncheons; a man fell to the floor, wounded and unconscious. Scores of people were rounded up and taken away, many of them to jails outside Minsk, as cells in the capital were already packed full of protesters. Some of the women said they were threatened with rape, or told they would be taken into the forest and shot. Most of them were jailed for a couple of weeks, but Kozulin was given a five-and-a-half year sentence for 'hooliganism' and incitement to mass disorder.

Members of the state youth organisation, the Belarussian Republican Union of Youth, held counter-demonstrations outside the Polish and American embassies. 'Stooges should be made into soap!' they chanted. 'Lukashenko is the power!'[40] For them, the election and its aftermath showed that the Belarussian population had chosen stability and prosperity over the mendacious temptations of the 'coloured revolutionaries' and the miseries of Western capitalism. The people had decided to listen to their Daddy, and the extremists had been exposed and defeated. At Lukashenko's inauguration ceremony, the re-elected president jeered at his Western detractors: 'Belarus has a strong immune system,' he said. 'Your awkward attempts to induce a revolutionary virus had the opposite effect and became an antidote to this coloured malaise.'[41]

Inside the cramped cells, as the tent campers waited for trial or release, they sang their favourite songs and chorused: *Long Live Belarus!* Locked up together, they still felt the glow of human solidarity from their Maidan warming them. One of them, Andrey Dyko, a journalist at the opposition newspaper *Nasha Niva* who had been given a ten-day sentence for 'using vulgar language in conversation with police', managed to smuggle a letter out of prison. Even though there had been no 'denim revolution', and hundreds had been arrested, Dyko believed that their week-long protest had at least managed to spoil Lukashenko's 'elegant victory': 'I don't know what is happening out there, outside the prison walls. I don't know who is still free. I am spending these ten days among people who have undergone sacrificial therapy, and these are bright days among bright people.'[42]

The arrests would continue, but for the Belarussian opposition, these had been days when they had dared, for the first time in years, to hope for better times to come. 'We knew these elections would only be the first step,' said the Young Front vice-chairman, Siarhei Lisichonak – although within days, he too had been detained by the KGB.

Other youth activists also realised that they had reached a critical point. Zubr issued a declaration stating that it was suspending its operations to join a national democratic movement, a kind of Belarussian version of the Polish Solidarity movement, which would unite the opposition – although such a thing didn't really exist at the time...

Despite Zubr's sudden demise, Alexander Atroshchankau vowed that the resistance would continue: 'I am sure we have made a crack in the system,' he insisted. 'The circle of people who are suffering from repression is getting wider. Before they were afraid, now they are angry. Nothing is finished yet. It's not over.'

Indeed, there was no shortage of people within the Belarussian opposition whose optimism was undiminished and whose determination remained strong. They believed that the events of March 2006 would inevitably attract new recruits to their proud but wounded resistance; people whose eyes had been opened to what was really going on in Belarus. 'We will act in the streets and underground,' declared one of the tent-camp veterans. 'And if Lukashenko attacks us, we will defend our Belarus. If necessary, we will fight. To the end, which means until victory.'

THE FIRST LEAP

Despite the defiant promises, it seemed to some observers that consecutive defeats for opposition movements in Azerbaijan and Belarus indicated that the wave of democratic revolutions had swept to a halt on the streets of Baku and Minsk, staunched by the determination of governments more powerful, more popular or more pitiless than those which had given way in Serbia, Georgia, Ukraine and Kyrgyzstan. The time of red roses and orange banners had come to an end. Even in some of the countries where the revolutionaries had triumphed, change was slow in coming and questions about democratic standards remained. With the resurgence of nationalist tendencies in Serbia, seemingly relentless political chaos in Ukraine and Kyrgyzstan, and persistent poverty in Georgia, it was suggested by some that the 'colour revolutions' were no more than empty gestures: seductive images with little genuine substance and few lasting benefits.

The failed attempts to incite uprisings in Azerbaijan and Belarus seemed to show that revolutionary youth movements could only make a critical impact when they were operating as the radical vanguard of a well-organised opposition with mass support. Their role was to inspire and provoke people into making what Aleksandar Marić of Otpor calls the 'first leap' towards democracy: to offer the hope that change was possible – even inevitable – and to give people the courage to make it happen. But they could not lead where others weren't willing to follow.

Nevertheless, the fearsome images of the Belarussian riot police grinding unarmed democracy protesters into the late winter snow, live on television, weren't enough to stop others trying to take the same risky path. A few months afterwards, I was sitting in a cosy, wood-panelled café in the capital of another former Soviet republic with an ugly history of sham elections. The country had a deeply cynical government which seemed determined to hold on to its apparently absolute power and its corruptly-acquired loot by any means – ultimately with violence, if the sacrifice of human blood was necessary to keep its leaders' greedy hands on their prize. Around the table in the café were a handful of fashionably-dressed, cosmopolitan young people, all in their mid-twenties and all connected in some way with international democracy campaigns or civil rights groups. They were plotting what they would do during the upcoming elections, which they had no doubt would be rigged despite the extravagant promises their government had been making to the Americans and the Europeans about the inviolable sanctity of democratic morals.

Some of these youths were already veterans of a small youth movement which had organised demonstrations in the city in the aftermath of the last disputed polls a couple of years beforehand, although their eager attempts to ignite mass unrest failed to capture the public imagination, and the riot police then stepped in to convince them that it would probably be better for their health if they stopped shouting about injustice quite so loudly. Their conversation switched easily between English, Russian and their native language as they sipped tea and sifted through the tactical options and potential outcomes – could it be like Georgia, or must it be like Belarus? How could they inspire their compatriots to make that first leap? One of them leaned forward, drew his friends closer, lowered his voice and demanded impatiently, '*What will it take to make a revolution in this country?*'

Their 'revolution', like so many others around that time, turned out to be stillborn – a desperate farce. But their conversation reminded me of another time in another place: Belgrade in the 1990s, long before the fall of Slobodan Milošević. The same intensity, the same desire – the same hope when all around seemed hopeless. The Serbian students who first spray-painted the sign of the clenched fist on the walls of Belgrade back in 1998 had no idea that almost a decade later, young people in countries they hardly knew would be trying to emulate them. What they achieved had become the catalyst for a global phenomenon which had helped to change the course of history, playing a decisive role in four revolutions, and influencing several more outbreaks of popular protest over a few dramatic years at the start of the twenty-first century.

For those who believed in the ideals of these revolutions, and who dreamed of repeating them in their own countries, the defeats which followed were simply setbacks on the long march towards liberation. Like the prison sentences and the beatings, they were not an ultimate deterrent: the radiant allure of the philosophy of peaceful resistance remained irresistible. For them, the triumph of democracy was inevitable; it could not be held back forever, even by force. Freedom, they believed, could not be stopped.

NOTES

CHAPTER ONE

1. *Danas*, 14 November 1998
2. *Nezavisna Svetlost*, 13 December 1998
3. *Danas*, 31 December 1998
4. Voice of America website, 10 December 1998
5. *Danas*, 31 December 1998
6. *Politika*, 13 January 1999
7. Institute for War and Peace Reporting, Balkan Crisis Report, 1 October 1999
8. International Republican Institute website, 2005
9. *Bringing Down a Dictator*, Steve York (director), 2001
10. Salon website, 18 May 2000
11. *New York Times*, 20 January 2002
12. *Independent*, 15 May 2000
13. *New York Times Magazine*, 26 November 2000
14. Ibid.
15. Institute for War and Peace Reporting, Balkan Crisis Report, 3 December 2003

CHAPTER TWO

1. *Campaign for Free and Fair Elections 'Kmara' – 2003*
2. Eurasianet, 10 June 2003
3. BBC News Online, 11 July 2003
4. *Che*, Alexander Koridze (director), 2003
5. *Bringing Down a Dictator*, Steve York (director), 2001
6. Eurasianet, 21 October 2003
7. Eurasianet, 30 October 2003

8. Eurasianet, 4 November 2003
9. Institute for War and Peace Reporting, Caucasus Reporting Service, 13 November 2003
10. BBC News Online, 10 November 2003
11. UrbanEnnui, Capitol Grill website, 24 November 2003
12. Radio Free Europe, 22 November 2003
13. Zurab Karumidze and James V. Wertsch (eds), *Enough: The Rose Revolution in the Republic of Georgia 2003*, Nova Science Publishers, New York, 2005
14. *Guardian*, 1 April 2004
15. Karumidze and Wertsch (eds), *Enough: The Rose Revolution*
16. *Washington Post*, 25 November 2003
17. *Washington Post*, 26 January 2004

CHAPTER THREE

1. Pora website, 2004
2. *Kyiv Post*, 28 September 2000
3. BBC News Online, 10 March 2001
4. BBC News Online, 1 March 2001
5. Institute for War and Peace Reporting, Balkan Crisis Report, 26 November 2004
6. Orysia Maria Kulick, *My House is No Longer on the Margins*, Fulbright Yearbook, 2004
7. Pora website, 2004
8. Agence France-Presse, 24 December 2004
9. Pora website, 2004
10. *Ukrainska Pravda*, 20 December 2004
11. Maidan website, 28 October 2004
12. *Financial Times*, 19 October 2004
13. *Kyiv Post*, 28 October 2004
14. *Zerkalo Nedeli*, 6 January 2005
15. *Kyiv Post*, 2 December 2004
16. Reuters, 3 December 2004
17. Neeka's Backlog website, 26 November 2004

18. *2000*, 21 May 2005
19. Reuters, 26 December 2005
20. Neeka's Backlog website, 26 November 2004
21. *Zerkalo Nedeli*, 6 January 2005
22. Ibid.
23. Ibid.
24. *Guardian*, 26 November 2004
25. Ibid.
26. *Guardian*, 27 November 2004
27. *New York Times*, 31 October 2004
28. Associated Press, 11 December 2004
29. Agence France-Presse, 17 January 2005
30. BBC News Online, 23 January 2005
31. *Guardian*, 24 January 2005
32. Pora website, 9 February 2005
33. Pora website, 19 April 2005

CHAPTER FOUR

1. BBC News Online, 10 May 2005
2. Associated Press, 26 December 2004
3. Associated Press, 8 January 2005
4. Associated Press, 26 December 2005
5. Radio Free Europe/Radio Liberty website, 15 March 2005
6. *Sunday Herald*, 27 March 2005
7. *MSN*, 29 March 2005
8. *International Herald Tribune*, 28 March 2005
9. *Christian Science Monitor*, 31 March 2005
10. Institute for War and Peace Reporting, Caucasus Reporting Service, 10 August 2005
11. Agence France-Presse, 30 October 2005
12. BBC World, 4 November 2005
13. *How Freedom is Won: From Civic Resistance to Durable Democracy*, Freedom House, 2005
14. BBC News Online, 10 July 2004

15. BelaPAN News Agency, 14 February 2001
16. Radio Free Europe/Radio Liberty website, 18 March 2002
17. *Time*, 3 September 2001
18. Belarussian Television, 28 September 2004
19. Transitions Online, 7 November 2005
20. *Washington Post*, 19 August 2002
21. Belarussian Television, 25 August 2005
22. Charter 97 website, 5 September 2005
23. BBC World Service, 2 October 2005
24. Charter 97 website, 23 December 2005
25. Reuters, 2 October 2005
26. Charter 97 website, 30 December 2005
27. *New York Times*, 26 February 2006
28. Agence France-Presse, 22 February 2006
29. Belarussian Television, 1 March 2006
30. *The Georgian Messenger*, 17 March 2006
31. Reuters, 2 March 2006
32. Associated Press, 2 March 2006
33. Agence France-Presse, 17 March 2006
34. Charter 97 website, 19 March 2006
35. LiveJournal website, 25 March 2006
36. Ibid.
37. Ibid.
38. Charter 97 website, 18 April 2006
39. Belarussian Television, 24 March 2006
40. Associated Press, 28 March 2006
41. Reuters, 8 April 2006
42. Charter 97 website, 31 March 2006

ACKNOWLEDGEMENTS

Special thanks are due to Tania Rakhmanova, Aleksandra Nikšić and Alex Kleimenov for their invaluable help with the research for this book. For their support, advice, hospitality and assistance in many countries, I also want to thank Natalia Antelava, Doug Aubrey, Iryna Chupryna, Pavol Demeš, Rajka Despotović, Sergei Devyatkin, Jane Ellis, Nini Gogiberidze, Milja Jovanović, Giorgi Kandelaki, Elena Kasko, Veronika Khokhlova, Monika Lajhner, Veran Matić, Marie Olesen, Gordan Paunović, Gavrilo Petrović, Isabella Sargsyan, Susanne Simon-Paunović, Sally Stainton, Katarina Subasić, Philippe Tschmyr and Yulia Yastremska. As always, thanks are also due to Audrey, Richard and Will Collin, to Lisa Eveleigh, and to Pete Ayrton and all at Serpent's Tail.

Fiction
Crime
Noir

Culture
Music
Erotica

dare to read at serpentstail.com

Visit serpentstail.com today to browse and buy
our books, and to sign up for exclusive news and
previews of our books, interviews with our
authors and forthcoming events.

NEWS

cut to the literary chase with
all the latest news about
our books and authors

EVENTS

advance information on
forthcoming events, author
readings, exhibitions
and book festivals

EXTRACTS

read the best of the outlaw
voices – first chapters, short
stories, bite-sized extracts

EXCLUSIVES

pre-publication offers,
signed copies, discounted
books, competitions

BROWSE AND BUY

browse our full catalogue,
fill up a basket and proceed
to our fully secure checkout
– our website is your oyster

FREE POSTAGE & PACKING ON ALL ORDERS…
ANYWHERE!

sign up today – join our club